Reactions to the Law Minority Religions

Much has been written about the law as it affects new and minority religions, but relatively little has been written about how such religions react to the law. This book presents a wide variety of responses by minority religions to the legal environments within which they find themselves.

An international panel of experts offer examples from North America, Europe and Asia demonstrating how religions with relatively little status may resort to violence or passive acceptance of the law; how they may change their beliefs or practices in order to be in compliance with the law; or how they may resort to the law itself in order to change their legal standing, sometimes by forging alliances with those with more power or authority to achieve their goals. The volume concludes by applying theoretical insights from sociological studies of law, religion and social movements to the variety of responses.

The first systematic collection focussing on how minority religions respond to efforts at social control by various governmental agents, this book provides a vital reference for scholars of religion and the law, new religious movements, minority religions and the sociology of religion.

Eileen Barker, FBA, FAcSS, OBE, is Professor Emeritus of Sociology at the London School of Economics, UK. She has spent the past five decades studying minority religions and social reactions to them. In 1988, she founded Inform in order to help enquirers with information that is as reliable, balanced, contextualised and up-to-date as possible. She has over 400 scholarly publications and is series editor of the Routledge Inform book series.

James T. Richardson is Emeritus Professor of Sociology and Judicial Studies at the University of Nevada, USA. He is a sociologist with legal training and has been researching new religious movements for five decades. He is the author of over a dozen books and over 300 articles in journals and chapters in edited collections. He has been a Fulbright Fellow in the Netherlands and a Rockefeller Scholar at the Bellagio Center in Italy as well as being an invited guest of universities in Europe, Australia and China.

Routledge Inform Series on Minority Religions and Spiritual Movements

Series Editor: Eileen Barker, London School of Economics and Political Science, UK

Inform is an independent charity that collects and disseminates accurate, balanced and up-to-date information about minority religious and spiritual movements.

The *Routledge Inform Series* addresses themes related to new religions, many of which have been the topics of Inform seminars. The series editorial board consists of internationally renowned scholars in the field.

Books in the series attract both an academic and interested general readership, particularly in the areas of Religious Studies, and the Sociology of Religion and Theology.

Prophecy in the New Millennium
When Prophecies Persist
Edited by Suzanne Newcombe and Sarah Harvey

Global Religious Movements Across Borders
Sacred Service
Edited by Stephen M. Cherry and Helen Rose Ebaugh

Spiritual and Visionary Communities
Out to Save the World
Edited by Timothy Miller

State Responses to Minority Religions
Edited by David M. Kirkham

Minority Religions and Fraud
In Good Faith
Edited by Amanda van Eck Duymaer van Twist

Reactions to the Law by Minority Religions
Edited by Eileen Barker and James T. Richardson

For more information about this series, please visit: www.routledge.com/religion/series/AINFORM

Reactions to the Law by Minority Religions

Edited by
Eileen Barker and
James T. Richardson

Routledge
Taylor & Francis Group

LONDON AND NEW YORK

First published 2021
by Routledge
2 Park Square, Milton Park, Abingdon, Oxon OX14 4RN

and by Routledge
52 Vanderbilt Avenue, New York, NY 10017

Routledge is an imprint of the Taylor & Francis Group, an informa business

British Library Cataloguing-in-Publication Data
A catalogue record for this book is available from the British Library

Library of Congress Cataloging-in-Publication Data
Names: Barker, Eileen, 1938- editor. | Richardson, James T., 1941- editor.
Title: Reactions to the law by minority religions /
edited by Eileen Barker and James T. Richardson.
Description: Milton Park, Abingdon, Oxon; New York, NY:
Routledge, 2021.
| Series: Routledge inform series on minority religions and spiritual
movements | Includes bibliographical references and index.
Identifiers: LCCN 2020038719 (print) | LCCN 2020038720
(ebook) | ISBN 9780367484323 (hardback) |
ISBN 9781003053590 (ebook)
Subjects: LCSH: Religious minorities—Legal status, laws, etc. |
Religious minorities—Legal status, laws, etc.—Europe. |
Conflict of laws.
Classification: LCC K3242 .R43 2021 (print) |
LCC K3242 (ebook) | DDC 342.08/52—dc23
LC record available at https://lccn.loc.gov/2020038719
LC ebook record available at https://lccn.loc.gov/2020038720

ISBN: 9780367484323 (hbk)
ISBN: 9781003053590 (ebk)

Typeset in Sabon
by codeMantra

For our grandchildren,
  Araceli, Beatrice, Charlie, Lucy, Olivia, and Thomas
  May you all live in a more tolerant world

Contents

List of figures   ix
Notes on contributors   xi

1 Fight, flight or freeze? Reactions to the law by minority religions   1
   EILEEN BARKER

2 Stand up for your rights: (minority) religions' reactions to the
   law in Estonia   23
   RINGO RINGVEE

3 Jehovah's Witnesses and the law: "Caesar's things to Caesar,
   but God's things to God"   37
   TONY BRACE

4 Scientology behind the scenes: the law changer   58
   ERIC ROUX

5 No stranger to litigation: court cases involving the Unification
   Church/Family Federation in the United States   79
   MICHAEL L. MICKLER

6 Legal challenges posed to the Unification Church in Europe:
   perspectives from a Unificationist advocate for religious freedom   97
   PETER ZOEHRER

7 The "Doukhobor Problem" in Canada: how a Russian
   mystical sect responded to law enforcement in British
   Columbia, 1903–2013   115
   SUSAN PALMER AND SHANE DUSSAULT

 8 Making sense of the institutional demarcation: Tenrikyō's
   response to legal environments in France   134
   MASATO KATO

 9 Strategies in context: the Essenes in France and Canada   152
   MARIE-ÈVE MELANSON AND JENNIFER GUYVER

10 Reactions to legal challenges by Aum Shinrikyō and its
   successor organisations   169
   RIN USHIYAMA

11 Religious persecution and refugees: legal and communication
   strategies of The Church of Almighty God in asylum cases   188
   MASSIMO INTROVIGNE AND ROSITA ŠORYTĖ

12 Minority religion reactions to the European Court of
   Human Rights   207
   EFFIE FOKAS

13 Minority religions respond to the law: a theoretical excursus   221
   JAMES T. RICHARDSON

   Index   237

Figures

1.1   Pastafarian driving licence with religious headwear   9

1.2   Falun Gong practitioners in Hong Kong do a mock forced organ harvest   16

2.1   The Tamme-Lauri Oak is the largest, and one of the oldest, trees in Estonia. It is estimated that the tree started to grow in 1326. It is the only surviving tree of an oak grove, once used for the pre-Christian nature worship that was suppressed in the 18th century. The tree came under heritage protection in 1939. In 1992 it was depicted on the Estonian 10 *kroon* banknote   27

3.1   Jehovah's Witness Dennis Christensen on trial in Russia. On 6 February 2019, Christensen was sentenced to 6 years' imprisonment for peaceful practice of his religion. The case has been referred by Jehovah's Witnesses to the European Court of Human Rights.'   46

4.1   First couple to be married in the newly registered Scientology Chapel   64

5.1   Rally outside the court of Reverend Moon's trial   82

6.1   The Reverend and Mrs. Sun Myung Moon   105

7.1   For many Sons of Freedom children, this was their first winter in New Denver. Peter Savinkoff (left, wearing the bunny rabbit jacket) was around 7 years old when this photo was taken in the winter of 1956/57. The fence that separated the children from their families during their monthly visit and moleniye – or prayer service – had only gone up the summer before   122

8.1   Tenrikyo Europe Centre   137

8.2   Association Culturelle Franco-Japonaise de Tenri   138

9.1   Maple Village in Cookshire-Eaton, QC, Canada   162

11.1   Members of The Church of Almighty God studying their Scripture   200

Notes on contributors

Eileen Barker is Professor Emeritus of Sociology with Special Reference to the Study of Religion at the London School of Economics, University of London, UK. In 1988, she founded INFORM (www.Inform.ac), an educational charity initially based at the LSE, but now at the Theology and Religious Studies Department of King's College, London. INFORM provides information about minority religions that is as objective, contextualised, and up-to-date as possible. She has over 400 publications translated into 28 different languages, including the award-wining *The Making of a Moonie: Brainwashing or Choice?* She is a frequent advisor to governments, other official bodies, and law-enforcement agencies throughout the world and has also made numerous appearances on television and radio.

Tony Brace is chair of The European Association of Jehovah's Witnesses Religious Freedom Subcommittee, which acts as spokesperson for the Governing Body of Jehovah's Witnesses on freedom of religion and belief in Europe and beyond. He is a third-generation Jehovah's Witness who has worked for 30 years in the legal department at the Witnesses' British headquarters, dealing with human rights matters relating to freedom of religion and belief. He has been involved in meetings with officials in Azerbaijan, Belarus, Cyprus, Rwanda and the United Kingdom as well as at the Council of Europe, the European Parliament and the UN in Geneva.

Shane Dussault is Research Assistant on the Children in Sectarian Religions and State Control project, directed by Susan Palmer of McGill's School of Religious Studies. He is the designer and administrator for the project's website: www.spiritualchildhoods.ca.

Effie Fokas is Senior Research Fellow at the Hellenic Foundation for European and Foreign Policy (ELIAMEP) and a Research Associate of the London School of Economics Hellenic Observatory. She was Principal Investigator of the European Research Council-funded project on Grassroots Mobilisations in the Shadow of European Court of Human

Rights Religious Freedoms Jurisprudence (Grassrootsmobilise), based at ELIAMEP. Her publications include *Islam in Europe: Diversity, Identity and Influence* (co-edited with Aziz Al-Azmeh) and *Religious America, Secular Europe? A Theme and Variations* (co-authored with Peter Berger and Grace Davie).

Jennifer Guyver is a PhD candidate in the School of Religious Studies at McGill University. She received a B.A. in Religious Studies from McGill University and an M.A. in Religious Studies from the University of Montreal. Her fields of study are secularism and public policy, religion and human rights, and the philosophy of Charles Taylor.

Massimo Introvigne is founder and Managing Director of the Center for Studies on New Religions (CESNUR) in Torino, Italy and editor of the daily magazine on religious liberty in China, *Bitter Winter*. Until 2016, he has been Professor of Sociology of Religions at Pontifical Salesian University, also in Torino. He served in 2011 as the Representative of OSCE (Organization for Security and Cooperation in Europe) for combating racism, xenophobia, and intolerance and discrimination against Christians and members of other religions. From 2012 to 2015, he was Chairperson of the Observatory of Religious Liberty instituted by the Italian Ministry of Foreign Affairs.

Masato Kato obtained a PhD in the Study of Religions in 2018 from SOAS University of London. From June 2018 to May 2020, he was a Postdoctoral Research Associate at the Centre for the Study of Japanese Religions, SOAS. His article, "Legitimating a Religion through Culture: Revisiting Peter Clarke's Discussion on the Globalisation of Japanese New Religions", is forthcoming in the *Journal of Contemporary Religion*.

Marie-Ève Melanson is a PhD candidate in the School of Religious Studies at McGill University. She received a B.A. in Social Work and an M.A. in Religious Studies from the Université du Québec à Montréal. Her fields of research are freedom of religion and minority rights. She works with Dr. Susan Palmer as a research assistant on the Children in Sectarian Religions research project. She received the Social Sciences and Humanities Research Council of Canada Joseph-Armand-Bombardier Scholarship in Honour of Nelson Mandela for her PhD research.

Michael L. Mickler is Vice-President and Professor of Church History at Unification Theological Seminary. He is Director of the Sunhak Institute of History which documents Family Federation activities in the United States. He is the author of *40 Years in America: An Intimate History of the Unification Movement, 1959–1999* (2000), *A History of the Unification Church in America, 1959–74: Emergence of a National Movement* (1993) and *The Unification Church in America: A Bibliography and Research Guide* (1987).

Susan Palmer is an Affiliate Professor in the Department of Religions and Cultures at Concordia University and an Affiliate Member of the School of Religious Studies at McGill University in Montreal, Quebec. She is the Principal Investigator of the Children in Sectarian Religions research project, supported by the Social Sciences and the Humanities Research Council. Palmer is the author or editor of twelve books as well as numerious journal articles and book chapters that involve sociological studies of new religious movements.

James T. Richardson is a Professor Emeritus of Sociology and Judicial Studies at the University of Nevada, Reno, where he taught sociology and social psychology and directed the master's and doctoral judicial studies program for trial judges. Dr Richardson is the co-author and editor of over a dozen books, including *Organized Miracles, Money and Power in the New Religions, The Satanism Scare, Regulating Religion: Case Studies from around the Globe, Saints under Siege: The Texas Raid on the Fundamentalist Latter Day Saints* and *The Sociology of Shari'a*.

Ringo Ringvee is a member of the Estonian Chancellor of Justice's Advisory Committee on Human Rights and editorial board member of the *International Journal for the Study of New Religions*. Since 1998, he has held a post at the Religious Affairs Department of the Estonian Ministry of the Interior and taught religion-related courses at higher educational institutions. His recent publications include "What do the censuses tell about minority religions? Some reflections on Estonia" in George D. Chryssides (ed.). *Minority Religions in Europe and the Middle East* (2019) and "Survival Strategies of New Religions in a Secular Consumer Society: A Case Study from Estonia" in *Nova Religio* (2017).

Eric Roux is Vice-President of the European Office of the Church of Scientology for Public Affairs and Human Rights and President of the European Interreligious Forum for Religious Freedom, an interfaith forum that advocates for freedom of religion and belief for all at European level. He has worked on the topic of religious freedom at national and international levels, and has been a speaker on this subject at many events, including at the OSCE, the Council of Europe, the European Parliament and the US Capitol.

Rosita Šorytė is co-founder and President of ORLIR, the International Observatory of Religious Liberty of Refugees, and a member of the scientific committee of the European Federation for Freedom of Belief. In 1992, she joined the Ministry of Foreign Affairs of Lithuania, where she worked as a diplomat for the following 25 years. She has been posted as the Permanent Mission of Lithuania to UNESCO (Paris, 1994–1996), as the Permanent Mission of Lithuania to the Council of Europe (Strasbourg, 1996–1998), and was Minister Counsellor at the Permanent Mission of Lithuania to the United Nations in 2014–2017, where she had already worked in 2003–2006. In 2013, she served as Chairperson of the

European Union Working Group on Humanitarian Aid on behalf of the Lithuanian *pro tempore* presidency of the European Union.

Rin Ushiyama is a British Academy Postdoctoral Fellow at the Department of Sociology, University of Cambridge, and a Research Fellow in Sociology at Murray Edwards College, University of Cambridge. He holds a PhD in Sociology (2017) from the University of Cambridge. A cultural and political sociologist of Japan, he has published scholarly articles on the social consequences of Aum Shinrikyo's violence in journals including the *British Journal of Sociology, Theory and Society* and the *International Journal of Politics, Culture, and Society*. Rin is currently completing an academic monograph, titled *Remembering Religious Terrorism: the Aum Affair in Japanese Collective Memory*.

Peter Zoehrer, an Austrian journalist who joined the Unification Church (UC) in 1972, is co-founder and Executive Director of Forum for Religious Freedom – Europe (FOREF). In 2005, Peter co-founded FOREF-Europe, and the NGO has since become a respected religious freedom monitor as well as a media forum for members of religious minority groups, their opponents, public media, legislators, government agencies and human rights defenders. FOREF's fundamental premise is that religious freedom is indivisible and that an attack on the freedom of one is an attack on the freedom of all. In December 2018, the Austrian Journalist Association (OEJC) granted him its 'Silver Pin' award.

1 Fight, flight or freeze?

Reactions to the law by minority religions

Eileen Barker

Introduction

While much has been studied about how the law affects minority religions (e.g., Barker 2004; Bielefeldt 2012; Durham and Ferrari 2004; Richardson 2004; Sandberg 2014), relatively little has been written on how the religions react to their legal environments. In most Western democracies, international, constitutional and national laws tend to enable minority religions to believe and practise in relative peace – so long as they do not indulge in criminal behaviour; but, even in such countries, many of the religions find aspects of one law or another interfering with their lives. As one moves eastward, the situation can become more fraught with difficulty until, *in extremis*, merely belonging to a minority religion can be punishable by death.

As part of the *Routledge/Inform Series*,[1] this volume complements several others in the collection, perhaps especially *Legal Cases, New Religious Movements, and Minority Faiths* (Richardson and Bellanger 2014) and *State Responses to Minority Religions* (Kirkham 2013). As is policy for the series, each volume approaches a particular issue concerned with minority religions by including authors who come from a wide range of perspectives. This entails inviting not only scholars and other professionals to contribute but also those who have a personal interest in the topic, such as members and former members of a variety of religions. Obviously enough, those who have been deeply involved with the issue in question are liable to have a more subjective approach than that of the professional. This, we believe, can enhance the understanding that the reader may gain about the different ways different people and organisations perceive and react to the social world. It might, moreover, be added that we have found that many of those who are or were in a minority religion are more than capable of expressing themselves in a scholarly manner. In this volume, as can be seen from the short biographies, we have included several current members. Unusually for the series, we have included two from the same movement – the Unification Church. They have, however, approached the topic from very different starting points, although both belong to the largest of the three movements that have followed different paths since the death of the Church's founder, the Rev Sun Myung Moon.[2]

Any attempt by the editors to produce coherent answers to questions raised by the topic in this or any other volume in the series would be counter-productive. The whole point of the exercise is to present readers with an (inevitably limited) selection of the many perspectives that interested individuals can have on a topic. Inform itself does not necessarily endorse any of the divergent opinions. No claim is made to exhaust the full range of possible responses. At least a dozen further volumes would be needed to attempt such an enterprise. This opening chapter merely considers, with examples, something of the variety of ways in which religions might adopt 'fight, flight, or freeze' responses, or combinations of such responses, to the law.

Violent reactions to the law

Only a tiny percentage of the tens of thousands of minority religions that exist at any one time will turn to violence,[3] and those that do are more likely to direct their violence towards their own members than the rest of society. On the rare occasions when they do resort to violence, however, they are likely to make headline news and, all too often, it is assumed that this is a typical characteristic of minority religions (Barker 2010; Richardson 2001).

In his book, *Terror in the Mind of God*, Mark Juergensmeyer argues that, while religions are not always innocent, they do not normally lead to violence – that, he states, "happens only with the coalescence of a peculiar set of circumstances – political, social, and ideological – when religion becomes fused with violent expressions of social aspirations, personal pride, and movements for political change" (2004: 10). Juergensmeyer might have added 'legal' to his list of circumstances, especially when the distinction between the law and the state has become blurred, and/or a religious minority entertains a political agenda of overthrowing the entire legal apparatus. Several jihadist terrorist movements, such as ISIS (Roy 2017) or Boko Haram (Thurston 2018), have been using violence to overthrow the present system in order to replace it with a caliphate ruled by sharia law. Another example could be The Lord's Resistance Army, which has been committing horrific atrocities in northern Uganda and South Sudan with the aim of restoring rights taken away from the Acholi people and establishing a theocracy (Allen and Vlassenroot 2010).

With a more focused objective, the Ku Klux Klan, originally formed in response to antislavery legislation in late eighteenth-century America, renewed its violence following the 1964 Civil Rights Act (Ridgeway 1990). There are some Christian minorities that have responded with violence to what they consider to be immoral laws; several religions objected strongly to the 1973 *Roe v Wade* court case legalising abortion in the United States

(Bader and Baird-Windle 2001) – most notably, perhaps, the loosely structured Army of God, which claimed biblical rationalisations for kidnapping, attempted murder and murder (Jefferis 2011).

Occasionally, methods involving violence or potential violence have targeted those attempting to apply the law – that is, the violence is directed against its implementers rather than the law itself. In a near-lethal example from 1978, members of Synanon put a four-foot rattlesnake in the letter box of a lawyer investigating the movement (Morantz c.2009). Examples resulting in deaths include Aum Shinrikyo's murder in November 1989 of Tsutsumi Sakamoto, a lawyer working on a class action lawsuit against the movement (Reader 2000).[4] Jim Jones ordered the murder of Congressman Ryan, who had arrived to investigate the Peoples Temple in Jonestown, Guyana, before ordering the suicides/deaths of the entire membership of over 900 (Hall 2004; Moore 2009).

When the Bureau of Alcohol, Tobacco, and Firearms (ATF) attempted a botched, no-knock 'dynamic entry' of the Branch Davidians' compound near Waco, Texas on 28 February 1993, the Davidians' immediate reaction was to shoot back, resulting in the deaths of four agents and six Davidians. The next day, FBI agents took charge of the case, which, because of the ATF agents' deaths, they called WACMUR (Waco Murder) (Wessinger 2017: 203). The movement's reaction to this resulted in a 51-day standoff, with their leader, David Koresh, refusing to surrender until he had finished writing out the message that God had revealed to him concerning the seven seals in the Book of Revelation (Tabor and Gallagher 1995). The FBI's subsequent storming of the Waco compound on 19 April 1995 provided Timothy McVeigh with a motivation for the Oklahoma City bombing, which resulted in the death of at least 168 men, women and children, exactly two years later (Wright 2007).

When the followers of Bhagwan Rajneesh bought a large property in Oregon, they reacted to local resistance against them, first, by taking over the adjacent town of Antelope (which had around 50 residents) and incorporating it as a city, so that they could have their own police force and pass local laws. They then tried to take over Wasco county to gain further legislative power by various means that included increasing the population of voters by inviting homeless people from around the country to the ranch, Rajneeshpuram, and then by sprinkling salmonella poisoning in the salad bars of restaurants, causing over 700 potential town voters to fall sick. There was also an unsuccessful plot to assassinate the Oregon State Attorney, Charles Turner, who had been investigating suspected sham marriages and immigration fraud by the Rajneeshees (Carter 1990). The documentary *Wild Wild Country*[5] presents a convincing picture of the gradual escalation of antagonism between the Rajneeshees and the local law makers at increasing levels. It also demonstrates how there were fears that the Rajneeshees would take over the whole state of Oregon and that there would be 'another Jonestown'.

It might be added that there are other examples when the *expectation* of violent reactions from a religious group can be used by law enforcers to justify their responding to the religion with what could appear to be a totally disproportionate act of violence. Following a siege lasting several months, on 8 August 1978 Philadelphia police entered the house of members of the MOVE, a black liberation group founded as the Christian Movement for Life by John Africa in 1972. In the confusion, a police officer was shot dead, and several other police and firefighters were wounded. Nine members of the MOVE were sentenced to between 30 and 100 years for the murder of the officer, although there is credible evidence suggesting that he was accidentally shot by another officer (Pilkington 2018). Nonetheless, according to the Philadelphia Special Investigation Committee Final Report, the death and reports that MOVE members were armed and dangerous had terrified their neighbours and threatened violence against public officials, and confirmed the belief that they would react with "deadly force when confronted" (Boyette and Boyette 2013: 318). This, the Report claimed, provided sufficient justification in 1985 for a police helicopter to bomb the MOVE house, killing 11 MOVE members, including five of their children, and destroying 65 houses in the neighbourhood (Boyette and Boyette 2013).

Violent reactions to the law by minority religions are not always directed outside their movement. Buddhist monks (most recently and frequently in Tibet and Vietnam) and members of other religions have set fire to themselves in protest against legal systems. The Ananda Marga reacted not only with hunger strikes, hijacking a plane and murder, but also with self-immolation in protest against the imprisonment of their leader, Prabhat Ranjan Sarkar (Prakash 2014: 22–3; Salusinszky 2019).

Passive resistance to the law

At an opposite extreme to violence, other religions have passively resisted complying with the law when they believe it to be in opposition to God's law or against their best interests. Throughout history, there have been those who, rather than denying their faith, have chosen to be thrown to the lions, face torture as a heretic during the Spanish Inquisition or, like the Cathars, be burned at the stake. Among examples to be found in modern times have been the Quakers and Jehovah's Witnesses who, taking seriously the commandment Thou shalt not kill,[6] have refused to take up arms or enlist for military service.[7] This has resulted in their being imprisoned, where they have not infrequently died (see Chapter 3 by Brace). Whilst Jews, gypsies and homosexuals had no choice when transported to concentration and other prison camps under Nazi Germany, Jehovah's Witnesses had, in theory at least, the option to salute the Nazi flag, to raise their arms with a 'Heil Hitler', to serve in the German army and to renounce their faith; in fact, very few did (King 1982). Figures vary, but about 10,000 Witnesses were imprisoned in Auschwitz and other concentration camps or prisons during the Nazi period, where an estimated 2,500–5,000 died. It is reported that both guards and officers would employ Witnesses as domestic servants because, although they would refuse to conform to military-type routines such as roll call or rolling bandages for soldiers at the front, the camp authorities considered them to be relatively trustworthy because they refused to escape or physically resist their guards.[8]

It is quite common for religions to respond in significantly different ways when faced with the same legislation. Feng Yang describes how Christians in mainland China have responded to Communist rule with three kinds of strategies: cooperation, accommodation and resistance.

> Each of these strategies has both active and passive aspects. While active cooperators embrace parts of Communist ideology and party-state politics, passive cooperators "walk the second mile" with the Communists to show Christian love. Active accommodators willingly support the party-state for perceived opportunities, whereas passive accommodators are "shrewd as snakes and innocent as doves" in findings ways to evangelise regardless of restrictions. Passive resisters try to avoid and escape from the authorities, but resisters take opportunities to challenge the authorities, demanding for rule of law and implementation of the constitutional promise of freedom of religious belief (or religion and belief).
>
> (Yang 2017: 79–80)

Hiding from the law

A less overt passive resistance is to hide *from* the law, either by escaping from the jurisdiction or by going underground. There are countless instances of individuals doing so in countries where simply belonging to a particular religious minority can be a criminal offence. This is the case in Iran, Saudi Arabia and several other Islamic-majority countries in Central Asia and the Middle East, and in an Orthodox Christian-majority country such as Russia, where the Supreme Court ruled on 20 April 2017 that the Jehovah's Witnesses organisation should be closed down and no longer allowed to operate legally.[9] In communist China, a number of lists have been drawn up of *xie jiao*, commonly translated as 'evil cult', but more accurately translated as heresy or unorthodox teachings (Irons 2018). Although the Chinese Communist Party (CCP) insists that these are criminal organisations,[10] not religions (and cannot therefore be protected under any laws of religious freedom), the lists include the Unification Church, the Children of God, The Church of Almighty God (CAG), 'The Shouters' and the Association of Disciples (Mentuhui),[11] all of which, by pretty well any definition, would be called religious (Introvigne 2020a). It is not only members of movements designated as *xie jiao* but also members of other unregistered religions who practice 'underground' (Yang 2006), not all of them passively (Wang 2018, 2019). Members of the Chinese police claim that most erstwhile adherents of Falun Gong have now given up the practice; I have, however, been informed by scholars and practitioners that many who publicly claim to have renounced their membership continue to practice in private;[12] Falun Gong itself claims that tens of millions still practise in China.[13] Many others have fled from the People's Republic to seek asylum in another country, where they may actively protest one way or another against the laws of their homeland (see below).

While some minority religions escape from jurisdictions they perceive as oppressive, others infiltrate them. During the Soviet period, several minority religions were involved in smuggling Bibles (Bourdeaux 1990) and/or underground witnessing (Gray 2019; Pranskevičiūtė-Amoson and Juras 2014), risking imprisonment and even death in some cases.[14] Many more flooded into the region as a reaction to the new Constitutions and laws associated with the dissolution of the former Soviet Union (Cardin 1998).

Fleeing the law

Sometimes, minority religions remove themselves to another jurisdiction when they are faced by laws that prevent them from practising their beliefs. The leadership and many followers of illegal minorities, such as Falun Gong and CAG (Introvigne 2020b), have fled China to seek asylum in countries throughout the world. Members of the Messianic Community, also known as the Twelve Tribes, left Germany for the Czech Republic when they found themselves unable to educate their children as they desired – both because of a law forbidding home-schooling and another one prohibiting corporal punishment (Twelve Tribes 2014).[15]

In Pakistan, the Criminal Law (Amendment) Act, passed in 1984, has declared that an Ahmadi:

> ... who directly or indirectly, poses himself as a Muslim, or calls, or refers to, his faith as Islam, or preaches or propagates his faith, ... or in any manner whatsoever outrages the religious feelings of Muslims shall be punished with imprisonment ... for a term which may extend to three years and shall also be liable to fine.
>
> ... Use of derogatory remarks, etc., in respect of the Holy Prophet: Whoever by words, either spoken or written, or by visible representation or by any imputation, innuendo, or insinuation, directly or indirectly, defiles the sacred name of the Holy Prophet Muhammad (peace be upon him) shall be punished with death, or imprisonment for life, and shall also be liable to fine.[16]

Since this Amendment, which declares the Ahmadi belief in the prophethood of Mirza Ghulam Ahmad to be blasphemous as it "defiles the name of Prophet Muhammad",[17] several hundred Ahmadis have been reported killed (Hashim 2017). In reaction to the ensuing persecution, most Ahmadi now live outside Pakistan, and the fourth caliph migrated to England, where the official headquarters of the Community is now based.

Article 13 of the current Iranian Constitution states that: "Zoroastrian, Jewish, and Christian Iranians are the only recognised religious minorities … free to perform their religious rites and ceremonies" (FIDH 2003: 11). Despite (or possibly because of) the fact that, unlike the Ahmadi, the Baha'i do not consider themselves to be Muslims, but an independent religion, they have been classified as both 'heretics' and 'unprotected infidels' by the Islamic regime, and are, thereby, forbidden to exercise their religion or to exist as an organised religious community. Baha'i have, furthermore, been denied the right to higher education, to pensions or unemployment benefits and have suffered confiscation of property, imprisonment and, not infrequently, death (ibid.: 11–14).[18] To take a recent example, on 15 June 2020, 12 men and 14 women, apparently simply by being Baha'is, were charged in the Revolutionary Court of Shiraz with:

> Propaganda against the regime and in favor of groups opposing the regime, running groups opposing the regime, membership in these groups, propaganda activities for, and cooperation with, hostile states; links to states hostile to the Islamic Republic and [supporting] global arrogance, and implementing their plans, [all the above taking] the form of the Bahai organization in Iran.[19]

Such a situation has led many to flee from Iran, some to Israel, the Baha'i international administrative and spiritual centre being located in Haifa. On the other hand, a considerable number have kept their heads down and remained in Iran, where, with more than 300,000 members, they form the largest religious minority.

Some minority religions, like the Wandering Jew, seem destined to flee from one jurisdiction to another. Marie-Ève Melanson and Jennifer Guyver's chapter tells how Olivier Manitara, the leader of the Christian Essene Church in France, after being found guilty of misuse of company assets, and having received a sentence conditional on his not communicating any of his ideas, decided that the Essenes should relocate. However, after some years in Canada, they were ordered by the local municipality to demolish all buildings dedicated for worship. Whilst they have tried fighting the ruling (so far unsuccessfully), this legal conflict led Manitara, once again, to ask his followers to relocate – this time to Panama.

Challenging the law

The Jehovah's Witnesses' political neutrality does not mean that they are not actively engaged in attempts to change the secular law. They are fully prepared to *use* the law against the law when their capacity to follow God's law is threatened. Indeed, Jehovah's Witnesses and the Church of

Scientology have been foremost among minority religions in changing the law and/or clarifying its content in a number of countries and at the European Court of Human Rights (Richardson 2017).

The chapter by Tony Brace describes some of the Witnesses' achievements in bringing about changes or reinterpretations of the law in cases relating to conscientious objection, compulsion to salute a nation's flag, and the right to refuse blood transfusions. Eric Roux's chapter on the Church of Scientology details the movement's legal battles to be recognised as a genuine religion. Its successes in this area have undoubtedly widened the definition of religion in legal parlance throughout much of the world, thereby enabling not only Scientology but also other religions to escape the penalties of not being registered and/or enjoy the benefits of recognition as a *bone fide* religion. Tellingly, Roux describes how, although Scientology has not yet been able to secure charitable status as a religion in England, it has succeeded in winning a case in which the Judge argued that one of its buildings could be recognised for the registration of marriage on the grounds that "the meaning given to worship in [an earlier case when registration was denied] was unduly narrow, but even if it was not unduly narrow in 1970, it is unduly narrow now".

Roux's chapter also covers a case concerning a list of 189 dangerous sects that had been included in a Belgium Parliamentary Commission Report (Duquesne and Willems 1997). Unlike the Chinese lists of *xie jiao* or the Russian lists of 'extremist movements',[20] membership of a religion on the list is not in itself a criminal act. Furthermore, the list was not officially accepted as part of the Belgian law. Nonetheless, as with a similar list in a French Government Report (Vivien 1995), the very fact that a religion had been included in an official report has placed its members at a considerable disadvantage if, for example, they want to rent an apartment or keep a job (L'Heureux et al. 2000), and has, as Roux recounts, been assumed to be 'proof' that such religions are, in some way, criminal – until the Court, in *Scientology v. Federal Prosecutor*, declared that the Parliamentary Commission had made a value judgement which it was not entitled to do by presenting a list of movements it considered harmful.

On what some might consider a slightly more frivolous note, while the Latvian Ministry of Justice has refused to include members of the Church of the Flying Spaghetti Monster in its official registry of religious organisations,[21] the Pastafarians (as members of the Church call themselves) have been successful in persuading the authorities in several countries and American states that they should be allowed to wear their religious headgear, a sieve or colander, for their driving licence photographs.[22] Furthermore, while the Temple of the Jedi Order, inspired by the Star Wars films, was unsuccessful in persuading the English Charity Commissioners that it is a religion,[23] it has succeeded in gaining tax-exempt status from the US Internal Revenue Service (Figure 1.1).[24]

The First Amendment of the USA has long been used by minority religions to appeal against legislation they believe discriminates against them.

Figure 1.1 Pastafarian driving licence with religious headwear. (Photograph courtesy of Niko Alm)

Frequently cited cases involving minority religions include *Reynolds v. US* (1879) in which the Court ruled that the law provided absolute freedom regarding beliefs, but not practices, when the Church of Jesus Christ of Latter-day Saints argued that it was their religious right to practice polygamy; *Sherbert v. Verner* (1963), when it was argued that, unless the government had a compelling state interest to do so, it should not place a substantial burden on someone – in this case, by expecting Seventh-day Adventists to work on a Saturday, their Sabbath; and *Wisconsin v. Yoder* (1972), when the Supreme Court found that Amish children could not be placed under compulsory education past 8th grade, as the parents' fundamental right to freedom of religion outweighed the state's interest in educating their children (Durham and Scharffs 2019: 232–43).

One topic that has by no means been fully resolved is whether the use of entheogens (substances that induce psychoactive effects) is legal when it is for religious purposes. Various laws have been passed throughout the centuries in attempts to control cannabis, cocaine, opium and other substances. In *Employment Division: Oregon v. Smith* (1990), the Supreme Court reversed an earlier decision by ruling that members of the Native American Church (who believe that the peyote plant embodies their deity and eating it is an act of worship and communion) could be denied unemployment benefits, having been dismissed for their use of peyote (Durham and Scharffs 2019: 244–50). Although the Native American Church's protest against the Oregon law had been unsuccessful in the Supreme Court, its case led to a widespread public reaction which resulted in the introduction of the 1993 Religious Freedom Restoration Act (RFRA), the application of which was later limited to Federal laws (ibid.: 250ff). Internationally, there remains a wide range of laws concerning the religious use of drugs, with minority religions often carrying out their rituals in secret. Santo Daime's ritualised consumption of ayahuasca has resulted in several unsuccessful legal suits fought by Daimistas as reactions to the arrest and prosecution of their members or confiscation of daime; its Oregon group has, however, been successfully proactive in pursuing the legal right to consume ayahuasca for ritual purposes (Dawson forthcoming; Haber 2011; Richardson and Shoemaker 2014).

Ringo Ringvee's chapter traces ways in which the Jewish community, Jehovah's Witnesses and indigenous Pagans have, in different ways, successfully managed to influence Estonian legislation so that it would permit alternative military service and medical treatment, the slaughter of unstunned animals for religious reasons, and the removal of terminology in the law that was derived from one particular religious tradition. Interestingly, all three cases were solved in out-of-court settlements with the government. Ringvee's chapter also explores a case involving the Cohabitation Act which allowed for the legal recognition of gender-neutral cohabitation. Although different religious associations expressed negative attitudes towards the new legislation, they failed to persuade the legislators to abandon it.

Not surprisingly, by no means all, or indeed most, laws are changed because of the reactions of minority religions, even when their attempts are being rejected by sympathetic officials. The Druze have tried long and hard, but unsuccessfully, to change Israel's controversial nation-state law, which the Druze argue makes them second-class citizens – despite the fact that the Justice Minister has insisted "The Druze are our brothers and the flesh and blood of the State of Israel".[25]

Susan Palmer and Shane Dussault's chapter tells how the Doukhobors, a radical Christian anarchist and pacifist movement dating back to the 1700s in Russia, refused enlistment in the Bolshevik army in the early 1890s and migrated to Canada. There, their defiance of government regulations resulted in mounting tensions with the British Columbian authorities. A splinter group, the Sons of Freedom, engaged in protest demonstrations that involved fire-bombing public schools and marching in the nude. In the early 1950s, their communities were raided and their children forced to live in a residential school where they were forbidden to speak Russian and were subjected to all manner of physical and sexual abuse. In 2005, these now-adult children applied to bring a class action suit against the B.C. government, demanding an apology and recompense for the abuse they had suffered in the school. However, this quest for justice and reconciliation ultimately failed.

Changing in compliance with the law

Rather than violently or passively resisting the law, some minority religions have taken the option of changing their beliefs or practices in compliance with the law. In 1890, ten years after publicly announcing and defending the practice of polygamy, the main branch of the Church of Jesus Christ of Latter-day Saints officially reversed its position (which had been ruled unlawful in Utah and other US states in 1862) and instead promoted the nuclear family (Van Wagoner 1986). Not all members of the Church agreed to the change, however, and numerous small groups have continued the practice in defiance of the law, generally living in small communities withdrawing from the rest of society to a greater or lesser degree (Bradley 2002).

The Children of God, later known as The Family International, was founded by David Berg (1919–1994) as part of the Californian Jesus movement in the late 1960s. From the mid-1970s, 'Flirty Fishers' followed Berg's interpretation of 'the Law of Love' by celebrating free sex between consenting adults as one of its methods of attracting men in clubs to become members of (or give financial support to) the movement (Williams 1998). Sexual experimentation was encouraged among children, and there were several instances of adults taking advantage of children. Such practices attracted widespread publicity and, although they were officially forbidden by the movement by the late 1980s, a woman, whose pregnant daughter was a member of the movement, went to court seeking custody of her infant grandchild on the grounds that the movement was an unsafe environment for the child. Following one of the longest English Family Court cases, during which Berg died, Lord Justice Ward ruled that the leaders had to denounce David Berg:

> They must acknowledge that through his writings he was personally responsible for children in The Family having been subjected to sexually inappropriate behaviour; that it is now recognized that it was not just a mistake to have written as he did, but wrong to have done so; and that as a result children have been harmed by their experiences.
>
> (Ward 1995: 293–4)

Peter Amsterdam, on behalf of the movement's leadership, promised to comply with the Judge's ruling, denounced some of Berg's teachings and apologised for mistakes of the past. In the concluding paragraph of his response to the Judge, he wrote:

> I conclude by acknowledging that we have learned a great deal from these proceedings...We are also appreciative that these hearings have underscored a number of areas in which the Family has needed to adopt different approaches towards our interaction with and understanding of society at large. We have undertaken to do this very determinedly, and have admitted to past mistakes and oversights on our part.
>
> (Amsterdam 1995)

Subject to a number of conditions, the mother was allowed to keep her child; several safeguarding policies were introduced and multiple public apologies were offered. The movement also became far more open to public scrutiny than had previously been the case (Barker 2016: 417–8).

Another example of adjusting to the law was evidenced in June 2012, when the Preston Down Trust (PDT) of the Plymouth Brethren Christian Church (PBCC), frequently referred to as the Exclusive Brethren, was refused charitable status on the grounds that it had not demonstrated that it was 'established for the public benefit'. After a protracted period of evidence gathering and exchanges between the lawyers, the PBCC succeeded in persuading the commissioners that: "The PBCC acknowledged past mistakes, demonstrated a willingness to make amends and proposed to address these issues by amending its trust deed, clearly setting out its doctrine and practices, including highlighting the concept of showing compassion to others" (Charity Commission 2014: para 16). The PDT was granted charitable status, as were around 100 other PBCC Trusts, on 'probationary' terms. Two years later, a Case Report stated that no further complaints had been received about the PDT and concluded that it had complied with the Commission's requirements. The Report included a section entitled "Lessons for other charities".[26]

Re-presentation of self

Migration to a new jurisdiction, whether to escape the laws of its country of origin or to carry out missionary work, does mean that a minority religion may have to re-present itself in order to be acceptable in the new surroundings. When the Children of God were 'litnessing'[27] throughout the world, they had, for example, to change illustrations to their literature showing scantily clad people to representations that would not offend against Islamic law. In his chapter, Masato Kato shows how, in order to keep a low profile in France, where *les sectes* have received a certain amount of unwelcome attention (Palmer 2011), the Japanese religion, Tenrikyō, established two legally separate institutions: their 'cultural association' catered to a growing French interest in Japanese language and culture and could serve as a way of meeting people and discreetly introducing them to their more low-key 'religious organisation'.

Aum Shinrikyo has already been mentioned as a religion associated with violence. Rin Ushiyama describes how, after its leader Asahara and other members were arrested for the release of sarin gas in the Tokyo underground in 1995, the movement re-presented itself by renaming itself as Aleph, still worshipping Asahara as a spiritual leader, but eschewing any kind of violence. It then split to form a new movement, Hikari no Wa, that seeks to distance itself from Aum Shinrikyo's past. Ushiyama's chapter elucidates how both groups have relied on civil lawsuits to challenge issues which they perceive to be illegal as they have developed, in their separate ways, in reaction to the legal consequences of Aum Shinrikyo's history.

Some ingenious re-presentations of minority religions have been manifesting themselves in China in recent years. For example, a temple built as a Buddhist place of worship with private funds was refused a religious venue registration certificate. The owner replaced the statues of deities with those of revolutionary leaders. The local Religious Affairs Bureau consequently designated the temple a 'red patriotic education base', and now "Party followers are swarming to the 'Chairman Mao Buddha Temple' to pray and worship" (Li 2019). Another innovator, fearing his temple would be closed or even demolished, installed statues of Mao Zedong, Zhou Enlai and Zhu De and had slogans promoting the core socialist values written on the walls of his temple. Not only was the temple allowed to stay open, the local government officials praised the director for "doing a good job" (Xin 2020).

Another way in which minority religions have reacted to the law by re-presenting themselves is simply by changing their name. Indeed, many new religions have taken on new names in order to disassociate themselves from a past that has met with legal or social disapproval. The Children of God started as 'Teens for Christ', became The Family of Love', then 'the Love Family', then simply 'The Family' then, finally, 'The Family International'. When the UK government banned the Islamist movement, Al-Muhajiroun, under its 2000 Terrorism Act, which gave the Home Secretary the right to proscribe an organisation if he believed it was concerned in terrorism, the official list of proscribed organisations, includes the following note:

> The Government laid Orders, in January 2010 and November 2011, which provide that "Al Muhajiroun", "Islam4UK", "Call to Submission", "Islamic Path", "London School of Sharia" and "Muslims Against Crusades" should be treated as alternative names for the organisation which is already proscribed under the names **Al Ghurabaa** and **The Saved Sect**. The Government laid an Order, in June 2014 recognising "Need4Khilafah", the "Shariah Project" and the "Islamic Dawah Association" as the same as the organisation proscribed as **Al Ghurabaa** and **The Saved Sect**, which is also known as **"Al Muhajiroun"**.
>
> (Home Office 2020: 8, *bold in original*)

Mobilising the law

Rather than challenging the law in order to change it (as we saw in the cases of the Jehovah's Witnesses and Scientologists), minority religions sometimes pro-actively take advantage of its existence by using it as a tool for their own, internal objectives. Michael Mickler's chapter traces something of the many legal disputes involving the Unification Church, as both plaintiff and defence, since its foundation in Korea in 1954 by the Rev Sun Myung Moon, who was himself sent to prison on a number of occasions (Barker 1984, 2017). Following Moon's death, his widow, his eldest living son and his youngest son all claimed to have inherited his legacy: Mrs Moon, now declares herself to be the 'Only Begotten Daughter' and, having retained the largest membership, leads the Family Federation for World Peace and

Unification (FFWPU);[28] the eldest son, Preston, whom his followers believe to be 'the Fourth Adam', leads the Global Peace Foundation (GPF);[29] and the youngest son, Sean, whose followers refer to as 'The King', leads the Sanctuary Church.[30] From the perspective of a senior member of the FF-WPU, Mickler reports on the use the movement has been making of the law in attempts to resolve family disagreements over the rightful ownership of the organisations' not inconsiderable assets.[31]

Peter Zoehrer, a long-term Austrian member of the FFWPU, describes how, having been deeply affected by the fact that Moon had been placed on a blacklist of undesirable foreign nationals for most European countries, he determined to devote himself to the cause of the religious rights of not only the Unification Church but also other minority religions throughout the world. And, indeed, Rev Moon was removed from the blacklist, the Unification Church was officially recognised as a confessional community, and Zoehrer was largely responsible for what is now an international human rights organisation, the Forum for Religious Freedom – Europe (FOREF).

Eliciting support

There are many reasons why minority religions frequently fail to get the better of the law. One is their lack of social standing; another is their lack of legal knowledge. In her chapter, Effie Fokas writes about a study in which she and her colleagues researched reactions amongst religious minorities concerning religion-related issues at the European Court of Human Rights. Despite the Court's record of defending religious minority rights, the research revealed significantly low levels of awareness of the relevant case law to be found amongst grassroots-level religious minorities.

Zoehrer may have been the prime impetus for the creation of FOREF, but he could not have managed it alone. His chapter shows how dependent he was on the cooperation of other individuals and organisations that were no part of the Unification Church. James Richardson's theoretically oriented final chapter introduces a discussion of 'cause lawyering', which provides one explanation of how some minority religions have been able to attract the assistance they need to function within various legal systems. Richardson describes how minority religions with a low standing in society and few contacts with decision-makers are at considerable disadvantage when involved in court cases. One source of support is for the religion to reach out to 'third-party participants' who can help by offering behind-the-scenes advice, making public statements on the religion's behalf and/or filing *amicus* briefs as a 'friend of the court' (Van den Eynde 2013). The Unification Church is but one of many minority religions that have wooed non-members to support their cause. When Moon was convicted in 1984 for filing false tax returns, "more than 40 *amica curiae* briefs were filed in the Moon appeal case alone ... combined, the briefs represented the voices of some 160 million Americans" (Sherwood 1991: 379). Among those organisations that submitted a brief were the American Civil Liberties Union, the American Baptist Churches in the USA, the National Council of Churches and the National Black Catholic Clergy Caucus (Robbins 1985: 245).

The Baha'i International Community has coordinated numerous campaigns on behalf of particular issues or concerns.[32] With representatives working in the UN and through collaboration with other bodies,[33] it has been successful in invoking an international reaction to its plight in Iran, eliciting the support of various governments and human rights organisations.[34] At the time of writing, the Korean religion, Shincheonji, has successfully been garnering support in the face of official enquiries into its alleged responsibility for spreading the COVID-19 virus (Introvigne et al. 2020).[35]

Massimo Introvigne and Rosita Šorytė, who have between them legal, sociological and diplomatic backgrounds and a wealth of experience in human rights activism, illustrate in their chapter the ways in which The Church of Almighty God (CAG) has turned to lawyers, scholars and human rights activists willing to help its members who have escaped from China to obtain asylum elsewhere. They also point out that CAG has cooperated with other persecuted minorities such as Falun Gong, Uyghur Muslims, Tibetan Buddhists and Protestant House Churches in their advocacy of democracy and human rights.

By far, the most visible, vocal and indefatigable opponent of not only the laws affecting *xie jiao,* but also the entire Chinese Communist Party (CCP) is Falun Gong (*The Epoch Times* 2004; Fisher 2003; Langone 2007; Palmer 2008; Tong 2009). It has lobbied throughout the world for international condemnation of the CCP's practices, forging personal contacts with influential sympathisers and employing street demonstrations and its various media outlets to spread its message.[36] The Australian Broadcasting Corporation has suggested that its Epoch Media Group has spent $millions supporting Donald Trump,[37] something that Falun Gong denies.[38] Perhaps most notably it has disseminated information and encouraged enquiries into 'organ harvesting', which they allege has involved tens of thousands of their imprisoned members having organs removed for purposes of transplantation.[39] In its 562-page judgement, an independent Tribunal chaired by Sir Geoffrey Nice QC declared itself satisfied that: "In the long-term practice in the PRC of forced organ harvesting it was indeed Falun Gong practitioners who were used as a source – probably the principal source – of organs for forced organ harvesting"' (Nice et al. 2020: 151).

Less gruesome than the gory street simulations of Falun Gong practitioners having their organs removed[40] are the truly spectacular international performances of its ballet company, Shen Yun,[41] which incorporate information designed to elicit support from a worldwide audience against the CCP.[42]

Figure 1.2 Falun Gong practitioners in Hong Kong do a mock forced organ harvest. (Photograph courtesy of Cory Doctorow via Flicker/CC BY 2.0)

Concluding remarks

A number of headings have been employed in this introduction. These should not be taken as in any way finite. Not only would many minority religions' reactions to the law fit under two or more of the headings, the same religion is likely to react in different ways in different jurisdictions in different countries at different times.

This volume too can offer no more than an all-too-brief introduction to the variety of reactions to the law that have been made by minority religions. It would be impossible to cover every aspect of the topic. Regions such as Africa and Latin America have been all but ignored; the international human rights work based at the Brigham Young University's J. Reuben Clark Law School by members of the Church of Jesus Christ of Latter-day Saints has not been touched upon;[43] then there is the role played by NGOs sponsored by minority religions that work in the field (Van den Eynde 2017), countering the suffering and persecution brought on by laws enacted by self-serving politicians (or the lack of laws protecting the vulnerable) – all such responses to legislation deserve to have further volumes dedicated to them.

Furthermore, there is still much that could be written about the dialectical dynamics of the reactions, and reactions to the reactions, of both 'sides'; and more needs to be written on how different sections of society (the economy, the polity, welfare provision, policing, etc.) react to the different responses of the religions. Despite the volume's inevitable limitations, however, it is hoped that the following chapters will offer many an insightful glimpse into some of the many ways in which minority religions respond to the legal environments within which they find themselves – ways in which they might fight, take flight or freeze.

Notes

1 www.routledge.com/Routledge-Inform-Series-on-Minority-Religions-and-Spiritual-Movements/book-series/AINFORM
2 Those who are interested in the differences between the three moments can refer to Vonck (2017), in which representatives of all three Unification movements make substantial contributions.
3 Counting the actual number in existence at any one time is well-nigh impossible, not least because of the problems of definition. It is, however, conceivable that the number could be far higher than often assumed. See Barker (1989: 148–55).
4 This was well before the release of deadly sarin gas in the Tokyo underground in 1995.
5 Netflix, 2018 www.netflix.com/title/80145240
6 Exodus 20: 13 KJV.
7 www.quaker.org.uk/resources/exhibitions/conscription; www.jw.org/en/library/magazines/g201307/is-protest-the-answer/
8 https://encyclopedia.ushmm.org/content/en/article/nazi-persecution-of-jehovahs-witnesses
9 www.hrw.org/news/2017/04/20/russia-court-bans-jehovahs-witnesses
10 hwww.duihuahrjournal.org/2020/05/detailed-court-statistics-on-article-300.html; www.duihuahrjournal.org/2020/06/detailed-court-statistics-on-article.html; www.duihuaresearch.org/2014/07/identifying-cult-organizations-in-china.html.
11 https://bitterwinter.org/attack-on-the-association-of-disciples-329-members-arrested/; www.refworld.org/docid/5a09b3520.html
12 Personal communications.
13 https://faluninfo.net/video/100-million-people-targeted-persecution/ @ 09.21
14 https://iskconnews.org/new-book-tells-incredible-history-of-soviet-era-iskcon-heroes,6141/
15 http://tcjonline.org/40-children-taken-from-christian-community-after-massive-german-police-raid/
16 www.refworld.org/pdfid/49b920582.pdf
17 www.hrw.org/news/2018/06/28/pakistan-ensure-ahmadi-voting-rights#
18 See also www.bic.org/focus-areas/situation-iranian-bahais/current-situation
19 https://sensday.wordpress.com/2020/06/16/in-shiraz-the-trial-of-26-bahais-begins-and-is-adjourned/
20 https: //hrwf.eu/why-a-2010-echr-ruling-jehovahs-witnesses-in-moscow-v-russia-is-relevant-now/
21 https: //eng.lsm.lv/article/society/society/worlds-tastiest-religion-refused-official-recognition-in-latvia.a206146/
22 www.google.com/search?sxsrf=ALeKk01_dTInr94skYQUFh-5YJfFwnzRzQ:1592744166647&source=univ&tbm=isch&q=pastafarian+colander&sa=X&ved=2ahUKEwjClpWy-pLqAhWSQ0EAHYX3A5IQsAR6BAgIEAE&biw=1536&bih=754
23 www.bbc.co.uk/news/uk-38368526
24 https: //psmag.com/economics/the-jedi-faithful
25 www.jns.org/we-will-not-change-nation-state-law-justice-minister-tells-druze/
26 https: //assets.publishing.service.gov.uk/government/uploads/system/uploads/attachment_data/file/846858/preston_down_trust_case_report_withdrawn.pdf
27 A combination of witnessing and distributing their literature.
28 http: //familyfed.org/
29 www.globalpeace.org/media-gallery/detail/5686/13208
30 www.sanctuary-pa.org/

31 .For an insight into the perspective of the GPA see Kwak (2019) and www.facebook.com/ProtectTheRightToBelieve/videos/285070722831501; and, for the perspective of the Sanctuary Church, see Moon (2018).
32 www.bic.org/global-campaigns-coordinated-bahai-international-community
33 www.bic.org/about/about-us#representatives
34 www.bic.org/focus-areas/situation-iranian-bahais/united-nations-documents-referencing-bahai-community; www.bic.org/focus-areas/human-rights; www.bic.org/about/about-us#representatives; www.bic.org/news/iranian-bahais-face-widespread-and-entrenched-discrimination-says-un-committee-0#Mml54pcz 94uFdlKM.97
35 https://news.thevoicebw.com/religious-leaders-defend-shincheonji-church-founder/;
36 www.theepochtimes.com/; http: //fofg.org/; https: //en.minghui.org/; https://faluninfo.net/over-600-lawmakers-from-30-countries-call-for-the-immediate-end-to-the-chinese-regimes-21-year-systematic-and-brutal-persecution-of-falun-gong/?utm_source=News&utm_campaign=0a69ffff4c-EMAIL_CAMPAIGN_ 2020_07_19_09_05&utm_medium=email&utm_term=0_480b7a73c3-0a69ff ff4c-8379561
37 www.youtube.com/watch?v=QzlMQyM8p74&feature=share@23.32ff; www.abc.net.au/news/2020-07-21/inside-falun-gong-master-li-hongzhi-the-mountain-dragon-springs/12442518?nw=0;
38 https://tvblackbox.com.au/page/2020/07/25/abc-responds-to-claims-of-influence-in-falun-gong-reporting/
39 https://faluninfo.net/forced-organ-harvesting-in-china-falun-gong/
40 www.en.minghui.org/emh/article_images/2006-9-27-carally-02.jpg
41 https: //web.archive.org/web/20161217013041/www.shenyunperformingarts.org/
42 www.youtube.com/watch?v=e8tpzgaZyzg: https: //web.archive.org/web/2016120 4231428/; www.shenyunperformingarts.org/spirituality/challenges-we-face
43 https://law.byu.edu/

References

Allen, Tim, and Koen Vlassenroot (eds). 2010. *The Lord's Resistance Army: Myth and Reality.* London: Zed Books.

Amsterdam, Peter. 1995. World Service's Response to Mr Justice Ward. September. https://media.xfamily.org/docs/fam/gn/gn-653.pdf

Bader, Eleanor J., and Patricia Baird-Windle. 2001. *Targets of Hatred: Anti-Abortion Terrorism.* New York: Palgrave Macmillan.

Barker, Eileen. 2017. The Unification Church: A Kaleidoscopic Introduction, in: Chris Vonck (ed.) *The Life and Legacy of Sun Myung Moon and the Unification Movements in Scholarly Perspective*, Special Issue, *Acta Comparanda, Subsidia* Volume VI, Faculty for Comparative Study of Religions and Humanism. Antwerp, Belgium: Wilrijk, pp. 19–55.

———. 2016. From the Children of God to The Family International: A Story of Radical Christianity and Deradicalising Transformation, in: Stephen Hunt (ed.) *The Handbook of Contemporary Christianity: Movements, Institutions & Allegiance.* Leiden: Brill, pp. 402–21.

———. 2010. Misconceptions of the Religious 'Other': The Importance for Human Rights of Objective and Balanced Knowledge. *International Journal for the Study of New Religions* 1(1): 5–25.

———. 2004. Why the Cults? New Religions and Freedom of Religion and Beliefs, in: Tore Lindholm, W. Cole Durham, and Bahia G. Tahzib-Lie (eds), *Facilitating*

Freedom of Religion or Belief: A Deskbook. Leiden, The Netherlands: Koninklijke Brill, pp. 571–93.

———. 1989. *New Religious Movements: A Practical Introduction*. London: HMSO.

———. 1984. *The Making of a Moonie: Brainwashing or Choice?* Oxford: Basil Blackwell.

Bielefeldt, Heiner. 2012. "Freedom of Religion or Belief: A Human Right under Pressure." *Oxford Journal of Law and Religion* 1(1): 15–35.

Bourdeaux, Michael. 1990. *Gorbachev, Glasnost and the Bible*. London: Hodder & Stoughton.

Boyette, Michael, and Randi Boyette. 2013 (1st edition 1989). *Let It Burn: MOVE, the Philadelphia Police Department, and the Confrontation that Changed a City*. San Diego, CA: Endpapers Press.

Bradley, Martha Sonntag. 2002. Polygamy-Practicing Mormons, in: J. Gordon Melton and Martin Baumann (eds.) *Religions of the World: A Comprehensive Encyclopedia of Beliefs and Practices* Volume 3. Santa Barbara: ABC CLIO, pp. 1023–4.

Cardin, Paul. 1998. Cults and New Religious Movements in the Former Soviet Union. *East-West Church & Ministry Report* 6(3): 1–5. https://eastwest report.org/articles/ew06301.htm

Carter, Lewis F. 1990. *Charisma and Control in Rajneeshpuram: The Role of Shared Values in the Creation of a Community*. Cambridge: Cambridge University Press.

Charity Commission for England and Wales. 2014, 3 January. *Summary of the Decision of the Charity Commission for England and Wales: Application for Registration as a Charity by the Preston Down Trust*. London. https://web archive.nationalarchives.gov.uk/20140506012144/http://www.charity commission.gov.uk/media/591725/preston_down_trust_summary_decision.pdf

Dawson, Andrew (forthcoming). Santo Daime: Work in Progress, in: Eileen Barker and Beth Singler (eds) *Radical Changes in Minority Religions*. Abingdon, Oxon: Routledge.

Duquesne, Antoine, and Luc Willems. 1997. *Enquete Parlementaire visant à élaborer une politique en vue de lutter contre les pratiques illégales des sectes et le danger qu'elles représentent pour la société et pour les personnes, particulièrement les mineurs d'âge*. Brussels: Belgian House of Representatives.

Durham, W. Cole, and Silvio Ferrari (eds). 2004. *Laws on Religion and the State in Post-Communist Europe*. Leuven: Peters.

Durham, W. Cole, and Brett G. Scharffs. 2019. *Law and Religion: National, International and Comparative Perspectives* (2nd edition). New York: Wolters Kluwer.

Epoch Times, The 2004. *Nine Commentaries on the Communist Party*. New York: The Epoch Times.

FIDH. August, 2003. *Discrimination against religious minorities in IRAN*. Paris: Report presented by the Fédération Internationale des Ligues des Droits de l'Homme and the Ligue de Défense des Droits de l'Homme en Iran. www.fidh. org/IMG/pdf/ir0108a.pdf

Fisher, Gareth. 2003. Resistance and Salvation in Falun Gong: The Promise and the Peril of Forbearance. *Nova Religio* 6(2): 294–311.

Gray, Julian. 2019. *The Faith that Broke the Iron Curtain: The Czechoslovakia Mission under Communism*. Seoul: Family Federation for world Peace and Unification International Headquarters.

Haber, Roy. 2011. The Santo Daime Road to Seeking Religious Freedom in the USA, in: Beatriz C. Labate and Henrik Jungaberle (eds.) *The Internationalization of Ayahuasca*. Berlin: LIT Verlag, pp. 301–18.

Hall, John R. 2004 (1st edition 1987). *Gone from the Promised Land: Jonestown in American Cultural History*. New Brunswick, NJ: Transaction.

Hashim, Asad. 2017. Three Ahmadis sentenced to death for blasphemy. *Al Jazeera News* 12 October. www.aljazeera.com/news/2017/10/ahmadis-sentenced-death-blasphemy-171012081709423.html?utm_source=website&utm_medium=article_page&utm_campaign=read_more_links

Home Office. 2020. *Proscribed Terrorist Organisations*. London: Home Office. https://assets.publishing.service.gov.uk/government/uploads/system/uploads/attachment_data/file/869496/20200228_Proscription.pdf

Introvigne, Massimo. 2020a. If Your Religion is a Xie Jiao, You Go to Jail – But What Is a Xie Jiao? *Bitter Winter* 11 June. https://bitterwinter.org/what-is-a-xie-jiao/

———. 2020b. *Inside the Church of Almighty God: The Most Persecuted Religious Movement in China*. Oxford: Oxford University Press.

Introvigne, Massimo, Willy Fautré, Rosita Šorytė, Alessandro Amicarelli, and Marco Respinti. 2020. Shincheonji and the COVID-19 Epidemic: Sorting Fact from Fictio. *The Journal of CESNUR* 4(3):70–86. https://cesnur.net/wp-content/uploads/2020/05/tjoc_4_3_5_corona.pdf.

Irons, Edward A. 2018. The List: The Evolution of China's List of Illegal and Evil Cults. *The Journal of CESNUR* 2(1): 33–57. https://cesnur.net/wp-content/uploads/2018/02/tjoc_2_1_3_irons.pdf.

Jefferis, Jennifer. 2011. *Armed for Life: The Army of God and Anti-Abortion Terror in the United States*. Santa Barbara, CA: Praeger.

Juergensmeyer, Mark. 2004. *Terror in the Mind of God: The Global Rise of Religious Violence*. Berkeley, CA: University of California Press.

King, Christine. 1982. *The Nazi State and the Nazi New Religions*. New York & Toronto: Edwin Mellen Press.

Kirkham, David M. (ed.). 2013. *State Responses to Minority Religions*. Aldershot: Ashgate.

Kwak, Chung Hwan. 2019. *Truth Shall Prevail: Understanding the Conflict Within the Unification Movement and Its Resolution*. Kindle edition.

Langone, Michael D. 2007. The PRC and the Falun Gong. *Cultic Studies Review. An Internet Journal of Research, News and Opinion* 6(3): 235–85.

L'Heureux, N. L., Irving Sarnoff, Joël Labruyère, Gabrielle Yonan, Robert Hostetter and Philippe Gast. 2000. *Report on Discrimination Against Spiritual and Therapeutical Minorities in France*. Paris: Coordination des Associations et Particuliers Pour la Liberté de Conscience.

Li, Guang. 2019. Mao Zedong Worshipped as Buddha. *Bitter Winter* 19 May. https://bitterwinter.org/mao-zedong-worshipped-as-buddha/

Moon, Hyung Jin Sean. 2018. *Rod of Iron Kingdom*. Newfoundland, PA: Rod of Iron Ministries.

Moore, Rebecca. 2009. *Understanding Jonestown and Peoples Temple*. Westport, CT: Praeger.

Morantz, Paul c. 2009. *The True Story of the Rattlesnake in the Mailbox*. www.paulmorantz.com/the_synanon_story/the-true-story-of-the-rattlesnake-in-the-mailbox/.

Nice, Sir Geoffrey, QC, et al. 2020, March 1. *The Independent Tribunal into Forced Organ Harvesting from Prisoners of Conscience in China:* JUDGMENT. https://chinatribunal.com/wp-content/uploads/2020/03/ChinaTribunal_JUDGMENT_1stMarch_2020.pdf

Palmer, David A. 2008. Heretical Doctrines, Reactionary Secret Societies, Evil Cults: Labelling Heterodoxy in 20th-Centruy China, in: Mayfair Yang (ed.) *Chinese Religiosities: The Vicissitudes of Modernity and State Formation.* Berkeley: University of California Press, pp. 113–34.

Palmer, Susan. 2011. *The New Heretics of France.* Oxford: Oxford University Press.

Pilkington, Ed. 2018. "This Is Huge": Black Liberationist Speaks Out after Her 40 Years in Prison. *The Guardian* 18 June. www.theguardian.com/us-news/2018/jun/18/debbie-sims-africa-free-prison-move-nine-philadelphia-police.

Prakash, Arun. 2014. Persecution: 6 Years 7 Months 4 Days. *PROUT* 25(6): 19–26. https://anandamarga.org/pdf/news/south-asia/prout/ProutJune2014.pdf.

Pranskevičiūtė-Amoson, Rasa, and Tadas Juras. 2014. Acting in the Underground: Life as a Hare Krishna Devotee in the Soviet Republic of Lithuania (1979–1989). *Religion and Society in Central and Eastern Europe* 7(1): 9–21.

Reader, Ian. 2000. *Religious Violence in Contemporary Japan: The Case of Aum Shinrikyo.* Richmond, Surrey: Curzon.

Richardson, James T. 2017. Update on Jehovah's Witness Cases before the European Court of Human Rights: Implications of a Surprising Partnership. *Religion, State & Society* 45(3–4): 232–48.

——— (ed.). 2004. *Regulating Religion: Case Studies from around the Globe.* New York & Dordrecht: Kluwer Academic/Plenum.

———. 2001. Minority Religions and the Context of Violence: A Conflict/Interactions Perspective. *Terrorism and Political Violence* 13(1): 103–33.

——— and François Bellanger (eds.) 2014. *Legal Cases, New Religious Movements, and Minority Faiths.* Aldershot: Ashgate.

——— and Jennifer Shoemaker. 2014. The Resurrection of Religion in America? The 'Tea' Cases, the Religious Freedom Restoration Act, and the War on Drugs, in: James T. Richardson and Francois Bellanger (eds.), *Legal Cases, New Religious Movements, and Minority Faiths.* London: Ashgate, pp. 71–88.

Ridgeway, James. 1990. *Blood in the Face: The Ku Klux Klan, Aryan Nations, Nazi Skinheads, and the Rise of a New White Culture.* New York: Thunder's Mouth Press.

Robbins, Thomas. 1985. Government Regulatory Powers and Church Autonomy: Deviant Groups as Test Cases." *Journal for the Scientific Study of Religion* 24(3): 237–52.

Roy, Olivier. 2017. *Jihad and Death: The Global Appeal of Islamic State.* London: Hurst & Company.

Salusinszky, Imre. 2019. *The Hilton Bombing: Evan Pederick and the Ananda Marga.* Carlton, Victoria, Australia: Melbourne University Press.

Sandberg, Russell. 2014. *Religion, Law and Society.* Cambridge: Cambridge University Press.

Sherwood, Carlton. 1991. *Inquisition: The Persecution and Prosecution of the Reverend Sun Myung Moon.* Washington, DC: Regnery Gateway.

Tabor, James D. and Eugene V. Gallagher. 1995. *Why Waco? Cults and the Battle for Religious Freedom in America.* Berkeley: University of California Press.

The Epoch Times. 2004. *Nine Commentaries on the Communist Party*. New York: The Epoch Times.

Thurston, Alexander. 2018. *Boko Haram: The History of an African Jihadist Movement*. Princeton, NJ: Princeton University Press.

Tong, James. 2009. *Revenge of the Forbidden City: The Suppression of the Falun Gong in China, 1999–2005*. Oxford: Oxford University Press.

Twelve Tribes (ed.). 2014. *When Spanking Stopped: All Hell Broke Loose*. Hiddenite, NC: Parchment Press.

Van den Eynde, Laura. 2017. Encouraging Judicial Dialogue: The Contribution of Human Rights NGOs' Briefs to the European Court of Human Rights, in: Amrei Müller (ed.) *Judicial Dialogue and Human Rights*. Cambridge: Cambridge University Press, pp. 339–400.

———. 2013. An Empirical Look at the Amicus Curiae Practice of Human Rights NGO before the European Court of Human Rights. *Netherlands Quarterly of Human Rights* 31(3): 271–313.

Van Wagoner, Richard S. 1986. *Mormon Polygamy: A History*. Salt Lake City, UT: Signature.

Vivien, Alain. 1995. *Les Sectes en France: Expression de la Liberté*. Paris: La Documentation Française.

Vonck, Chris (ed.). 2017. *The Life and Legacy of Sun Myung Moon and the Unification Movements in Scholarly Perspective*, Special Issue, *Acta Comparanda, Subsidia* Volume VI, Faculty for Comparative Study of Religions and Humanism. Antwerp, Belgium: Wilrijk.

Wang, Ray. 2019. *Resistance under Communist China: Religious Protestors, Advocates and Opportunists*. Cham, Switzerland: Palgrave Macmillan.

———. 2018. Authoritarian Resilience versus Everyday Resistance: The Unexpected Strength of Religious Advocacy in Promoting Transnational Activism in China. *Journal for the Scientific Study of Religion* 56(3): 558–76.

Ward, Alan. 1995. Judgement of Lord Justice Ward in the matter of ST (a minor). W 42 1992 in The High Court of Justice Family Division 19 October. London.

Wessinger, Catherine. 2017. The FBI's "Cult War" against the Branch Davidian, in Sylvester A. Johnson and Steven Weitzman (eds.) *The FBI and Religion: Faith and National Security before and after 9/11*. Berkeley, CA: University of California Press, pp. 324–321.

Williams, Miriam. 1998. *Heaven's Harlots: My Fifteen Years as a Sacred Prostitute in the Children of God Cult*. New York: Eagle Brook.

Wright, Stuart. 2007. *Patriots, Politics and the Oklahoma City Bombing*. Cambridge: Cambridge University Press.

Xin, An. 2020. Chairman Mao Replaces Buddha in Temples. *Bitter Winter* 3 July. https://bitterwinter.org/chairman-mao-replaces-buddha-in-temples/

Yang, Fenggang. 2017. From Cooperation to Resistance: Christian Responses to Intensified Suppression in China Today. *The Review of Faith & International Affairs* 15(1): 79–90.

———. 2006. The Red, Black, and Gray Markets of Religion in China. *The Sociological Quarter* 47, 93–122.

2 Stand up for your rights

(Minority) religions' reactions to the law in Estonia

Ringo Ringvee

Introduction

The freedom of religion or belief is stipulated in the 1992 Constitution and further guaranteed and protected by different legal acts. The Churches and Congregations Act sets the legal framework for religious associations as legal entities. The first Churches and Congregations Act was adopted in 1993, and it reflected the neoliberal aspiration for individual freedom and optimistic faith in the free market and freedom to choose (Ringvee 2013).

Religious entities are equal before the law and have all same exceptions and privileges with no distinction based on historical presence, impact on culture or membership numbers. The path that was set in the early 1990s continued in the current Churches and Congregations Act and approved in 2002. It can be argued that with freedom of religion or belief, Estonia does well, and these freedoms are followed both in legislation and in practice. This, however, does not mean that there have not been problems related to *forum externum* of religious freedom. In cases of violation of freedom of religion or belief, an individual or a collective may turn for relief to governmental ministries and agencies, the Chancellor of Justice, the courts and, finally, to the European Court of Human Rights.

There have been a few court cases regarding religious practices in prison environments, mostly about religious diet and burning of incense in prison cells (Ringvee 2020). Besides court cases, there also has been involvement by the Chancellor of Justice on questions of possible violation of constitutional rights. In Estonia, several possible problems regarding religious freedom were avoided in the drafting process of legislation by taking into account the particularities of various religious associations. At the same time, there has been a high sensitivity to possible violations of religious freedom. Presidents of the Republic have refused to accept that the Nonprofit Associations Act (1996) and the Churches and Congregations Act (2001–2002) violate the autonomy of religious associations.

The following cases are about religious minorities' involvement in the legislative process in Estonia. Included in historical order are discussions of the Jehovah's Witnesses, the association of Native Religions and the

Jewish community. These examples show that religious minorities have more success in cases where they *stand up for* their rights to practice their religion than when religious actors *stand against* some social or political changes that they consider to be against only their beliefs or values. The latter example is shown in the futile fight against gender neutral or same sex marriages. At the same time, the right for alternatives to compulsory military service in which the Jehovah's Witnesses could participate, or standing for the right to slaughter animals in a religiously prescribed manner for the Jewish community have been successful.

Jehovah's Witnesses

The Watchtower Bible and Tract Society started their activities in Estonia in 1926. In 1927, the Watchtower Society started to air multi-lingual radio programmes in Estonia. The weekly gatherings and discussions of themes of the Society's publication became established by 1931, and in 1934, the Watchtower Society was established as a legal entity. When the state of emergency was declared in 1934, censorship was enforced, and the Jehovah's Witnesses' radio programmes were cancelled and several of their publications were banned and confiscated. In 1935, the Watchtower Society was liquidated after being accused of being a danger to the interests of the Estonian state both internally and in foreign policy.

Although banned as an organization, the Jehovah's Witnesses were not persecuted and continued their work to a lesser extent during the following years. The Soviet occupation in 1940 forced core members of the Jehovah's Witnesses' organization with foreign citizenship to leave the country. The small community of Estonian Witnesses continued their activities on a smaller scale. The situation of Witnesses in Estonia changed in 1951 when the operation 'Sever' by the Soviet authorities targeted the Jehovah's Witnesses in all the new territories of the Soviet Union (western Ukraine and western Byelorussia, Bessarabia, and the Baltic States). In April 1951, altogether 8,576 Jehovah's Witnesses from these territories were deported to Siberia (Polian 2003, 169–71). Among them were 54 Estonian Witnesses with their 227 family members. The deported Witnesses had returned to Estonia by the 1960s, and this small community of Witnesses continued its activities underground until the reestablishment of Estonia's independence in 1991.

In the 1990s, Jehovah's Witnesses became one of the fastest growing religious movements in Estonia. In the late 1960s, there were around 60 Witnesses in Estonia, 1000 in the early 1990s and around 4,000 by the 2000s. After this rapid growth, the numbers of Jehovah's Witnesses have now stabilized in Estonia and, according to the official statistics of the Watch Tower Society, there were 4,036 'publishers'[1] and 6,265 attendees in the Memorial service in 2018 (Service Year Report 2019, 3).[2] According to available statistics, Jehovah's Witnesses are the fifth largest denomination in Estonia (Ringvee 2019).

Conscientious objection

The first issue that emerged for Estonian governmental agencies in its relations with Jehovah's Witnesses was conscientious objection. According to § 124 of the 1992 Estonian Constitution, conscientious objectors have to perform alternative service in accordance with the law. The first law to set a procedural framework for alternative service was the Military Service Act in 1994, three years after the restitution of Estonia as an independent state. The idea of what alternative service should be or look like was rather vague in the early 1990s Estonia. Persons who chose alternative service were required to prove or convince the Defence Forces Agency that the claims of the person were true. To be sure that a person who claimed to be a Jehovah's Witness was indeed a witness, communications between the Jehovah's Witnesses and Estonian Defence Forces started. The problem was that the 1994 Military Service Act understood alternative service as unarmed service at the Defence Forces premises, wearing uniform. The law did not provide alternative service suitable for the religious convictions of Jehovah's Witnesses. The first court case involving a person's refusal of both military service as well as the legally defined alternative service on religious grounds started in March 1996 and ended in August 1996 with a ruling from the Supreme Court. However, the sentence of five months of imprisonment was not enforced, and a year-long probation was set instead. On 1 May 1996, *The Watchtower* published an article, "Paying Back Caesar's Things to Caesar," explicitly arguing for performing alternative service in a civilian capacity (Jehovah's Witnesses 1996). In the early summer of 1996, Jehovah's Witnesses in Estonia started intense negotiations with the Ministry of Defence regarding alternative service in a non-military form, which were successful in allowing a form of alternative service acceptable to the Witnesses. In November, 12 Witnesses started their alternative service in Rescue Board (Vabar 1996), the approved service alternative. The current Military Service Act from 2012 in § 62 (1) now states:

> A person in alternative service shall not, against his will, be required to handle weapons or other means of warfare, practice the use thereof or participate in the maintenance thereof, or handle other means or substances which are intended for the extermination or injury of a person.

Blood transfusion

In July 1997, a newly born baby with a serious haemolytic disease died three days after birth in Tallinn children's hospital. Both parents had refused blood transfusion for the child. The medical personnel in the maternity hospital and then at the children's hospital were dealing for the first time with a situation where parents refused medical treatment. The mother of the child had refused the blood transfusion for religious reasons as a Jehovah's Witness, while father's refusal concerned the quality of the blood and security of the transfusion. The mother wrote a letter to the doctors in which she accepted all possible consequences of the decision not to allow transfusion of blood or blood components. In this situation, the medical personnel respected the parents' rights and the child died. The death of the child was followed by two court cases. The first was against eight doctors of the maternity hospital. The prosecutor withdrew the charges against the doctors in April 2010 with the conclusion that the doctors did not know what would have been the legally correct action. However, the parents were charged with negligent homicide. The court case was delayed due to new pregnancy of the charged mother. Her child was born in Sweden in January 2001, also having the haemolytic disease. This time, a blood transfusion was not used and the child survived. The defence team of the parents in the court included alongside an Estonian attorney of law a barrister, Richard Daniel, Daniel, retained by the Watch Tower's UK office (Väljaots 2001). In March 2001, the court made a decision and the parents were acquitted. In the decision, the court noted that there was no proof that the blood transfusion would have saved the child's life.

After the court's decision, a representative of the Jehovah's Witnesses' public relations commented that no Witness was going to reject their child because it had received a blood transfusion, but that the person concerned needed sympathy and attention. However, he stressed that "Nobody can deny us the freedom of speech, the right to say that I do not want this or that kind of treatment. It is a different thing if a doctor can accept my decision." A defence attorney for the parents noted that perhaps a process was needed that would allow the state to take steps to impose a temporary guardianship which would take the burden both from the doctors and from people with religious convictions (Kaljulaid 2001). And indeed, new legislation started to take into account patients' rights to decide on their medical treatment, and temporary or special guardianship became regulated.

The Law of Obligations Act, that passed Parliament in September 2001 and entered into force in July 2002, set in Chapter 41 the regulations for the contract for provision of health care services. In § 766, the Law of Obligations Act places a duty on the provider of health care services to inform patients and obtain their consent. In 2009, Parliament adopted a new Family Law Act that introduced the status of a special guardian to be appointed by the court "to a person under curatorship of a parent or to whom a guardian has been appointed for the act which cannot be performed by the parents or the guardian." Although the Act is meant for the administration of property, this provision also has important implications regarding medical treatment. From now on, a special guardian can be appointed for the performance of a single act only, meaning that parent's parental rights are not taken away entirely but suspended for the single act, after which the rights of special guardianship will terminate.

The native religions

The House of Taara and Native Religions is a religious association representing indigenous Estonian religious tradition. *Maausk*, the Estonian term for the Native Religion meaning Earth (or Land) religion or faith, is the indigenous world-view or world-understanding of the native Estonians as an ethnic group once divided into different tribes living on the southern corner of the Baltic Sea and Finnish Gulf for thousands of years.[3] Maausk as known today emerged in the late 1980s as part of a process of national reawakening. There were different groups of people who became interested in discovering and reviving the old Estonian religion and world-view and/ or the native Taara-religion of the 1920s and 1930s.[4] Among those groups interested in Estonians pre-Christian past in the late 1980s were students of folklore, ethnology and art, members of folklore choirs, activists of folklore movements and others. In 1995, the statute of the House of Taara and Native Religions (*Taarausuliste ja Maausuliste Maavalla Koda*) was registered in the Estonian churches and congregations register. The *Maavalla Koda* represented both Taara-religion and the *Maausk*-tradition and consisted of three local Houses (*Koda*). In the following years, three Taara-religion's religious associations, groves (*hiis*), became legal entities as religious associations as well (Figure 2.1).

Taara-religion in the first half of the twentieth century, as well as Maausk from the late 1980s onwards, confronted Christianity, which was and has been considered alien to Estonia by the followers of these two religions.

Figure 2.1 The Tamme-Lauri Oak is the largest, and one of the oldest, trees in Estonia. It is estimated that the tree started to grow in 1326. It is the only surviving tree of an oak grove, once used for the pre-Christian nature worship that was suppressed in the 18th century. The tree came under heritage protection in 1939. In 1992 it was depicted on the Estonian 10 *kroon* banknote (photograph courtesy of Marju Kõivupuu).

Maavalla Koda became a noticeable actor in the society from the late 1990s onwards through the critiques of governmental policies on religion that were perceived as favouring Christianity. This was particularly obvious in religious education in public schools, which has been an issue in Estonia since the 1920s, and it has been a subject of discussion and argument since the 1990s.

At the initiative of the *Maavalla Koda*, an informal entity called the Roundtable of Religious Associations (*Usuliste ühenduste ümarlaud*) was formed in 2001. The Roundtable included, besides *Maavalla Koda*, the Estonian Jewish Community, the congregation of Muslims, Baha'is, the International Society for Krishna Consciousness and two Buddhist congregations. The reason for the initiative was the new curriculum proposed for religious education public schools. Non-Christian traditions, especially *Maavalla Koda*, considered the curriculum to be Christianity-centred and thus problematic for other religious traditions than mainstream Christianity. Besides the discussions and debates regarding the position of religious education in Estonian schools, there were also other debates regarding the relations between the state and religious actors in 2001. Drafting of a new Churches and Congregations Act started formally in 1996 when the Parliament twice adopted the Non-Profit Associations Act, which the President of the Republic refused to accept. Finally, the decision of the Supreme Court led Parliament to remove articles that were thought to violate the autonomy of religious associations (Kiviorg 2011, 36–7; Ringvee 2012, 100–1).

After five years of effort, the draft of a new Churches and Congregations Act was presented in the Parliament in 2001. The drafting process had been long and included representatives from different religious associations, both Christian and others. The Parliament adopted the new Churches and Congregations Act in 2001. However, in the Parliament, a new paragraph was added to the text without any discussion with any religious actor that denied registration for a religious association whose administrative or economical decisions were made or confirmed by the association's higher bodies situated outside Estonia. The President of the Republic refused to declare the newly adopted Act as constitutional, and it was sent back to Parliament. While removing the controversial article, Parliament added a new provision that would have extended the range of subjects dealing with property reform of which only one religious association, the Estonian Evangelical Lutheran Church would have benefitted. The new version of the Act was adopted by Parliament, but again, the President of the Republic refused to accept it, considering the extension of range of subjects of property reform to be violating the equality principle of the Constitution.

Parliament removed the problematic paragraph and adopted the Act for the third time on 12 February 2002. Two days later, *Maavalla Koda* sent a letter to the President of the Republic asking him not to sign the adopted Churches and Congregations Act. According to *Maavalla Koda*, the requirement in paragraph seven to use the terms *kirik* (church), *kogudus* (congregation), *koguduste liit* (association of congregations) and *klooster* (monastery) in the official names of religious associations forced them to use the terms of another religious tradition, something that was unacceptable according to their religious tradition, and thus violating religious freedom principles.[5] This argument was repeated in an appeal to the President from the Roundtable of Religious Associations on 20 February 2002. *Maavalla Koda* had turned attention to this problematic use of fixed terms from one tradition already in 2000 in their letter to the Parliament's Justice Commission.[6] A week before the Act was adopted, *Maavalla Koda* asked the Justice Commission to halt the process with reference to the requirements to use terms 'congregation', 'association of congregations' or 'church' as the official names of religious associations. The Justice Commission declined their request. The chairman of the Justice Commission explained in his answer to *Maavalla Koda* the logic of the Act in which the terms 'church', 'congregation' and others were understood as neutral, technical terms. According to the concept of the law, there had to be a direct reference in the name of the association to the type of the association it belongs to, and it was concluded that to change this would create confusion.[7] The logic was derived from commercial law where the type of enterprise had to be mentioned by name. The President's Office replied to *Maavalla Koda* that their recommendations had been discussed but rejected, and the new Churches and Congregations Act was accepted by the President on 27 February 2002.

In May 2002, the *Maavalla Koda* asked the Chancellor of Justice to control the accordance of paragraphs 2, 7 and 11 of the Churches and Congregations Act with the Constitution and presented expert opinions from the University of Tartu and Institute of Estonian Language. The expert opinions supported *Maavalla Koda*'s claim that the terms 'church', 'congregation' and 'monastery' were derived from and connected to the Christian tradition. *Maavalla Koda* sent a notice to the Chancellor of Justice, stating that if the Act were not amended, their associations are going to be liquidated as they could neither define nor register themselves using the terms of another religious tradition. The request from *Maavalla Koda* resulted in consultations between the bureau of Chancellor of Justice and the religious affairs department at the Ministry of Interior. On 2 March 2003, there were parliamentary elections in Estonia, and a new Parliament was sworn in a month later.

The Chancellor of Justice was concerned about the violation of the constitutional rights of *Maavalla Koda*, while the religious affairs department had been critical of the initial amendment when it was originally introduced in Parliament. In June 2003, the Chancellor of Justice informed *Maavalla Koda* that it agreed with the Ministry of the Interior and would initiate a change to the 2002 Churches and Congregations Act to return it to the condition in which it had been before the change brought by the 2002 Churches and Congregations Act. The amendments regarding the mandatory use of the terms were drafted, and finally, in April 2004, the draft was discussed in the justice commission of the Parliament. The justice commission asked a representative from the Estonian Council of Churches to participate at the commission's session. There, the Council supported the possibility of using other historical terms in the name instead of church, congregation or monastery. Finally, on 28 June 2004, Parliament adopted the amendments to the Churches and Congregations Act, and the statute of *Maavalla Koda* was reregistered in the register of religious associations on 7 January 2005.

This amendment in the 2002 Churches and Congregations Act could be considered a quite substantial one. It restored the practice that was introduced in the 1993 Churches and Congregations Act, allowing religious associations to use their own terms in their names. The official standardization may be logically well justified, as exemplified in the Justice Commission's answer to *Maavalla Koda*, but this change may violate the realization of the freedom of religion or belief. The amendment of the 2002 Churches and Congregations Act did not completely restore the situation to what it had been before 2002, but retained a minor limitation on the use of terms by saying, 'A religions association may [...] use a corresponding own-designation in its name, if such a designation derives from the historically established practice of the religious association name-use.' The word 'historically' is debatable, however, because the 'historically established practice' derives from 1995 when the *Taarausuliste ja Maausuliste Maavalla Koda* statute was registered for the first time. In the 1920s and 1930s, Taara-religion used the term *hiis* (grove) for their religious associations, and this has remained the case with two independent Taara-religion associations.

Religious slaughter

The ritual slaughter of animals in accordance with religious regulations became an issue for the first time in the 1930s when the Animal Protection Society turned to the Supreme Court, applying for a ban on ritual slaughter of animals (Rohtmets 2018, 157–9). World War II and the subsequent Soviet occupation interrupted these discussions. Ritual slaughter was not mentioned in the Animal Protection Act that was adopted in 1992. For the first time, ritual slaughter was mentioned in the Animal Protection Act that was adopted in 2001; it allowed the slaughter of animals outside slaughterhouses for religious reasons. The process of slaughtering was regulated by government regulation, and the Veterinary and Food Board had to be informed. Also, there had to be an official of the Board present at the site. The reason for this regulation was the adoption of the EU Council's Directive 93/119/EC from 1993 on the protection of animals at the time of slaughter or killing during Estonia's accession period for membership in the European Union. In 2009, the Council's Regulation 1099/2009 replaced the previous directive, and in 2012, Estonia started to amend the Animal Protection Act and the changes to be adopted regulated animal testing and slaughter.

In the 1930s, the Animal Protection Society had been active in drafting a law for the protection of animals, a legal act that was never adopted. More than 80 years later, the situation regarding animal protection has changed considerably, and animal right groups and organizations have more influence. When the Ministry of Agriculture started drafting amendments regarding the Animal Protection Act in 2012, religious communities were neither informed nor involved in the process. The animal protection organizations, being more active in animal rights issues in general, had the opportunity to present input during the drafting process. The intended amendments that concerned religion, however, aimed to withdraw the possibility of slaughter prior to stunning with no exemptions.

In June 2011, the Minister of Agriculture sent the draft of the amendments for approval to the Ministry of Social Affairs, to the Ministry of Finance, to the Ministry of Environment and to the Ministry of Science and Education pursuant to the procedure. In the accompanying explanatory memorandum, it was explained that the animal protection organizations had stressed that the slaughtering of animals prior to stunning was prohibited in the member states of the European Union like Sweden, Luxembourg and the Netherlands, and also in Australia. The memorandum also referred to new scientific knowledge about animal suffering and the DiaRel report on religious slaughter (DialRel 2010). In addition to that, the explanatory memorandum noted that slaughtering prior to stunning was considered not to be important for religious communities as only two authorisations for such a type of slaughtering had been requested since 2001. The explanatory memorandum referred also to the Minister's negative response back in 2011 to an inquiry about establishing an industrial *halal* slaughterhouse in Estonia (Loomakaitseseaduse 2012). However, during the preliminary approval round, it was revealed that these amendments might affect some religious communities. Here, the Ministry of the Interior, responsible for matters related to religion and religious communities, stepped into the process.

The Ministry of the Interior did not approve the draft. According to an opinion from the Ministry of the Interior, the amendment on prohibiting slaughter prior to stunning violated the Constitutional principle of religious freedom as it was going to outlaw certain practices essential for some religious communities, referring to Jewish and Muslim religious communities, but also to the rights of followers of the indigenous religious tradition represented by *Maavalla Koda*. At this stage also, the religious communities were informed about the planned changes in the law. The Jewish community in Estonia expressed its concerns about the situation. At the same time, the international Jewish community became alarmed and reacted in the media, and negotiations between different interest groups began. These discussions included representatives from the Jewish and the Muslim communities as well as from the indigenous *Maavalla Koda*. The Jewish community had the leading role, and the attention in the Jewish press reflected the ongoing discussions in Europe regarding *shechita* slaughter. In 2012, Slovenia and the Netherlands had made legislative decisions regarding ritual slaughter. In the latter case, the legislative ban on slaughtering animals prior to stunning them had passed the House of Representatives in 2011 but did not pass the Senate.[8]

On 24 August 2012, the Ministry of Agriculture organized a roundtable meeting with all parties involved. Besides civil servants from the Ministry of Agriculture, the Ministry of the Interior, the Ministry of Food, the Veterinary and Food Board, academics from the University of Agriculture, representatives from the Estonian Animal Protection Union and the Estonian Animal Protection Society as well as representatives of the Jewish and Muslim communities and the indigenous *Maavalla Koda* were present. The aim of the meeting was to find a consensus between the different parties and interests. The outcome was realized in a new draft that respected freedom to practice religion by allowing slaughtering an animal before stunning. At the same time, the new draft required slaughter to take place in an official slaughterhouse with permission from the Veterinary and Food Board and that animal should be stunned 'immediately' after the cut. But what would 'immediately' mean in this context? The animal protection organization stance had been that 'immediately' would mean not more than five seconds. The proposal from the Jewish community extended the time from the cut to the stunning to 30 seconds and the Muslims proposed 40 seconds. *Maavalla Koda* considered that demand to stun animals at all violated tradition. The Estonian courts ruled that in practice 'immediately' has to be interpreted to mean 'as soon as possible.' In December 2012, Parliament adopted amendments to the Animal Protection Act including some affecting religious communities and associations.[9]

In 2012, slaughtering outside a slaughterhouse became unlawful although slaughtering an animal for religious reasons prior to stunning remained an option with mandatory post-cut stunning. According to the Act, the animal has to be stunned immediately after slaughtering, and the traditions of religious associations have to be respected. The explanatory memorandum to the amendments explains that 'immediately' in this context means 'as soon as possible' as it is understood in the Constitution and by the Supreme Court's rulings. The memorandum noted that stunning should not be postponed more than 40 seconds, referring to the Netherlands practice.[10]

Conclusion

The cases from Estonia show that minority religions' reactions to legislative changes need not be futile. This, however, does not mean that religious actors would be successful in every attempt to change or influence legislation. For example, in 2014, religious actors tried in vain to influence Parliament not to adopt the Registered Partnership Act that allows the registration of gender-neutral cohabitation. Reactions from the ecumenical Estonian Council of Churches, with separate statements from the Estonian Evangelical Lutheran Church, the Estonian Orthodox Church of Moscow Patriarchate, the Estonian Jewish Congregation and some smaller Christian Charismatic associations, did not succeed in derailing the adoption of the Act in the Parliament. When comparing the latter case with the success of the ones described above, it could be claimed that religious actors have more support and are more successful when lobbying for their rights than against these.

The religious minorities' strategies for achieving their goals have been different. The Jehovah's Witnesses' approach is probably the most distinctive, having on the one hand a very low-public profile, whilst on the other hand oriented effectively to problem solving through communication and through direct relations with governmental bodies. In this approach, the legal capacity available in the Jehovah's Witnesses local organization as well as legal help from abroad have been quite important in keeping the negotiations with governmental bodies on a professional level. At the same time, the issues that Jehovah's Witnesses have been concerned about have not been new or peculiar to Estonia, but in the cases of blood transfusion and conscientious objection, the Witnesses have had extensive experience elsewhere, although the final decision depended on political will within Estonia.

International mobilization of the Jewish community for the right to practice their religion has been important in recent decades, as it was in 2011 and 2012 when Parliamentary discussions on religious slaughter were debated in several European countries. In Estonia, the Animal Protection Act was going to be amended with a ban on slaughter, including religious slaughtering prior to stunning by referring to the EU directive on animal welfare. In the Estonian case, it should be noted that the reaction from the Jewish community was most vocal in protesting against the draft of the new legislation not because of a regular practice or actual need for *shechita* slaughtering in Estonia, but more on account of the principle being able to practice their religion. Although in the 2012 Act religious freedom for ritual slaughter triumphed over animal rights, the post-cut stunning exemption for religious reasons remains an issue that will be discussed again in the future.

The third case treated in this chapter illustrates the possibility of standing for religious freedom in Estonia beyond the negotiations taking place in political and governmental corridors. Pure ignorance of the part of lawmakers with no particular ill will could lead to a situation where the native or indigenous religious association *Maavalla Koda* turned to the Chancellor of Justice. The problem was the lawmakers' intention to connect the name of the association to the type of religious association by making the terms used in the Act a mandatory part of association's name. *Maavalla Koda* asked the Chancellor to issue an opinion as to whether the 2002 Churches and Congregations Act requirement to use term 'congregation', 'association of congregations', 'church' or 'monastery' in the official names was in compliance with the Estonian Constitution. At the same time, representatives of *Maavalla Koda* were vocal in the public arena, accusing the state of forcing a situation that would lead to their association's disestablishment. As a result of the interference of the Chancellor of Justice, the Churches and Congregations Act was amended in 2004 to allow the use of historical terminology.

Estonian cases where religious communities have stood for their rights and challenged the changes in legislation with success seem to be the result of several factors. Estonian legislation on religions is historically liberal. The legal framework is egalitarian, meaning that all religious associations are equal before the law. State neutrality has been governmental policy. In reality, some religious associations have more social capital than others, but religion has never been explicitly politicised. The normal state of affairs in Estonian society regarding religion and religious institutions is general indifference. Estonia seems to illustrate well John Stuart Mill's notion, "that religious freedom has hardly anywhere been practically realized, except where religious indifference, which dislikes to have its peace disturbed by theological quarrels, has added its weight to the scale" (Mill 2003, 79).

Notes

1 Publishers is the name given to those baptised Witnesses who participate in organized preaching activity. Only individuals who are approved and active as publishers are officially counted as members.

2 Although Jehovah's Witnesses do not celebrate Christmas and other days that they believe have Pagan origins, they do mark the death of Jesus with their annual Memorial Day service.

3 About *Maavalla Koda* www.maavald.ee/en/about-maavalla-koda, accessed 30 January 2020.

4 The first native religion since the thirteenth-century Christian conquest of Estonia emerged in the 1920s as *Taara-usk* or Taara-religion. *Taara-usk* became a registered religious society in 1930 and had around 700 members by 1940, when it was liquidated by the Soviet authorities. After this, *Taara-usk* was practised underground in family circles.

5 www.maavald.ee/koda/usuvabadus/kirikute-ja-koguduste-seadus/76-presidendile-14022002-ja-vastus, accessed 30 January 2020.

6 www.maavald.ee/koda/usuvabadus/kirikute-ja-koguduste-seadus/75-rk-oiguskomisjonile-13062000, accessed 30 January 2020.

7 www.maavald.ee/koda/usuvabadus/kirikute-ja-koguduste-seadus/91-riigikogu-oiguskomisjonile-04022002-ja-vastus, accessed 30 January 2020.

8 www.reuters.com/article/us-dutch-religion-slaughter/dutch-vote-to-ban-religious-slaughter-of-animals-idUSTRE75R4E420110628, accessed 30 January 2020;

www.haaretz.com/jewish/.premium-netherlands-rejects-bill-banning-kosher-slaughter-1.5182799, accessed 30 January 2020.
9 www.riigiteataja.ee/akt/118122012002, accessed 30 January 2020.
10 www.riigikogu.ee/download/b4f1776f-839d-4738-a707-c3aa30953e47, accessed 30 January 2020.

Bibliography

DialRel. 2010. Improving Animal Welfare during Religious Slaughter. Recommendations for Good Practice. DialRel Reports No. 2.4, http://webcache.google usercontent.com/search?q=cache:mHJT7HjTDGwJ:www.dialrel.eu/images/recom-light.pdf+&cd=1&hl=en&ct=clnk&gl=ee, accessed 30 January 2020.

Jehovah's Witnesses. 1996. Paying Back Caesar's Things to Caesar. *The Watchtower*, 117(9): 15–20.

Kaljulaid, Tanel. 2001. Eile lõppes ülekohtune kannatamine. *Eesti Päevaleht*, 15 märts, www.epl.ee/news/arvamus/tanel-kaljulaid-eile-loppes-ulekohtune-kannatamine.d?id=50871385, accessed 30. January 2020.

Kiviorg, Merilin. 2011. *Law and Religion in Estonia*. Alphen aan den Rijn: Kluwer Law International.

Leppik, Kristi. 2010. Arst võib lapse ravil vanema luba eirata. *Postimees* 14 June. https://tervis.postimees.ee/275919/arst-voib-lapse-ravil-vanema-luba-eirata, accessed 30 January 2020.

Loomakaitseseaduse. 2012. Loomakaitseseaduse ja sellega seonduvalt teiste seaduste muutmise seadus, 4.1-1/1131, 11 June 2011, http://eelnoud.valitsus.ee/main/mount/docList/b03534ee-0f8a-4ebd-b871-44885792a43e#MKZiulWE, accessed 30 January 2020.

Mill, John Stuart. 2003. *On Liberty*. Edited by David Bromwich and George Kateb with essays by Jean Bethke Elshtain, Owen Fiss, Richard A. Posner, Jeremy Waldron. New Haven and London: Yale University Press.

Polian, Pavel. 2003. *Against Their Will. The History and Geography of Forced Migrations in the USSR*. Budapest, New York: Central European University Press.

Ringvee, Ringo. 2020. Regulating Religion in Estonian Prisons Since the 1990s, in: Julia Martinez-Ariño and Anne-Laure Zwilling (eds) *Religion and Prison in Europe. A Contemporary Overview*. Cham: Springer, pp. 135–148.

Ringvee, Ringo. 2019. What Do the Censuses Tell about Minority Religions? Some Reflections on Estonia, in: George D. Chryssides (ed.) *Minority Religions in Europe and the Middle East. Mapping and Monitoring*. Oxon & New York: Routledge, pp. 11–25.

Ringvee, Ringo. 2016. From Controversial Bible Students to Respected Bible Translators? Some reflections on the reception of Jehovah's Witnesses in the Baltic States. *Acta Comparanda*, Subsidia III, pp. 151–63.

Ringvee, Ringo. 2015. Jehovas Zeugen im Baltikum – ein historiografischer Überblick, in: Gerhard Besier and Katarzyna Stoklosa (eds) *Jehovas Zeugen in Europa – Geschichte und gegenwart*. Berlin: LIT, pp. 13–42.

Ringvee, Ringo. 2013. Regulating Religion in a Neoliberal Context: The Transformation of Estonia, in: Tuomas Martikainen and François Gauthier (eds) *Religion in the Neoliberal Age: Political Economy and Modes of Governance*. Farnham: Ashgate, pp. 143–60.

Ringvee, Ringo. 2012 Dialogue or Confrontation? New Religious Movements, Mainstream Religions and the State in Secular Estonia. *International Journal for the Study of New Religions*, 3(1), pp. 93–116.

Rohtmets, Priit. 2018. *Riik ja usulised ühendused*. Tallinn: Siseministeerium.

Service Year Report 2019. *2019 Service Year Report of Jehovah's Witnesses Worldwide*. Pennsylvania: The Watch Tower Bible and Tract Society of Pennsylvania.

Vabar, Sven. 1996. Jehoova tunnistajad teenivad aega päästekompaniis. *Päevaleht*, 14 November, https://epl.delfi.ee/arvamus/jehoova-tunnistajad-teenivad-aega-paastekompaniis?id=50732887, accessed 30 January 2020.

Väljaots, Jaan. 2001. Vereülekanne poleks meie last päästnud. *Õhtuleht*, 27 February, www.ohtuleht.ee/103069/8220vereulekanne-poleks-meie-last-paastnud-8221, accessed 30 January 2020.

3 Jehovah's Witnesses and the law

"Caesar's things to Caesar, but God's things to God"

Tony Brace

Introduction

Jehovah's Witnesses believe that the Bible is the inspired Word of God and use it to inform their worship and way of life. BeDuhn has described them as: "...building their system of belief and practice from the raw material of the Bible without predetermining what was to be found there" (BeDuhn, 2003: 165). However, as Richardson points out in the final chapter of this book: "All minority religious groups must finds ways to function within the society in which they have chosen to operate," and Jehovah's Witnesses highlight two passages of Scripture that impinge on this truism: Matthew 22:21, "Pay back, therefore, Caesar's things to Caesar, but God's things to God";[1] and Romans 13: 1, 4, "Let every person be in subjection to the superior authorities, for there is no authority except by God ... it is God's minister to you for your good."

Following these strictures, Jehovah's Witnesses obey national laws. They diligently pay taxes and respect legal requirements, and they do not engage in protest movements, civil disobedience or attempts to overthrow governments. However, this default position begs the question of what are, respectively, Caesar's and God's things. Jehovah's Witnesses place a number of matters in the latter category. They see sharing their faith with non-affiliates as an essential part of their worship, though they respect the right of others to choose not to engage with them.[2] They interpret Jesus' instruction to be "no part of the world" (John 15:19; 17:14, 16) as enjoining political neutrality, so they do not vote or seek public office, and neither do they lobby nor campaign for changes in legislation. They see veneration of national symbols as a forbidden act of idolatrous worship in which they cannot engage.[3] And they will not take up arms, place themselves under military control, or do anything to harm their fellow-man.[4] If called upon to transgress what they see as God's law, they will not obey, whatever the consequences.[5] However, because they see the courts as part of 'God's minister,' they will appeal to them to construe law in such a way as to allow their freedom of conscience and religion: freedoms that 'Caesar' himself designates as fundamental human rights, protected by national constitutions and international treaties.[6]

Accordingly, Jehovah's Witnesses have pursued litigation to the highest level in a number of lands, and have taken cases to international tribunals in defence of their rights and freedoms. More often than not they have succeeded, and they list 89 victories and friendly settlements before the European Court of Human Rights as well as 20 successful communications to the UN Human Rights Committee (CCPR) and five favourable opinions from the Working Group on Arbitrary Detention.[7] On occasion, their litigation has led to changes in laws or in application of laws. Jehovah's Witnesses' willingness to "appeal to Caesar"[8] has established precedents that apply beyond their religious community and benefit other minorities. Three examples are discussed in detail below: conscientious objection to military service—an example of Caesar requiring something that God forbids (Europe and Korea); public manifestation of belief—Caesar both forbidding something God requires and requiring something God forbids (United States and elsewhere); and religious autonomy—Caesar becoming entangled in what belongs to God (Canada). Finally, there is a short section on choice of medical treatment, a matter of Caesar being asked to defend what belongs to God.

Conscientious objection to military service

As conscientious objectors, during both World Wars, Jehovah's Witnesses were stigmatised and imprisoned in many countries. During World War I, five of the so-called Richmond Sixteen conscientious objectors in Britain were International Bible Students (as Jehovah's Witnesses were then termed), and *English Heritage*, which now cares for Richmond Castle where they were imprisoned, says of this group:

> Secretly taken by night in irons to France by a roundabout route, on the beach at Boulogne the men were tied with barbed wire to posts almost as if they were being crucified and made to watch the execution of a British deserter by firing squad. Then they were told that if they did not obey orders the same fate awaited them.[9]

None relented. They were later court martialled and sentenced to death, commuted to ten years penal servitude. During World War II, 1,249 male and 344 female Witnesses, including the writer's parents, were imprisoned in Britain for conscientious objection to war service.[10] In Germany, on 15 September 1939, Witness August Dickmann, a prisoner in Sachsenhausen concentration camp, was the first conscientious objector of the war to be executed on the direct orders of Himmler.[11] Elsworth Jones (2008: 261) documents a further 271 German and Austrian Jehovah's Witnesses who were ultimately executed as conscientious objectors, and the Witnesses' own archives list 282.[12]

Following the war, Jehovah's Witnesses in Europe sought either exemption from military service or alternative civilian service, appealing both to constitutional provisions and to the commitment in Article 1 of the European Convention on Human Rights to secure freedom of thought, conscience, and religion under Article 9. However, until the case of *Bayatyan v. Armenia*,[13] the European Court followed the thinking of the then Commission in *Grandrath v. Germany* (1964),[14] "...that Article 9, read in the light of Article 4 § 3 (b),[15] does not guarantee a right to refuse military service on conscientious grounds" (section judgment, 27 October 2009, para. 63). Nevertheless, decisions by the Court and friendly settlements gradually established that Jehovah's Witnesses' religious ministers, albeit unpaid volunteers, are entitled to the same exemptions as ministers of other faiths (*Tsirlis and Kouloumpas v. Greece*,[16] *Gütl v. Austria; Lang v. Austria; Löffelmann v. Austria*,[17] *Religious Organization of Jehovah's Witnesses v. Romania (friendly settlement)*).[18]

Jehovah's Witnesses did not give up in their efforts to persuade the court to apply the Convention in a way that respected their religious conscience. *Thlimmenos v. Greece* considered an application brought on behalf of Iakovos Thlimmenos, one of Jehovah's Witnesses who was convicted of a felony because of his conscientious objection to military service, and automatically barred from admission to the profession of chartered accountant. The Grand Chamber of the European Court of Human Rights decided that the legislation:

> ...violated the applicant's right not to be discriminated against in the enjoyment of his right [to freedom of religion] under Article 9 of the Convention... by failing to introduce appropriate exceptions to the rule barring persons convicted of a felony from the profession of chartered accountants.[19]

In a partially dissenting opinion to the preliminary consideration, six distinguished members of the then Commission, including Sir Nicolas Bratza who later became President of the Court itself, considered (at para. 4) that: "...the freedom to 'manifest... in observance' the well-known religious conviction of Jehovah's Witnesses by refraining from personal military service is a freedom which attracts the guarantees of Article 9..." This set the scene for the subsequent decision of the Court's Grand Chamber in its reconsideration of *Bayatyan*. The Court there ruled, by 16 to 1:

> ...opposition to military service, where it is motivated by a serious and insurmountable conflict between the obligation to serve in the army and a person's conscience or his deeply and genuinely held religious or other beliefs, constitutes a conviction or belief of sufficient cogency, seriousness, cohesion and importance to attract the guarantees of

Article 9 ... The applicant in the present case is a member of Jehovah's Witnesses, a religious group whose beliefs include the conviction that service, even unarmed, within the military is to be opposed. The Court therefore has no reason to doubt that the applicant's objection to military service was motivated by his religious beliefs, which were genuinely held and were in serious and insurmountable conflict with his obligation to perform military service...

The Court reiterates that, as enshrined in Article 9, freedom of thought, conscience, and religion is one of the foundations of a 'democratic society' within the meaning of the Convention. This freedom is, in its religious dimension, one of the most vital elements that go to make up the identity of believers and their conception of life, but it is also a precious asset for atheists, agnostics, sceptics, and the unconcerned. The pluralism indissociable from a democratic society, which has been dearly won over the centuries, depends on it.

Although individual interests must on occasion be subordinated to those of a group, democracy does not simply mean that the views of a majority must always prevail: a balance must be achieved which ensures the fair and proper treatment of people from minorities and avoids any abuse of a dominant position. Thus, respect on the part of the State towards the beliefs of a minority religious group like the applicant's by providing them with the opportunity to serve society as dictated by their conscience might, far from creating unjust inequalities or discrimination as claimed by the Government, rather ensure cohesive and stable pluralism and promote religious harmony and tolerance in society.[20]

Wanting to ensure that 'Caesar' respected 'God's things' to the full, a number of further applications were pursued, and the cases of *Adyan v. Armenia*, and *Mushfig Mammadov and others v. Azerbaijan* saw the European Court of Human Rights specifying the requirement for a State Party to the Convention: "... to guarantee a system of alternative service that struck a fair balance between the interests of society as a whole and those of the applicants, as required by Article 9 of the Convention..."[21] and commenting:

... a system that is limited in its scope to the religious beliefs only of members of the clergy who perform ecclesiastical duties and students of religious establishments does not offer persons who claim conscientious objector status (such as the applicants in the present case) the possibility of benefiting from this status for the purposes of safeguarding their interests as protected by Article 9 of the Convention.[22]

In parallel with these developments in Europe was consideration of the same issue in the Republic of (South) Korea. For decades, this country made a practice of imprisoning conscientious objectors, to such an extent that the HRWF Report *For South Korea without Prisoners of Conscience* (Fautré, 2007) quoted Im Jong-in, a member of the Korean National Assembly, as asserting that 95 per cent of the conscientious objectors in prison anywhere in the world at that time were in Korea. The overwhelming majority of these prisoners were Jehovah's Witnesses.

Universal mandatory military service has been the norm in South Korea since the Korean war, with the authorities claiming an ever-present threat of invasion. However, as in other parts of the world, Jehovah's Witnesses in Korea have consistently been conscientious objectors, and Fautré reports that on 21 June 1939, there were nationwide arrests of adherents in Japan, the then colonial power, followed by similar arrests in Korea eight days later. The Korean Military Service Act was enacted in 1949, and revised in 1957, when the penalty for conscientious objectors was increased to a maximum of three years' imprisonment. In 1973, the Punishment of Violation of Military Service Act increased the maximum penalty to ten years and allowed for multiple prosecutions of conscientious objectors. It is estimated that a total of more than 16,000 Jehovah's Witnesses were imprisoned under these laws. However, on 21 May 2004, Judge Lee Jong-ryoel found three Witnesses not guilty under the legislation: the first recorded not-guilty verdict in Korea (Schroeder, 2011).

Jehovah's Witnesses challenged Article 88 of the Military Service Act, which deals with draft evasion, but on 26 August 2004, the Korea Constitutional Court upheld the constitutionality of this article by 7 to 2, stating: "The right to request alternative service arrangement cannot be deduced from the [constitutionally guaranteed] freedom of conscience." The applicants, Yoon Yeo-bum and Choi Myung-jin, having subsequently been convicted, and with their convictions upheld on appeal to the Supreme Court of Korea, submitted a communication to the UN Human Rights Committee (HRC) on 18 October 2004, under Article 18 of the International Covenant on Civil and Political Rights (ICCPR) (1976), which provides: "Everyone shall have the right to freedom of thought, conscience and religion."

On 3 November 2006, the HRC found in favour of Yoon and Choi, informing the national government that it was under obligation to provide an effective remedy and to "avoid similar violations of the Covenant in the future."[23] Brett comments: "The committee definitively laid to rest suggestions that conscientious objection is not recognized in the covenant," and Boyle states: "...for the first time an international body has ruled on the status of conscientious objection under the International Covenant which has been ratified by the great majority of states in the world" (Schroeder, 2011).[24] Korea proved reluctant to accept the obligations outlined by the HRC, which went on to make similar findings in favour of Jehovah's Witnesses in respect of 538 further complainants named in three ICCPR communications.[25] An additional complaint by 600 applicants is pending before the Working Group on Arbitrary Detention.[26]

With a growing international consensus that conscientious objection to military service should be accommodated, Jehovah's Witnesses filed another application with the Constitutional Court, which ruled on 28 June 2018 that: "...the failure to provide alternative service for conscientious objectors is unconstitutional and alternative service should be implemented no later than 31 December 2019."[27] Deciding a subsequent application to the Supreme Court by Oh Seung-heon, one of Jehovah's Witnesses who had been charged under Article 88(1) of the Military Service Act for failing to enlist in the military "without justifiable grounds," the Court decided:

> This issue cannot be simply resolved by the individual giving up on acting upon his conscience... Therefore, compelling a genuine conscientious objector to perform military service which involves the use of arms and military training, and punishing him for refusing to perform this duty would amount to an excessive restriction upon freedom of conscience or a threat to the fundamental contents of this freedom... Forcing conscientious objectors to perform military duty and imposing restrictions upon their failure to perform this duty by means of criminal punishment cannot be justified in the light of the constitutional system of upholding fundamental rights such as freedom of conscience and is in violation of the principle of liberal democracy, which calls for tolerance and embracing minorities. Therefore, if one's objection to military service is due to a genuinely held conscience, it constitutes a "justifiable ground" under Article 88(1) of the Military Service Act.[28]

Pursuant to these two decisions, 65 Jehovah's Witnesses had been released by 28 February 2019, pending legislation.[29] At the time of writing, the Korean legislature is in the process of passing amended laws offering alternative national service to conscientious objectors. Time will tell whether the legislation meets international standards and, from the point of view of Jehovah's Witnesses, whether it will constitute one of Caesar's things that they shall willingly 'pay back'.

Public manifestation of belief

In the first half of the twentieth century, numerous municipalities and States in the United States of America attempted to control religious expression by limiting the right of citizens to canvass from house to house and to offer religious publications. Efforts were made to compel children in publicly funded schools to recite a quasi-religious pledge of allegiance and to salute the national flag. Such legislation constrained what Jehovah's Witnesses viewed as 'God's things'; and in their view also transgressed rights guaranteed by the US Constitution. Attempts to defend their position in the first instance and appellate courts proving unsuccessful, a string of cases was taken to the Supreme Court, with the support of the Witnesses' headquarters in New York. To take three examples:

Cantwell v. Connecticut,[30] concerned three Jehovah's Witnesses, Newton, Jesse, and Russell Cantwell, who were arrested and subsequently convicted for failure to obtain a certificate from the state secretary before soliciting funds from the public and for allegedly inciting a breach of the peace. They had been going from house to house with books and pamphlets on religious subjects, a portable phonograph, and a set of records, each of which, when played, introduced one of the books. Each appellant asked the person who answered the door for permission to play a record. If permission were granted, he asked the person to buy the book described and, if refused, he solicited such contribution towards the publication of the pamphlets as the listener was willing to make. If a contribution were received, a pamphlet was offered on condition that it would be read. The Witnesses maintained that the requirement to obtain a certificate deprived them of their liberty without due process of law, in contravention of the Fourteenth Amendment to the United States Constitution; and that the fundamental concept of liberty embodied in that Amendment embraces the right to religious freedom, as guaranteed under the First Amendment.[31] On 20 May 1940, the United States Supreme Court reversed the decision of the lower courts, agreed that the Fourteenth Amendment was contravened by the local statute, and upheld the First Amendment's guarantees of religious freedom. This established the principle that no State can enact any law that contravenes the right to religious freedom.

In *Murdock v. Pennsylvania*, eight Jehovah's Witnesses had been convicted and fined for violation of an ordinance that required them to obtain a licence before engaging in selling or distributing printed material. The Witnesses went from door to door offering religious literature and playing a phonograph record. It was their practice to request a contribution for the books and pamphlets, but to accept lesser sums or to provide the volumes free of charge in the case of an interested person who had no funds. The judgments were reversed and the Supreme Court held that a State may not impose a charge for the enjoyment of a right granted by the Federal Constitution. Specifically, the Court stated:

> This form of religious activity occupies the same high estate under the First Amendment as do worship in the churches and preaching from the pulpits. It has the same claim to protection as the more orthodox and conventional exercises of religious [*sic*]. It also has the same claim as the others to the guarantees of freedom of speech and freedom of the press.[32]

Benefits to others than Jehovah's Witnesses are encapsulated in the Court's further comments:

> Freedom of speech, freedom of the press, freedom of religion are available to all, not merely to those who can pay their own way; ... Plainly a community may not suppress, or the state tax, the dissemination of views because they are unpopular, annoying or distasteful. If that device were ever sanctioned, there would have been forged a ready instrument for the suppression of the faith which any minority cherishes but which does not happen to be in favor.[33]

Demonstrating that rights once established can again be contested, and the willingness of Jehovah's Witnesses to mount a challenge when Caesar forbids what God requires, is the much more recent case of *Watchtower Bible and Tract Society v. Village of Stratton, Ohio*. The municipality adopted an ordinance requiring door-to-door 'canvassers' to obtain a permit from the mayor's office before going to private residences to promote any cause. Jehovah's Witnesses challenged the ordinance, which affected their evangelising outreach. The Supreme Court held that requiring a permit to engage in such activity is unconstitutional, violating the First Amendment to the United States Constitution. Again demonstrating the wider effect of the litigation, and its benefits to those who (unlike Jehovah's Witnesses) engage in other forms of activism, the Court commented:

> To require a censorship through license which makes impossible the free and unhampered distribution of pamphlets strikes at the very heart of the constitutional guarantees; ... there is a significant amount of spontaneous speech that is effectively banned by the ordinance. A person who made a decision on a holiday or a weekend to take an active part in a political campaign could not begin to pass out handbills until after he or she obtained the required permit. Even a spontaneous decision to go across the street and urge a neighbor to vote against the mayor could not lawfully be implemented without first obtaining the mayor's permission.[34]

In Canada, following cases brought by Jehovah's Witnesses in Quebec challenging 'seditious libel' convictions for distributing a pamphlet exposing in strong language (a) the persecution of Jehovah's Witnesses, (b) disregard for law by public officials, and (c) instigation of persecution by certain clergymen, the Supreme Court ruled in the case of *Boucher v. Canada* (1951):

> Freedom in thought and speech and disagreement in ideas and beliefs, on every conceivable subject, are of the essence of our life. The clash of critical discussion on political, social and religious subjects

has too deeply become the stuff of daily experience to suggest that mere ill-will as a product of controversy can strike down the latter with illegality.[35]

Again in Canada, the case of *Blainville v. Beauchemin* (2003) involved a municipal by-law requiring a permit for any 'door-to door' soliciting, which had been applied to Jehovah's Witnesses. The Quebec Court of Appeal decided:

> Jehovah's Witnesses have adopted a model throughout the world inspired by primitive Christian congregations and further to which they visit households in neighbourhoods to encourage people to maintain high standards of morality and spirituality, inviting them to read the Bible and share their religious beliefs... If a person is compelled by the state or the will of another to a course of action or inaction which he would not otherwise have chosen, he is not acting of his own volition and he cannot be said to be truly free... the obligation to obtain a permit prior to conducting door-to-door soliciting of neighbours to invite them to discuss religion appears to me so contrary to our system of government that I cannot conceive cases where any such authorization could be validly required.[36]

In Norway, in January 1950, Herman Lubbe and six other Jehovah's Witnesses were present in the main street of Oslo, holding up copies of *The Watchtower* magazine and talking to those showing interest. The police fined them for violating the prohibition of "distributing advertisements without permission from the police." The Supreme Court decided in *Lubbe v. Norway*:

> ...it is evident that the authorities—after several discussions concerning the different proposals—have chosen a wording for the regulations (§ 3, paragraph 1) that precludes the word advertisements 'and the like' from being interpreted as something that includes newspapers, proclamations or the distribution of a publication like *The Watchtower*.[37]

In 1952, one of Jehovah's Witnesses in the Netherlands was fined for offering *The Watchtower* on a public street outside of the designated days and hours provided by municipal decree. He appealed, contending that the decree was a limitation to the right of distribution. In *Havenaar v. Netherlands* (1953), the Supreme Court found in his favour, stating:

> ...next to the fundamental right to put down thoughts and feelings in printed matter, also the right is recognized to publish the same to the public by distributing the contents, and this right to distribution

is exercised among other things by the means of distribution that exists in the gratuitously offering of printed matter... the limitations to that means may never go so far as boiling down to a prohibition in general.[38]

In Serbia, Jehovah's Witnesses brought the case of *Blagojević v. Belgrade* (1983) following the administrative conviction of Mira Blagojević and Mileva Popović. This examined whether the distribution of religious literature in the vicinity of a bus station violated laws banning the spreading of propaganda, the promotion of hostility, and the disruption of peace. The Supreme Court held (Figure 3.1):

[The] Court does not find any elements of violation, because offering religious magazines and talking about one's faith cannot be considered as spreading false news and as claims which can arouse hostility and can disturb citizens. Thereby the Court finds that the accused have been wrongly accused for the cited violation.[39]

In *A.S. v. Poland* (1995), brought by Jehovah's Witnesses regarding State control of printing and distributing religious literature, the Supreme Court of Poland ruled:

Printing and distributing religious publications is [*sic*] the case of Jehovah's Witnesses is an extraordinarily important Evangelic activity... The guarantee of not intervening by the State authorities in the matters of

Figure 3.1 Jehovah's Witness Dennis Christensen on trial in Russia. On 6 February 2019, Christensen was sentenced to 6 years' imprisonment for peaceful practice of his religion. The case has been referred by Jehovah's Witnesses to the European Court of Human Rights.' (Photograph courtesy of Jehovah's Witnesses)

religious worship was expressed by the Constitution of People's Republic of Poland from 1952 as well as the Decree from August 5, 1949 about the protection of freedom of conscience and religion, granting each citizen freedom in this regard... Acts characterised by violating norms of penal law contrary to constitutional norms that preclude free carrying out of religious practices within the scope of guaranteed by the Constitution to all citizens freedom of conscience and religion, as an expression of a justified disobedience towards law, cannot be treated as a crime.[40]

In Turkey, the case of *Atalay v. Turkey [2]* (1980) concerned ten Jehovah's Witnesses who were criminally charged for "establishing and managing an illegal organization originating from foreign countries to form a new state order based on a religious rule against the secularism principles," and for "holding meetings, preaching, and distributing religious literature." The first part of the charge is bizarre in view of the political neutrality observed by the Witnesses. The Turkey Cassation Court not only disposed of that but also upheld the Witnesses' religious practices stating:

> If, some day, the belief of the accused will be realized and a Godly rule will be established on the earth after the Doomsday, punishing the accused since they believed that will not prevent the result. [On the other hand] if this expectation is produce of imagination and an unfounded belief, we do not need to be concerned that the belief of the accused will harm our secular state order... spreading and teaching of religious beliefs are within the limits of the freedom of religion and conscience. Since secularism means the independence of states towards all religions, it is a clear truth that the accused did not commit the crime of propaganda only because they are adherents of that belief. Moreover, it is possible to say that even no inspiration for political ends was observed except religious emotions.[41]

Turning to Caesar requiring what God forbids, the United States case *West Virginia State Board of Education v. Barnette* questioned a requirement that all teachers and pupils "shall be required to participate in the salute honoring the Nation represented by the Flag," and that refusal be dealt with by expelling the child from school. The child was then considered "unlawfully absent," and his parents were liable to prosecution. This mandated an act that Jehovah's Witnesses believed to be forbidden by God, and they were unable to comply with the requirement. Despite an earlier ruling upholding the obligation, the Supreme Court found in their favour and pronounced:

> If there is any fixed star in our constitutional constellation, it is that no official, high or petty, can prescribe what shall be orthodox in politics, nationalism, religion, or other matters of opinion or force citizens to confess by word or act their faith therein.[42]

That the benefits of this transcend Jehovah's Witnesses is self-evident, and the Court applied its reasoning in the instant case as follows:

> We think the action of the local authorities in compelling the flag sa-
> lute and pledge transcends constitutional limitations on their power
> and invades the sphere of intellect and spirit which it is the purpose of
> the First Amendment to our Constitution to reserve from all official
> control.[43]

Similar decisions regarding the manifestation of belief by respectfully declining to salute the flag or to sing the national anthem have been reached
after application by Jehovah's Witnesses to the courts of several other lands.
In *Donald v. Hamilton Board of Education* (1945), the Ontario Supreme
Court, Canada, held that singing the national anthem or saluting the flag is
a subjective religious matter and commented that other countries hold that
the issue is one of conscience.[44]

The Supreme Court of India concluded in *Bijoe Emmanuel v. Kerala,
India Supreme Court* (1986) as follows:

> The objection of the petitioners is not to the language or the sentiments
> of the National Anthem... They desist from actual singing only because
> of their honest belief and conviction that their religion does not permit
> them to join any rituals except it be in their prayers to Jehovah their
> God... The petitioners have not asserted these beliefs for the first time
> or out of any unpatriotic sentiment. Jehovah's Witnesses, as they call
> themselves, appear to have always expressed and stood up for such
> beliefs all the world over.[45]

In Costa Rica, the Supreme Court decided in *Fernandez v. Ingeniero Alejandro Quesada Ramirez School* (2003):

> To not sing the National Anthem does not threaten morals, public or-
> der, and does not damage third parties. The text of article 32 of the In-
> ternal Rules for Students should conform to the Political Constitution,
> which is above these Rules. The duty to sing the National Anthem is
> conditioned to [subject to] superior human rights, such as freedom of
> thinking and religious freedom.[46]

In the Philippines, the Supreme Court ruled in *Ebralinag v. Schools of
Cebu* (1995):

> ... the suggestion implicit in the State's pleadings to the effect that the
> flag ceremony requirement would be equally and evenly applied to all
> citizens regardless of sect or religion and does not thereby discrimi-
> nate against any particular sect or denomination escapes the fact that

"[a] regulation, neutral on its face, may in its application, nonetheless offend the constitutional requirement for governmental neutrality if it unduly burdens the free exercise of religion"... the view that the flag is not a religious but a neutral, secular symbol expresses a majoritarian view intended to stifle the expression of the belief that an act of saluting the flag might sometimes be—to some individuals—so offensive as to be worth their giving up another constitutional right—the right to education. Individuals or groups of individuals get from a symbol the meaning they put to it. Compelling members of a religious sect to believe otherwise on the pain of denying minor children the right to an education is a futile and unconscionable detour towards instilling virtues of loyalty and patriotism which are best instilled and communicated by painstaking and non-coercive methods... Provided that those influences do not pose a clear and present danger of a substantive evil to society and its institutions, expressions of diverse beliefs, no matter how upsetting they may seem to the majority, are the price we pay for the freedoms we enjoy.[47]

Finally, the Tanzania Appeal Court decided in *Kamwela v. Minister of Education* (2013) that students who refuse to sing the National Anthem at school because it would be against their genuine and sincerely held religious belief cannot be expelled, suspended, or subjected to other disciplinary action for their refusal.[48]

Religious autonomy in Canada

This example of Caesar becoming entangled in what belongs to God begins with a Mr Randy Wall, who was part of the Highwood Congregation of Jehovah's Witnesses in Calgary, Alberta, Canada. In December 2013, two congregation elders gave him Bible-based counsel regarding allegations from his wife and two youngest sons, who complained of severe emotional abuse. Mr Wall admitted the accusations. The elders warned him that being verbally abusive (what the Bible terms "reviling") is a serious sin for which he could be removed (disfellowshipped) as a member of the congregation, and the counsel was ostensibly accepted.

Shortly thereafter, the elders again counselled Mr Wall. This time, his wife and adult daughter accused him of continuing verbal abuse and of twice being drunk, on one occasion to the point where the police were called. Mr Wall confessed to what were, according to Scripture, serious sins—drunkenness and repeated verbal abuse. The congregation elders determined that he was not genuinely repentant of his sins and disfellowshipped him from the congregation, following the Bible command "remove the wicked person from among yourselves" (1 Corinthians 5:13). On 23 April 2014, the Highwood Congregation was informed by oral announcement that Mr Wall was no longer one of Jehovah's Witnesses. After such an announcement, individual Jehovah's Witnesses, based on their religious conscience, choose to avoid further association with the person concerned until he is formally reinstated into the congregation.

Dissatisfied with the decision, Mr Wall brought an application for judicial review before the Alberta Court of Queen's Bench. The Congregation challenged the application on the basis the Court lacked jurisdiction to examine a Bible-based, ecclesiastical decision. In effect, such a decision belongs to God, and Caesar should not interfere.

The Queen's Bench judge held that the Court had jurisdiction to review the merits of the elders' religious decision, in effect deciding that a secular court could step into the shoes of the elders, and if necessary, experts could interpret and apply Scripture in court. An appeal was taken to the Supreme Court of Canada, which on 31 May 2018, unanimously held that Jehovah's Witnesses' disfellowshipping arrangement should remain free from court intervention. The Court approved an earlier US appellate decision, *Anderson v. Watchtower Bible and Tract Society* (2007) that held "a decision to disfellowship ... is clearly an ecclesiastical matter"[49] and stated:

> ... Fundamental constitutional principles give the members of the Highwood Congregation the right to determine their coreligionists... A civil court must decline to review membership decisions of a religious association. The decision of dispute resolution procedures religious entities themselves construct to resolve membership disputes should be respected.[50]

This case thus joined a line of Supreme Court decisions upholding freedom of conscience and religion in Canada.

Choice of medical treatment

The European Court of Human Rights, in a case brought by Jehovah's Witnesses against Russia, accurately observed:

> Jehovah's Witnesses believe that the Bible prohibits ingesting blood, which is sacred to God, and that this prohibition extends to transfusion of any blood or blood components that are not the patient's own. The religious prohibition permits of no exceptions...[51]

This religious prohibition, based (*inter alia*) on the decision of the Council of Jerusalem as recorded at Acts 15:28, 29, is often misunderstood or misrepresented. It was correctly summarised by an English judge in a 1992 case involving a woman whose mother was one of Jehovah's Witnesses but who had never embraced the faith. Baroness Butler-Sloss LJ stated:

> Jehovah [*sic*] Witnesses accept and take advantage of the same medical treatment as those who do not subscribe to their beliefs and are as

anxious as anyone else to recover from any illness from which they may suffer. There is no question of a right to die. This acceptance of medical treatment in its widest sense is subject to the requirement not to accept transfusions of blood or blood derivatives.[52]

Accordingly, Jehovah's Witnesses seek to exercise choice in medical treatment and their right under the Common Law, which forms the basis of numerous legal systems around the world, is identical to that of other patients. It was set out by Donaldson MR in the same case:

> An adult patient who ... suffers from no mental incapacity has an absolute right to choose whether to consent to medical treatment, to refuse it or to choose one rather than another of the treatments being offered... This right of choice is not limited to decisions which others might regard as sensible. It exists notwithstanding that the reasons for making the choice are rational, irrational, unknown or even non-existent.

While much can be, and has been, written on this matter, not least on the role of parents making decisions for children, one Canadian lawsuit involving Jehovah's Witnesses has set the tone for litigation beyond the Witness community and has contributed to legislation in many lands. That is, the Ontario Supreme Court case of *Malette v. Shulman* (1990). Georgette Malette, aged 57, was admitted to hospital as an emergency patient after a car accident. A nurse found a signed Advance Directive in the patient's purse which identified her as one of Jehovah's Witnesses and stated that she would reject blood transfusions in any circumstances. Owing to the severity of her injuries, the doctor treating her concluded that a blood transfusion was indicated to save her life, and although he was made aware of the patient's Advance Directive, he administered several transfusions.

Mrs Malette brought action against the doctor, the hospital, its Executive Director, and four nurses, alleging that the administration of blood transfusions in the circumstances of her case constituted negligence and assault and battery and subjected her to religious discrimination. The Trial Court awarded damages and the doctor appealed. On 30 March 1990, the province's Supreme Court dismissed the appeal, ruling that in administering the blood transfusions, the doctor violated the patient's rights over her own body. An honest, and even justifiable, belief that the treatment was medically essential did not relieve him of liability for his intentional actions. The patient's carrying of an Advance Directive regarding blood transfusions in the form of a card was evidence of her beliefs. The Court stated:

> The right of a person to control his or her own body is a concept that has long been recognized at common law. The tort of battery has traditionally protected the interest in bodily security from unwanted physical interference. Basically, any intentional nonconsensual touching which is

harmful or offensive to a person's reasonable sense of dignity is action-able... The right of self-determination, which underlies the doctrine of informed consent, also obviously encompasses the right to refuse medi-cal treatment. A competent adult is generally entitled to reject a specific treatment or all treatment, or to select an alternate form of treatment, even if the decision may entail risks as serious as death and may appear mistaken in the eyes of the medical profession or of the community. Re-gardless of the doctor's opinion, it is the patient who has the final say on whether to undergo the treatment... For this freedom to be meaningful, people must have the right to make choices that accord with their own values...

Our concern here is with a patient who has chosen, in the only way possible, to notify doctors and other providers of health care, should she be unconscious or otherwise unable to convey her wishes, that she does not consent to blood transfusions. Her written statement is plainly intended to express her wishes when she is unable to speak for herself. There is no suggestion that she wished to die. Her rejection of blood transfusions is based on the firm belief held by Jehovah's Witnesses, founded on their interpretation of the Scriptures...[53]

This case has been cited, and approved, around the world including in the seminal English case of *Bland*,[54] to support the idea that a patient has au-thority over his or her own body and that this authority does not end if the patient loses consciousness but may be encapsulated in a written advance decision to refuse clearly specified treatment. Legislation such as the Men-tal Capacity Act 2005 in England and Wales adds to the Common Law by giving statutory authority to such advance decision documents. If, as Jehovah's Witnesses believe, their body is one of God's things, Caesar has upheld their right to use it according to their beliefs and to choose medical treatment accordingly. All patients who wish to give informed consent be-fore being treated, and to have a documented advance decision respected, have reason to be grateful for this development.

Conclusions

So how do Jehovah's Witnesses function within the confines of the legal structures and procedures of the societies within which they operate? Russian scholar Sergei Ivanenko stated: "Jehovah's Witnesses are known throughout the world as impeccably law-abiding people..."[55] Haynes wrote:

We all owe the Jehovah's Witnesses a debt of gratitude. No matter how many times they're insulted, run out of town or even physically at-tacked, they keep on fighting for their (and thus our) freedom of reli-gion. And when they win, we all win.[56]

Jehovah's Witnesses pay Caesar's things to Caesar. But they are unwilling to give Caesar what they believe rightfully belongs to God. This conscientious stand has contributed to the enjoyment of freedom of conscience and belief for all. Charles Braden (1949: 381), in his book *These Also Believe*, said of the Witnesses: "They have performed a signal service to democracy by their fight to preserve their civil rights, for in their struggle they have done much to secure those rights for every minority group in America."

Jehovah's Witnesses do not litigate because of a love of confrontation. Nor do they see themselves primarily as human rights defenders. Their aim in pursuing legal cases is to enable them to follow the Biblical command: "...go on leading a calm and quiet life with complete godly devotion and seriousness" (1 Timothy 2:2). Like the Bible writer who penned those words; who saw the "superior authorities" as "God's minister"; and who himself appealed to Caesar, they are happy to pay Caesar's things to Caesar, while also being determined to pay God's things to God. They have found that, with persistent effort, the courts of many nations, as well as supra-national institutions, have respected their persistent applications, in which they ask for no more than is theoretically guaranteed though not always accorded. The God whom they worship does not allow them to pursue political activism, even if they are subjected to ill-treatment that, in the words of the late Glen How OC QC, crosses the "threshold of shock".[57] However, their understanding of Scripture does allow them, indeed motivates them, to use the legal system in their defence; and their determination has served to confirm treasured rights that benefit all, especially minorities who suffer misunderstanding and misrepresentation. It is a service to their fellow man that they quietly rejoice to have rendered; part of what they see as following the command: "Thou shalt love thy neighbour as thyself" (Matthew 22:39 *KJ*).

Notes

1 Repeated verbatim at Mark 12:17, Luke 20:25.
2 Matthew 28:18–20; 10:14.
3 Exodus 20:4–6; Daniel 3: 1, 4, 5, 16–18; 1 John 5:21.
4 Isaiah 2:4; Matthew 22:37–39; 26:52; 2 Corinthians 10:2–5.
5 While largely outside the scope of this chapter, Jehovah's Witnesses have been imprisoned for following the dictates of conscience in many countries and have even suffered the death penalty, for instance, under the Nazi regime in Germany and in Malawi during the regime of Dr Banda.
6 For example: International Covenant on Civil and Political Rights, Article 18; European Convention on Human Rights, Article 9; Constitution of the United States, First Amendment; Constitution of the Russian Federation, Article 28.
7 As of 1 January 2020.
8 Acts 25:11.
9 Quoted in Third Party Intervention by EAJW at European Court of Human Rights in the case of *Bayatyan v. Armenia*, 2010.
10 *Ibid.*
11 *The New York Times*, September 16, 1939, p. 26.

12 Central Europe branch office of Jehovah's Witnesses, Selters, Germany: personal communication.
13 Application no. 23459/03.
14 Application no. 2299/64.
15 For the purpose of this Article, the term 'forced or compulsory labour' shall not include: ... (b) any service of a military character or, in case of conscientious objectors in countries where they are recognised, service exacted instead of compulsory military service.
16 Application nos. 19233/91; 19234/91.
17 Application nos. 49686/99; 28648/03; 42967/98.
18 Application no. 63108/00, 11 July 2006.
19 Application no. 34369/97, para. 48.
20 Application no. 23459/03, Grand Chamber Judgment, 7 July 2011, paras. 110, 111, 118, 126.
21 *Adyan*, Application no. 75604/11, para. 72.
22 *Mushfig Mammadov*, Application no. 14604/08 and three others, para. 96 (unofficial translation from French).
23 Communications nos. 1321/2004, 1332/2004 (2007) CCPR/88/D/1321-1322/2004, 23 January 2007, para. 10.
24 www.jstor.org/stable/43751909 (accessed October 2020).
25 www.jw.org/en/news/legal/by-region/south-korea/?start=10 (accessed January 2020).
26 As of 1 January 2020.
27 2011Hunba379 of 28 June 2018.
28 *Oh v. Korea*, Korea Supreme Court, 2016Do10912 of 1 November 2018, pp. 6, 9, 10.
29 www.jw.org/en/news/jw/region/south-korea/All-Witnesses-Imprisoned-for-Conscientious-Objection-in-South-Korea-Now-Free/ (accessed January 2020).
30 310 US 296 (1940).
31 Text available at www.senate.gov/civics/constitution_item/constitution.htm (accessed January 2020).
32 319 US 105 (1943) at p. 109, also 63 S.Ct. 870.
33 *Ibid.*, pp. 111, 116.
34 536 US 150 (2002) at. pp. 162, 167.
35 [1951] S.C.R. 265, p. 288.
36 CarswellQue 14753 (2003), paras. 19, 35, 48.
37 Rt.1950.601, p. 2.
38 HR 17 maart 1953, NJ 1953, 389 m.nt. BVAR, AB 1953, biz. 586 (concl. A-G Langemeijer; Havenaar/Staat), p. 2.
39 Case number 480/83, 1983, p. 1.
40 II KRN 137/95, pp. 2, 3.
41 Case Number 1980/115, March 24, 1980, p. 7.
42 319 US 624 (1943) at p. 642.
43 *Ibid.*
44 [1945] O.R. 518 (C.A.).
45 (1986) 3 Supreme Court Cases 615, paras. 2, 3.
46 2003-03018, p. 3.
47 Case Number 95770, 95887, 29 December 1995, pp. 10, 12, 14.
48 Case Number 3/2012, 12 July 2013.
49 WL 161035, 15 (Tenn. Ct. App.).
50 *Highwood Congregation of Jehovah's Witnesses (Judicial Committee) v. Wall*, 2018 SCC 26, pp. 8, 25.
51 *Jehovah's Witnesses of Moscow and others v. Russia*, Application no. 302/02, 10 June 2010,

52 *re T* [1992] 3 WLR 782.
53 72 O.R.2d 417 (Ont. Ct. App. 1990), paras. 17, 19, 32.
54 *Airedale NHS Trust v. Bland*, House of Lords [1993] W.L.R. 316, at 342.
55 https://wol.jw.org/en/wol/d/r1/lp-e/101997607#h=1:0-51:0 (accessed January 2020).
56 www.jw.org/en/library/magazines/g20030108/Supreme-Court-Rules-for-Freedom-of-Speech/ (accessed January 2020).
57 Personal communication.

References

BeDuhn, Jason David. 2003. *Truth in Translation*. Lanham, MD: University Press of America.

Braden, Charles Samuel. 1949. *These Also Believe*. New York: Macmillan.

Elsworth Jones, Will. 2008. *We Will Not Fight—the Untold Story of World War One's Conscientious Objectors*. London: Aurum Press.

Fautré, Willy. 2007. *For South Korea without Prisoners of Conscience*. Brussels: Human Rights without Frontiers International.

The Holy Bible. Exodus 20:4–6; Isaiah 2:4; Daniel 3: 1, 4, 5, 16–18; Matthew 10:142; 2:37–39; 26:52; 28:18–20; Mark 12:17; Luke 20:25; Acts 25:11;12 Corinthians 10:2–5; 1 John 5:21.

Jehovah's Witnesses' Official Website. www.jw.org/en/library/magazines/g200301 08/Supreme-Court-Rules-for-Freedom-of-Speech. New York: Watch Tower Bible and Tract Society of Pennsylvania (accessed January 2020).

———. www.jw.org/en/news/jw/region/south-korea/All-Witnesses-Imprisoned-for-Conscientious-Objection-in-South-Korea-Now-Free/ (accessed January 2020).

———. www.jw.org/en/news/legal/by-region/south-korea/?start=10 (accessed January 2020).

The New York Times. 1939. Germans Execute Objector to War, 17 September, p. 26.

Schroeder, Judah B. 2011. The role of Jehovah's Witnesses in the emergent right of conscientious objection to military service in international law, *Kirchliche Zeitgeschichte* 24(1): 169–206. www.jstor.org/stable/43751909 (accessed October 2020).

United States Senate Website. www.senate.gov/civics/constitution_item/constitution. htm Washington D.C. (accessed January 2020).

Watchtower Online Library. https://wol.jw.org/en/wol/d/r1/lp-e/101997607#h=1: 0-51:0 New York: Watch Tower Bible and Tract Society of Pennsylvania (accessed January 2020).

Legislation and international instruments

Constitution of the Russian Federation.
Constitution of the United States.
European Convention on Human Rights (1950, 2010).
International Covenant on Civil and Political Rights (1976).
Mental Capacity Act 2005 (England and Wales).
Military Service Act (Republic of Korea) 1949, 1957.
Punishment of Violation of Military Service Act (Republic of Korea) 1973.

Cases

A.S. v. Poland, Supreme Court of Poland, II KRN 137/95, pp. 2, 3.

Adyan v Armenia, ECtHR Application no. 75604/11.

Airedale NHS Trust v Bland, U.K. House of Lords [1993] W.L.R. 316.

Anderson v. Watchtower Bible and Tract Society, Tennessee Court of Appeal, WL 161035, 15 (Tenn. Ct. App.).

Atalay v. Turkey, Cassation Court of Turkey, Case Number 1980/115, March 24, 1980.

Bayatyan v. Armenia, 2010, ECtHR Application no.23459/03.

Bijoe Emmanuel v. Kerala, India Supreme Court (1986) 3 Supreme Court Cases 615.

Blagojević v. Belgrade, Supreme Court of Serbia, Case number 480/83, 1983, p. 1.

Blainville v. Beauchemin, Quebec Court of Appeal (Canada), CarswellQue 14753 (2003).

Boucher v. Canada, Supreme Court of Canada [1951] S.C.R. 265.

Cantwell v. Connecticut, U.S. Supreme Court, 310 U.S. 296 (1940).

Donald v. Hamilton Board of Education, Ontario Supreme Court (Canada) [1945] O.R. 518 (C.A.).

Ebralinag v. Schools of Cebu, Philippines Supreme Court, Case Number 95770, 95887, 29 December 1995.

Fernandez v. Ingeniero Alejandro Quesada Ramirez School, Costa Rica Supreme Court 2003–03018.

Grandrath v. Germany, ECtHR Application no. 2299/64.

Gütl v. Austria, ECtHR Applications no. 49686/99.

Havenaar v. Netherlands, Supreme Court of the Netherlands, HR 17 maart 1953, NJ 1953, 389 m.nt. BVAR, AB 1953, biz. 586 (concl. A-G Langemeijer; Havenaar/Staat).

Highwood Congregation of Jehovah's Witnesses (Judicial Committee) v. Wall, Supreme Court of Canada, 2018 SCC 26.

Jehovah's Witnesses of Moscow and others v. Russia, ECtHR Application no. 302/02.

Kamwela v. Minister of Education, Tanzania Appeal Court, Case Number 3/2012, 12 July 2013.

Lang v. Austria, ECtHR Application no. 28648/03.

Löffelmann v. Austria, ECtHR Application no. 42967/98.

Lubbe v. Norway, Supreme Court of Norway, Rt.1950.601.

Malette v. Shulman, Ontario Court of Appeal (Canada) 72 O.R.2d 417 (Ont. Ct. App. 1990).

Murdock v. Pennsylvania, U.S. Supreme Court, 319 U.S. 105 (1943) also 63 S.Ct. 870.

Mushfig Mammadov and Others v. Azerbaijan, ECtHR Application no. 14604/08 and 3 others.

Oh v. Korea, Korea Supreme Court, 2016Do10912 of 1 November 2018.

In re T. (Adult: Refusal of Treatment), England and Wales Court of Appeal, [1992] 3 WLR 782.

Religious Organization of Jehovah's Witnesses v. Romania (friendly settlement), ECtHR Application no. 63108/00.

Thlimmenos v. Greece, ECtHR Application no. 34369/97.

Tsirlis and Kouloumpas v. Greece, ECtHR Applications nos. 19233/91; 19234/91.
UN Human Rights Committee Communications nos. 1321/2004, 1332/2004 (2007) CCPR/88/D/1321–1322/2004.
Watchtower Bible and Tract Society v. Village of Stratton, Ohio, U.S. Supreme Court, 536 U.S. 150 (2002).
West Virginia State Board of Education v. Barnette, U.S. Supreme Court, 319 U.S. 624 (1943).
Yoon and Choi, Constitutional Court of South Korea, 2011Hunba379 of 28 June 2018.

4 Scientology behind the scenes
The law changer

Eric Roux

Introduction

In almost 70 years of existence, the Church of Scientology has been confronted by the law probably more than any other religious movement in modern times. It has developed an extraordinary record of interaction with legislation, whether in courts or through its interaction with governments and government agencies. These interactions have sometimes created significant changes in the law regarding freedom of religion, religious recognition and related topics. In many countries, this has been achieved through case law, with the Church of Scientology's efforts contributing to the development of new definitions of religion that fit with contemporary religious diversity, but also through advocacy before national and supranational governmental organizations. Herein, I will give several examples of how the Church of Scientology reacted to the law through court cases in order to force changes. I also will describe a successful advocacy crusade of the Church within the Council of Europe that resulted in dramatically changed legislation at supranational level.

The Italian case

Italy is emblematic for several reasons. First, the major issue involved a criminal case, and the accusations in it are similar to those repeated in various criminal cases that Scientology has had to face in Europe. It is also emblematic because it occurred in a country which is known for the predominance of the Catholic Church to an extent rarely seen elsewhere.

The case started in 1986, when the carabinieri (Italian police) organized a huge series of simultaneous raids against churches of Scientology in Italy, and placed under arrest 75 'leaders' of the Church under various criminal charges (extortion, fraud, running a criminal conspiracy, abuse of weak people) that eventually were revealed to be false. In 1991, most of the 'leaders' were acquitted in a first instance trial. The prosecutor appealed the decision, and on 5 November 1993, the Court of Appeal of Milan rendered a very harsh decision against the Scientologists. That decision was appealed before the Court of Cassation, and in 1995, the Court of Cassation squashed the Court of Appeal decision and sent the case back to that Court. The Court of Appeal persisted in its initial decision in 1996 by once again strongly condemning the Scientologists as criminals. The case went back to the Court of Cassation, which, in October 1997, issued a landmark decision recognizing the religious bona fides of Scientology.

The court, in reaching that conclusion, acknowledged the earlier recognition of the Church as a religion in the United States: "...since the Church of Scientology has been recognized in the U.S. as a religious denomination, it should have been recognized in Italy and thus allowed to practice its worship and to conduct proselytising activities..." (*Bandera and others v. Italy* 1997).

It also took into account the work of the scholars who had given their opinion on the case: Scholars of religion, the Court noted, acknowledge that Scientology is a religion whose aim is "the liberation of the human spirit through the knowledge of the divine spirit residing within each human being" (*Bandera and others v. Italy* 1997).

Interestingly, the Italian Court of Cassation, in its decision, entered strong comparisons to other religious practices and concluded that "the circumstance that the religion has brought into being lucrative activities does not distinguish it from other religions nor in itself deprive it of its intrinsic religiosity". It also concluded that:

> Because any religion (...) carries out the catechesis of neophytes and catechumens in special courses, imposes practices, places prohibitions, marks and teaches ways and paths of improvement and ascesis, often very difficult and afflictive, towards and in search of God, so that the books to be read, the courses to be followed, the practices to be performed and the ways of improvement imposed by the [Church of Scientology's] association in question cannot be defined as illicit based [on such grounds].
>
> (*Bandera and others v. Italy* 1997)

In its final decision recognizing the religious nature of Scientology, the Court noted that the procedure adopted by the Court of Appeal (which relied on what they thought was the 'common consideration' for rejection of the religious nature of Scientology) was wrong. It decided that the criteria that should be taken into account for religious recognition were, in addition to the opinion of religious scholars and the fact that it was recognized in the United States, "the conviction of thousands of members of the association with regard to its religiosity, a fact certainly not irrelevant in order to form the common consideration in this regard" (*Bandera and others v. Italy* 1997).

This was the first time in Italy that a Supreme Court decision opened the door to recognition of religions, which were not 'traditional' in the country, by setting objective criteria based on a pragmatic, positive, open and modern approach to freedom of religion or belief. The Court sent the case back to the Court of Appeal of Milan, which acceded to the Superior Court's jurisdiction and recognized the religious nature of Scientology on 5 October 2000.

Italy also recognized the religious nature of Scientology in numerous tax case determinations. For example, in 1991, the Criminal Court of Milan recognized that the Church of Scientology could not be subject to commercial taxes due to the religious and not-for-profit nature of its activities. Earlier, the first tax jurisdiction to render a positive decision on Scientology was the Tax Commission of Monza on 27 March 1990:

> The Commission considers that the religious nature of Scientology is an established fact, which applies equally to the theory of its teachings, to the salvific contents of the latter such as the religious rites practiced, and to the ecclesiastical character of the way the organization carries out its activities.
>
> (Tax Commission of Monza 1990)

More recently, since 2000, 37 decisions related to tax issues in Italy have recognized the religious nature of Scientology, including three by the Court of Cassation.

Welcome to Australia and beyond

The Australian High Court's decision regarding the Scientology religion in *Church of the New Faith v. Commissioner of Payroll Tax* (1983) is a landmark judgment which established the standard definition of religion and religious charities in Australia and New Zealand and, in fact, throughout the Commonwealth of Nations.

The Church of Scientology in the State of Victoria had been asked to pay a tax on salaries, while other religions were exempted of such tax. The Church went through all levels of jurisdiction, including the Supreme Court of Victoria, before finally appealing to the High Court of Australia, the equivalent of the Supreme Court in the United States.

The High Court determined the following: "The Church of Scientology has easily discharged the onus of showing that it is religious. The conclusion that it is a religious institution entitled to tax exemption is irresistible" (*Church of the New Faith v. Commissioner of Payroll Tax* 1983: 40). It adopted the following definition of religion:

> First, belief in a supernatural Being, Thing or Principle; and second, the acceptance of canons of conduct in order to give effect to that belief, though canons of conduct which offend against the ordinary

laws are outside the area of any immunity, privilege or right con-
ferred on the grounds of religion. Those criteria may vary in their
comparative importance, and there may be a different intensity of
belief or of acceptance of canons of conduct among religions or
among the adherents to a religion. The tenets of a religion may give
primacy to one particular belief or to one particular canon of conduct. Variations in emphasis may distinguish one religion from other
religions, but they are irrelevant to the determination of an individual's or a group's freedom to profess and exercise the religion of his,
or their, choice.

(*Church of the New Faith v. Commissioner
of Payroll Tax* 1983: 10)

This 60-page decision opened the door for other minority religions in Australia to be recognized, including indigenous religions hitherto denied by
the churches of the colonizers, and for them also to benefit from tax exemption. This decision has been cited in a series of decisions in other nations
of the Commonwealth. For example, the New Zealand Inland Revenue, in
its June 2001 report of the Policy Advice Division on *Tax and Charities: A
Government Discussion Document on Taxation Issues Relating to Charities and Non-Profit Bodies*, stated:

With respect to the advancement of religion, there is no distinction in
case law between one religion and another or one sect and another, so
the advancement of any religious doctrine could be considered charitable.... For purposes of the law, the criteria of religion are the belief in
a supernatural being, thing or principle and the acceptance of certain
canons of conduct in order to give effect to that belief.

(2001: Chapter 3.15: 18)

Similarly, in February 2005, the English Lords of Appeal in *Secretary of
State for Education and Employment and others (Respondents) ex parte
Williamson (Appellant) and others* relied on the Australian Scientology decision as an 'illuminating' case for the definition of religion, in a case not
related to Scientology:

Courts in different jurisdictions have on several occasions had to attempt the task [of reaching a definition of religion], often in the context
of exemptions or reliefs from rates and taxes, and have almost always
remarked on its difficulty. Two illuminating cases are the decisions of
Dillon J in *In re South Place Ethical Society* [1980] 1 WLR 1565 and
that of the High Court of Australia in *Church of the New Faith v.
Commissioner of Pay-Roll Tax (Victoria)* (1983) 154 CLR 120, both
of which contain valuable reviews of earlier authority. The trend of

authority (unsurprisingly in an age of increasingly multi-cultural societies and increasing respect for human rights) is towards a 'newer, more expansive, reading' of religion.

(2005)

The Supreme Court of the United Kingdom

The Supreme Court of the United Kingdom also recognized the conclusions of the Australian High Court to decide on Scientology. On 11 December 2013, the UK Supreme Court rendered a decision regarding the case of a couple who had been denied the right to marry in their Church by the Registrar General. The Registrar General, who is responsible for the civil registration of births, adoptions, marriages, civil partnerships and deaths in England and Wales, based his refusal on a precedent by a Court of Appeal: the 'Segerdal' decision which had stated in 1970 that the Church of Scientology was not a 'place of meeting for religious worship' within the meaning of the Places of Worship Registration Act 1855 (*R v. Registrar General* 1970). Thus, the only way for the Scientology couple to have the decision overturned was to challenge it before the Supreme Court. The decision that followed has been recognized as a milestone for minority religions.

> In a manner which might well resonate for some time, Lord Toulson [the leading judge], in *Hodkin* [2013: 19, name of the decision], has taken the debate about the nature of religion into new territory. Lord Toulson recalibrated the vocabulary, from the idea of definitions or the search for essentials, to the more open quest for a description of religion.
>
> (Cranmer et al. 2016: 27)

To reach his conclusion (which was unanimously agreed by the whole Court), the leading Judge in the Supreme Court stated that "from the considerable volume of common law jurisprudence, [he] would select two cases for particular attention" – one of the two being the above-mentioned judgment of the High Court of Australia cited above. He also reviewed the 'Segerdal' decision and in that regard judged:

> 60. On the approach which I have taken to the meaning of religion, the evidence is amply sufficient to show that Scientology is within it; but there remains the question whether the chapel at 146 Victoria Street is "a place of meeting for religious worship".
>
> 61. In my view the meaning given to worship in Segerdal was unduly narrow, but even if it was not unduly narrow in 1970, it is unduly narrow now.
>
> (*R v. Registrar* 2013: 19)

Then, with regards to the definition of religious worship:

> 62. I interpret the expression 'religious worship' as wide enough to in-
> clude religious services, whether or not the form of service falls within
> the narrower definition adopted in Segerdal. This broader interpreta-
> tion accords with standard dictionary definitions. The Chambers Dic-
> tionary, 12th ed (2011) defines the noun 'worship' as including both
> 'adoration paid to a deity', etc., and 'religious service', and it defines
> 'worship' as an intransitive verb as "to perform acts of adoration; to
> take part in religious service". Similarly, the Concise Oxford English
> Dictionary, 12th ed (2011), defines 'worship' as including both "the
> feeling or expression of reverence and adoration of a deity" and "reli-
> gious rites and ceremonies".
>
> 63. The broader interpretation accords with the purpose of the statute
> in permitting members of a religious congregation, who have a meet-
> ing place where they perform their religious rites, to carry out religious
> ceremonies of marriage there. Their authorisation to do so should not
> depend on fine theological or liturgical niceties as to how precisely they
> see and express their relationship with the infinite (referred to by Scien-
> tologists as 'God' in their creed and universal prayer). Those matters,
> which have been gone into in close detail in the evidence in this case, are
> more fitting for theologians than for the Registrar General or the courts.
>
> 64. There is a further significant point. If, as I have held, Scientology
> comes within the meaning of a religion, but its chapel cannot be regis-
> tered under PWRA because its services do not involve the kind of ven-
> eration which the Court of Appeal in Segerdal considered essential, the
> result would be to prevent Scientologists from being married anywhere
> in a form which involved use of their marriage service. They could have
> a service in their chapel, but it would not be a legal marriage, and they
> could have a civil marriage on other 'approved premises' under section
> 26(1)(bb) of the Marriage Act, but they could not incorporate any form
> of religious service because of the prohibition in section 46B(4). They
> would therefore be under a double disability, not shared by atheists, ag-
> nostics or most religious groups. This would be illogical, discriminatory
> and unjust. When Parliament prohibited the use of any 'religious service'
> on approved premises in section 46B(4), it can only have been on the
> assumption that any religious service of marriage could lawfully be held
> at a meeting place for religious services by registration under PWRA.
>
> (*R v. Registrar* 2013: 19)

Thus, the Court unanimously overruled the 'Segerdal' decision and ordered
the Registrar to register the Chapel of the Church of Scientology of London
as a place of worship. This decision has completely redefined the scope of
what is a religion and means that minority religions should not be discriminated against in the United Kingdom (Figure 4.1).

Figure 4.1 First couple to be married in the newly registered Scientology Chapel. (Photograph courtesy of the happy couple, Alessandro and Louisa Calcioli.)

The United States Internal Revenue Service decision

After years of battle against the Internal Revenue Service (IRS) in the United States, Scientology won in 1993 what they called 'the war'. It was celebrated by Scientologists all over the world with these words: "The war is over!" The IRS had finally ruled that Scientology was a genuine religion and so became tax exempt in the United States. After years of conflict between the IRS and the Church of Scientology on the topic of tax exemption for religious organizations, and after discussion with the ecclesiastical leader of the Church of Scientology, Mr David Miscavige, the IRS carried out the most thorough investigation it had ever done for any applicant claiming eligibility for religious tax exemption. This included a full and extensive review of all operations and financial records and a complete review of all aspects of the policies of the Church as well as its practices at national and international levels. By the end of its investigation, IRS had inspected more than 1 million pages of data regarding the Church of Scientology.

To render its tax-exemption rulings, the IRS had to decide that Scientology is a genuine religion; that the Churches of Scientology and their related charitable and educational institutions are operated exclusively for religious purposes; that the Churches of Scientology and their charitable and educational institutions operate for the benefit of the public interest and not for the interests of private individuals and that no part of the net earnings of these Churches of Scientology and their charitable and educational institutions are used for the financial benefit of any individual or non-charitable entity. For this determination, the IRS employs a 'facts and circumstances' test, looking at the following criteria:

- A distinct legal existence;
- A recognized creed and form of worship;
- A definite and distinct ecclesiastical government;
- A formal code of doctrine and discipline;
- A distinct religious history;
- A membership not associated with any other Church or denomination;
- An organization of ordained ministers;
- Ordained ministers selected after completing prescribed studies;
- A literature of its own;
- An established place (or places) of worship;
- Regular congregations;
- Regular religious services;
- Sunday schools for religious instruction of the young; and
- Schools for the preparation of its ministers.

All materials related to this ruling, more than 14 linear feet of documents, are available for inspection by the members of the public at the IRS National office.

Surprisingly in France

The strong opposition of some French government agencies against Scientology (and the strong discrimination Scientologists have faced in that country) has led many to state that France did not consider Scientology to be a religion. However, many French courts have recognized the religious nature of the Church since the 1980s. As Professor Marco Ventura stated:

> French case law always confined itself to findings by the Paris Court of Appeal which had, back in 1980 already stated that "Scientology activities seem to correspond to activities normally pertaining to the definition usually given to a religion, since the Court observes that in Scientology, despite a lack of metaphysical concern normally attached to the great traditional Western religions, the subjective element of faith comes with an objective factor which is the existence of a human community, however small, the members of which are bound with a system of beliefs and of practices relating to sacred things". In the subsequent cases, regardless of the conclusions that were reached, French Courts never denied the religious nature of the Church of Scientology.
>
> (Ventura 2015: 19)

In 1981, two decisions by the Court of First Instance of Paris reached the same conclusion (*Valentin v. Prosecution* 1981; *Laarhuis v. Prosecution* 1981). In 1987, in a divorce case, the Dijon's Court of Appeal ruled that the fact that one of the members of a divorcing couple had abandoned Catholicism for Scientology was protected by the right to freedom of religion and should not affect negatively the opinion of the Court (1987).

In an emblematic case, *Church of Scientology of Paris v. Interpol*, the Court of First Instance of Nanterre ruled in 1994 that "Its [Scientology's] object is thus a religious discipline, insofar as its members are united by a system of beliefs and practices relating to sacred things. Moreover, this religious character has been recognized in various judicial decisions in various countries" (*Scientology v. Interpol* 1994:18). Then, in 1996, the Administrative Court of Paris had been asked by the Church to cancel a ruling by the City of Clichy-la-Garenne which had forbidden the distribution of religious literature by Scientology. In his decision, the judge ruled that this ruling by the City of Clichy-la-Garenne was a violation of the right to freedom of religion of the Scientologists and their Church and cancelled it (*Church of Scientology v. Clichy-la-Garenne* 1996). On 28 July 1997, the Court of Appeal of Lyon stated that:

> To the extent that a religion can be defined by the coincidence of two elements, an objective element, the existence of even a small community, and a subjective element, a common faith, the Church of Scientology can claim the title of religion and freely develop, within the framework of the existing laws, its activities including its missionary activities, even of proselytizing.
>
> (*Veau et al. v. the General Prosecutor* 1997: 21)

This decision triggered some controversy as the then Minister of Interior complained that courts had no power to decide what is a religion and what is not. This political controversy led the Prosecutor's Office to appeal the decision before the Court of Cassation. The Court of Cassation ruled that, indeed, this part of the judgment was 'superabundant', in the sense of not necessary, but upheld the judgment of the Court of Appeal (*General Prosecutor v. Scientology* 1999).

The Belgian victory

On 11 March 2016, in a landmark decision, the Criminal Court of Brussels found in favour of the defendants and completely dismissed all charges against the Church of Scientology of Belgium, the Church of Scientology International European Office for Public Affairs and Human Rights and 11 Scientologists who were current or former staff members (*Scientology v. Federal Prosecutor* 2016: 122). This 173-page judgment was issued after a two-month criminal trial that ended in December 2015, following an

18-year investigation. It unequivocally rejected all charges and acquitted all defendants.

The two Church entities and the 11 Scientologists had been subjected for 18 years to numerous charges including fraud, extortion, running a criminal enterprise, violating privacy and the illegal practice of medicine. The prosecution had called for the Church entities to be disbanded, along with prison terms for the defendant members.

For almost two decades, the media, the prosecutor in charge of the case and even the State Security (Belgian intelligence services) had accused the Church of being a 'cult' and had based all their accusation mainly on this non-legally defined concept. The Court found that the charges brought against the defendants were 'deficient', 'incoherent', 'contradictory', 'inconsistent', 'vague', 'imprecise', 'unclear' and 'incomplete'. The Court also determined the criminal investigation and accusations violated the defendants' right to their presumption of innocence because the prosecutor had placed their religion on trial inappropriately by presuming that the defendants were guilty solely because they were members of the Church of Scientology:

> In other words, before it is the trial of each of the defendants prosecuted before this Court, it is primarily the trial of Scientology, in its ideological meaning, that the Prosecution intended to try. (...) "Like a Catholic priest accused of paedophilia or fraud to charities, or a terrorist responsible of terrorist attacks, whose criminal behaviours would not be judged according to the teachings of the Bible or the Koran or some of their excerpts, although sometimes very explicit, the acts of the defendants cannot be considered criminal on the sole basis of the ideological or doctrinal writings of their faith, putting the burden on them to prove to the contrary."
>
> (*Scientology v. Federal Prosecutor* 2016: 150)

The background to this trial involved a 670-page Belgium Parliamentary Commission Report that stigmatized 189 religious organizations, including Baha'is, Buddhists, Scientologists, Seventh-day Adventists, Mormons, Amish and Pentecostals, all of which were labelled as 'dangerous cults' without any investigation, cross examination or right to reply by the religions themselves. This report was used as 'evidence' by the prosecution, and the Church of Scientology challenged these assertions before the court as illegal. The Court stated that:

> The Court shares the views of the defence...: it seems obvious that by presenting in particular a list of 189 movements it considered harmful, the Parliamentary Commission made a value judgment which it was not entitled to do, violating the presumption of innocence which must benefit everyone. (...) According to the Court, it is at the level of the

conclusions drawn from its works that the Commission exceeded its powers and eventually violated certain fundamental rights guaranteed in particular under the European Convention on Human Rights, including the presumption of innocence which was just censured.

(2016: 122)

The Spanish battle

Scientology and Scientologists in Spain have endured many difficulties before reaching the position they occupy today. In 1988, the Guardia Civile raided a symposium of the International Association of Scientologists and arrested 72 members, including the President of the Church of Scientology International, Mr Heber Jentzsch. The investigatory judge, Jose-Maria Vasquez Honrubia, started from the premise that Scientology should be banned and he stated that he feared Scientologists could hypnotize him during his investigations. He even accused the Church of Scientology of being behind the death of the dictator Franco, based on secret service reports that a Scientology boat was not far from the place where sickness killed him (in fact, Franco died in his bed in Madrid while the boat in question was on the Mediterranean coast). Thirteen years later, in 2001, all Scientologists without exception were acquitted in a final decision of the Spanish Criminal Court. On 7 December 2001, the Spanish *newspaper El Pais* wrote:

> The acquittal by the Provincial Court of Madrid of members of the Church of Scientology, after 17 years of persecution by the judiciary, to which is added the intolerable slowness of our judicial system, highlights the improper use of a criminal device to oppose models of moral and religious conduct that are dissimilar to contemporary trends, or that, by their novelty or because they deviate from the most fashionable practices, raise suspicion for being abnormal phenomena. If we add to this misuse of criminal law, as was the case in this trial, the accusation of a prosecutor unable to provide evidence and an instruction without the guarantees that constitute our rule of law, it must result in an acquittal, even if it is somewhat late.

(Perseguidos Absueltos 2001)

But in ensuing years, Scientology still had to fight to be recognized as a religion at the National level. When its registration was rejected by the Ministry of Justice, which in Spain operates the registry of religious entities, Scientology challenged the rejection in court. Finally, on 31 October 2007, the National Court in Madrid (Audiencia Nacional) issued a unanimous decision affirming the right to religious freedom in Spain by recognizing that the National Church of Scientology of Spain is a religious organization entitled to the full panoply of religious rights that flow from entry in the government's Registry of Religious Entities. In its Ruling, the Audiencia Nacional stated:

> The positive conclusion favourable to its consideration as a religious entity emerges 'prima facie' from its bylaws as well as from the doctrine/teachings presented, and also from the fact that the association is similar to others that are rightfully registered in official registries in countries of similar jurisprudence and culture.
>
> *(Scientology v. Ministry of Justice* 2007)

Based on these findings, the Court "declare[d] the right of the [National Church of Scientology of Spain] to its registration in the Registry of Religious Entities of the Ministry of Justice" (2007). This decision was the first of its kind in Spain and opened the door to other 'non-traditional' religions and religious minorities being included in the Register of Religious Entities of Spain.

The Germans

Germany has had a long history of discrimination by the executive branch against Scientologists since the 1990s. Nevertheless, its Courts have a long history of recognizing Scientology as a religious organization entitled to the protection of freedom of religion or belief guaranteed by the German Constitution, its fundamental law.

In 1985, the Court of Stuttgart rendered a decision about the case of a member of the Church of Scientology who had been distributing religious literature in the street. He had been fined and forbidden to continue by the local police on the grounds that he did not have authorization for commercial activity. The Court found that the defendant was not only exercising his right to freedom of speech and freedom of religion but also that his activity could not be characterized as commercial, as it was religious:

> The Court has no evidence that would suggest that the books, pamphlets and other materials for study and information offered for sale would not serve these religious purposes; the same applies to courses, seminars and auditing subject to financial contribution, and all of them - according to the description of the person concerned and of his Church - directly constitute religious activities and practices, serve equally directly religious purposes, and are underpinned by religious motives. The Court has no doubt as to the characterization of this purpose;
>
> (...)
>
> Whereas the interested person acted in the service of a goal directly religious (...) [he] must be acquitted.
>
> (Court of Stuttgart 1985)

In 1988, the Superior Court of Hamburg decided that the Church of Scientology of Hamburg had to be recognized as a Church in the meaning of the Constitution:

> The association seeking registration must be recognized as a Church within the meaning of Article 140 of the Basic Law (Constitution) and Article 137 WRV (Constitution of the Weimar Republic).
>
> The characteristics required for a group to be recognized as a religion under the above-mentioned law are, however, uncertain. Nevertheless, the criteria that can be demanded of a Church are undoubtedly present in the present case. We are dealing with an association that is not only united for ideological purposes but also pursues a transcendental goal. This is evident not only in view of its statutes, but also its ecclesiastical rules, all elements included in the application for registration.
>
> (Court of Hamburg 1988)

In 1989, the Regional court of Frankfurt decided a case brought by a former member of the Church of Scientology who wanted to be reimbursed for money paid to receive auditing (a spiritual and religious practice of Scientology). She based her case on the fact that auditing was a psychological therapy violating the law on healers and the law on advertising medicine. The court found that auditing was part of the religious practice of Scientology, that it could not be confused with any medical or psychological practice and that the plaintiff had known this from the beginning:

> Auditing does not intervene in the field of medical therapeutics. It has its origins in the defendant's religious vision, which is protected by the Fundamental Law, and is the core of spiritual / religious practice and the manner in which Scientology ministers can contribute to the salvation of their members. Like most religious and philosophical communities, the Respondent herself describes Scientology as an approach to mankind, understood in its unity, unity of body and soul.
>
> (Regional Court of Frankfurt 1989)

A similar decision had already been rendered in 1976 by the Court of First Instance of Stuttgart.

In November 1997, the Federal Administrative Court of Germany issued a landmark judgment, stating that Scientology services were of a spiritual nature and not for commercial purposes. This decision followed an attempt by Baden-Württemberg to cancel the registration of a Scientology mission on the grounds that it violated the state's statutes and engaged in non-religious business activities.

> The Federal Administrative Court denied in 1997 the arguments used by the Administrative Courts to reject the religious nature of the

Church of Scientology, finding the religious nature of the organization to be compatible with the payment of the spiritual services that were offered. The Federal Court also recognized that one "has to rely especially on the fact that the ideas of the Church of Scientology (especially the auditing) that are manifested in the framework of services in kind, and the association's services are only proposed by its religious organization and subdivisions and that its religious reference is recognized by its members". This clarification later allowed Courts like the Higher Court of Hamburg in 1998, the Administrative Court of Stuttgart in 1999 and the Court of Social Affairs of Nuremberg in 2000 to ascertain the religious nature of the Church of Scientology.

(Ventura 2015: 7)

Thus, there are dozens of decisions in Germany recognizing the religious nature of Scientology, which makes Scientology unique in regard to case law on religious issues in Germany.

Other decisions of note

There are many other countries with case law related to freedom of religion and belief or religious recognitions involving Scientology. The European Court of Human Rights has three times ruled in favour of the Church of Scientology against the Russian Federation for the latter's refusal to register the Church of Scientology on its religious entities register (*Kimlya and Others v. Russia* 2009; *Church of Scientology of Moscow v. Russia* 2007; *Church of Scientology of St Petersburg and Others v. Russia* 2014). These decisions have frequently been cited in subsequent decisions of the Court with respect to Article 9 of the European Convention on Human Rights, protecting freedom of religion or belief.

A decision that created an important precedent was taken in 1979 by the European Commission of Human Rights (the predecessor of the European Court of Human Rights) recognizing the collective and community dimension of the Church of Scientology's subjectivity. According to the Commission, by filing a petition pursuant to the European Convention of Human Rights, the Church of Scientology in its dimension as an "ecclesiastical body" acted "actually in the name of the believers" and "the consequence must be that such a body is capable of owning and exerting, personally, as a representative of believers, the rights which are provided in Article 9" (*X and Church of Scientology v. Sweden* 1979: 70). This was the first time that the Commission recognized freedom of religion as a collective right that could be defended by a Church, as such.

In the Netherlands, the Court of Amsterdam recognized Scientology: "due to the goal pursued, auditing and training were not different from the religious activities of other ecclesiastical institutions" (*Church of Scientology of Amsterdam v. the Inspector of the Tax Services* 2013).

In Austria, on 1 August 1995, the Independent Administrative Court of Vienna, Austria, stated that:

> In addition to the fact that after several decades of thorough investigations, Scientology has been granted the status of a bona fide religion and charitable organization by the IRS, less than two years ago in the United States, the country with the greatest number of Churches of Scientology, sufficient evidence was also given by [the Church] to convince us that the Church of Scientology of Austria is a religion.
>
> (1995: 27)

The battle within the Council of Europe

After describing various court cases where the Church of Scientology has brought innovation and precedents in international case law, I will now describe some efforts of the Church as a law changer through advocacy before national or supranational governmental organizations.

On four different occasions between 1990 and 2011, attempts were made to bring about restrictions on religious minorities (derogatorily named 'sects' or 'cults') through the Parliamentary Assembly of the Council of Europe (PACE). On each occasion, the Church of Scientology was present and instrumental in working with NGOs, parliamentarians and other concerned people in order to counter the discriminatory proposals put before the Assembly and the Committee of Ministers (the highest authoritative body of the Council of Europe). International 'Observatories on Sects' was a common theme in these proposals (a proposal that would have targeted and placed under special observation 'sects' with the intention of isolating them and classifying them as groups with no religious protection). Each time, the discriminatory measures were diluted or not accepted. What may be the last of these efforts is described here.

On 7 September 2011, Rudy Salles, who was at that time a member of the National Assembly in France and part of the French delegation to PACE, was appointed as the Assembly's Rapporteur for a Report on the "protection of minors against sectarian influence". French 'anti-cult' movements had been seeking to create a 'European Observatory on sectarian movements' for many years without success. European governments have broadly held the position that common criminal law can take care of the few cases involving so-called 'sects' and that investing energy and money for creating special observatories for such a non-problem would be wasteful and discriminatory. Nevertheless, on 3 March 2014, the report drafted by Rudy Salles put forth such a measure (amongst other discriminatory proposals) on the PACE agenda for voting on 10 April during the plenary session. The draft report proposed a resolution and a recommendation, both of which were effectively attempting to export the French anti-sect model and policies to the European level and the 47 countries of the Council of Europe, including the creation of a European Observatory of Sects at the level of the Council of Europe. The report also contained a proposal to provide resources to so-called traditional religions in order to have them support the effort:

> When it comes to preventing and combating excesses of sects, some Council of Europe member states grant significant leeway to civil society and the 'traditional' Churches (Catholic, Orthodox and Protestant). In this case, it is necessary to provide these stakeholders with sufficient resources for effectively performing their tasks in terms of advising and assisting the victims of such excesses and their relatives.
>
> (Salles 2014)

Realizing what it could mean for the rights of minority religions across Europe if such recommendations were implemented, I alerted many other movements of the risks stemming from this initiative. While none were aware of this French initiative, they immediately realized how this draft resolution was contrary to international standards on freedom of religion or belief. This led to a coalition of religious movements and NGOs from all over the world. More than 80 NGOs, faith-based or not, wrote to the President of PACE to protest against the draft report and the proposed resolution.

As stated in the Council of Europe Human Rights blog:

> Readers will remember that Israeli President Simon Peres, Turkey's Deputy Prime Minister and many others were outraged by an assembly resolution last year which they thought threatened the ancient practice of male circumcision.
>
> The assembly deftly rebuffed the criticism and faint whispers of anti-Semitism, claiming it only wished to start a dialogue.
>
> Now, in a capital letter-headlined article published by World Religion News, the assembly has been warned that the new debate it has opened on 'sect observatories' has stoked the ire of yet more religious groups.
>
> (Anon 2014)

Campaigning with the Church of Scientology were NGOs from the Evangelicals, Muslims, Sikhs, Catholics, Hindus, but also many humanist or non-affiliated NGOs, such as the Moscow Helsinki Group, at that time headed by its co-founder Lyudmila Alexeyeva, considered a hero in the fight for freedom in the Soviet Union, who personally wrote to the President of PACE to alert her to the danger of such legislation. Protesters also included well-known figures as Dr Aaron Rhodes, former Executive Director of the International Helsinki Committee and Co-Founder of the Freedom Rights

Project, and Vincent Berger, former Jurisconsult of the European Court of Human Rights and Law Professor at the College of Europe.

The campaign included meeting with dozens of members of the various national delegations of the Council of Europe, making sure that they understood what legislation such as that drafted by Rudy Salles meant in terms of human rights. It also included organizing side events on the premises of the Parliamentary Assembly in Strasbourg which dozens of members of PACE attended.

Finally, on 10 April 2014, PACE decided to uphold its standards in terms of freedom of religion or belief and voted down the recommendations proposed by Salles and transformed his proposal into a resolution protecting the rights of religious minorities, reversing completely what had been written in the draft. The original draft resolution contained the following proposal which were ultimately rejected:

The Assembly therefore calls on member States to:

- 6.1. Sign and/or ratify the relevant Council of Europe conventions on child protection and welfare;
- 6.2. Gather accurate and reliable information about cases of excesses of sects affecting minors, where appropriate in crime and/or other statistics;
- 6.3. Set up or support, if necessary, national or regional information centres on sect-like religious and spiritual movements;
- 6.4. Provide teaching in the history of religions and the main philosophies in schools;
- 6.5. Make sure that compulsory schooling is enforced and ensure strict, prompt and effective monitoring of all private education, including home schooling;
- 6.6. Carry out awareness-raising measures about the scale of the phenomenon of sects and excesses of sects, in particular for judges, ombudsmen's offices, the police and welfare services;
- 6.7. Adopt or strengthen, if necessary, legislative provisions punishing the abuse of psychological and/or physical weakness and enabling associations to join proceedings as parties claiming damages in criminal cases concerning excesses of sects;
- 6.8. Support, including in financial terms, the action of private bodies which provide support for the victims of excesses of sects and their relatives and, if necessary, encourage the establishment of such bodies.

(Salles 2014)

The entire section above was replaced by:

- 6. "The Assembly therefore calls on the member states to sign and/or ratify the relevant Council of Europe conventions on child protection and welfare if they have not already done so".

(PACE 2014)

The Assembly also rewrote several articles to align them with international human rights standards and reinforce the protection of freedom of religion of minority religions in the Council of Europe region. As examples:

- 5. The Assembly believes that any religious or quasi-religious organisation should be accountable in the public sphere for any contraventions of the criminal law and welcomes announcements by established religious organisations that reports of child abuse within those organisations should be reported for investigation to the police. The Assembly does not believe that there are any grounds for discriminating between established and other religions, including minority religions and faiths, in the application of these principles.
- 9. The Assembly calls on member States to ensure that no discrimination is allowed on the basis of which movement is considered as a sect or not, that no distinction is made between traditional religions and non-traditional religious movements, new religious movements or 'sects' when it comes to the application of civil and criminal law and that each measure which is taken towards non-traditional religious movements, new religious movements or 'sects' is aligned with human rights standards as laid down by the European Convention on Human Rights and other relevant instruments protecting the dignity inherent to all human beings and their equal and inalienable rights.

(PACE 2014)

Finally, the international journal, *The Economist*, in its online edition, summarized it this way:

Yesterday was a big day in the annals of the Parliamentary Assembly of the Council of Europe (PACE), a body of legislators which is supposed to act as an important guardian of the continent's democratic freedoms. (...) [It] saw a victory in PACE for purist advocates of religious liberty, as a long-planned move to curb the activities of "sects" was unexpectedly knocked off course.

(...)

At stake was a resolution which in its original form would have denounced "new religious movements" (to use an alternative, and less loaded description of the groups sometimes described as "sects") and urged European governments to monitor such bodies and restrict their influence on youngsters. To critics, this seemed like a move to extend the policy of France—which takes a relatively harsh view of small religious groups and has an agency dedicated to countering them—across the whole of Europe. The initiative's prime mover was a French politician, Rudy Salles, and it found support in some east European countries which have one prevailing religion and regard new players in the field as unwelcome foreign imports.

(...)

It's not often that Jehovah's Witnesses, secularists and humanists find themselves on the same side, and rejoicing for the same reason, but this seems to be one such moment.

(Erasmus 2014)

To conclude

If one seeks to understand why the Church of Scientology and Scientologists have been since its inception at the forefront of legal and legislative battles related to freedom of religion or belief, I would propose examining the scriptures of the religion. Amongst many texts that cover the subject of religious freedom, one is the Code of Scientologist, first issued in 1954 and then revised in 1969 and in 1973. In its final version, the code states:

> As a Scientologist, I pledge myself to the Code of Scientology for the good of all.
> (...)
> 8. To support true humanitarian endeavours in the fields of human rights.
> 9. To embrace the policy of equal justice for all.
> 10. To work for freedom of speech in the world.
> 11. To actively decry the suppression of knowledge, wisdom, philosophy or data which would help Mankind.
> 12. To support the freedom of religion.
> (...)
> 15. To stress the freedom to use Scientology as a philosophy in all its applications and variations in the humanities.
> (...)
> 20. To make this world a saner, better place.

(Hubbard 1973)

Furthermore, the Scientology Creed, written in 1954, states:

> We of the Church believe:
> (...)
> That all men have inalienable rights to their own religious practices and their performance.

(Hubbard 1954)

That should be a good basis to understand why freedom of religion and belief is so important to Scientology and why this religion became 'law changers' in the field of religion.

References

Anon. 2014, March. Something for the weekend. [Blog post]. Retrieved from www. humanrightseurope.org/2014/03/something-for-the-weekend/ on 27 June 2014.

Bandera and others v. Italy. Italian Court of Cassation. Decided 1997. Retrieved from www.cesnur.org/testi/Milano.htm on 26 January 2020.

Church of Scientology of Amsterdam v. the Inspector of the Tax services. Court of Justice of Amsterdam. Decided 2013. Retrieved from https://uitspraken. rechtspraak.nl/inziendocument?id=ECLI:NL:GHAMS:2013:3338 on January 26, 2020.

Church of Scientology v. Clichy-la-Garenne. Administrative Court of Paris. Decided 1996.

Church of Scientology of Moscow v. Russia. ECtHR. Decided 2007.

Church of Scientology of St Petersburg and Others v. Russia. ECtHR. Decided 2014.

Church of the New Faith v. Commissioner of Payroll Tax. High Court of Australia. Decided 1983.

Court of Appeal of Dijon. Judgment 040558. Decided 1987.

Court of Stuttgart. Judgment 49 711 292249. Decided 1985.

Cranmer F., Hill M., Celia Kenny C., Sandberg R. 2016. *The Confluence of Law and Religion: Interdisciplinary Reflections on the Work of Norman Doe.* Cambridge, United Kingdom: Cambridge University Press.

Erasmus. 2014 April 10. Europe, sects and freedom, One man's sect… Secularists and small religious groups hail a quiet victory in Strasbourg. *The Economist. com.* Retrieved from www.economist.com/erasmus/2014/04/11/one-mans-sect on 19 November 2019.

General Prosecutor v. Scientology. French Court of Cassation. Decided 1999.

Hubbard, L.R. 1954. *The Creed of the Church of Scientology.* Retrieved from www.scientologyreligion.org/background-and-beliefs/the-creed-of-the-church-of-scientology.html on 19 November 2019.

———. 1973. *The Code of a Scientologist.* Retrieved from www.scientology religion.org/background-and-beliefs/the-code-of-a-scientologist.html on November 20, 2019.

Independent Administrative Court of Vienna. Decided 1995.

Kimlya and Others v. Russia. ECtHR. Decided 2009.

Laarhuis v. Prosecution. Court of First Instance of Paris. Decided 1981.

New Zealand Inland Revenue, Report of the Policy Advice Division 2001. *Tax and Charities: A Government Discussion Document on Taxation Issues Relating to Charities and Non-Profit Bodies.*

PACE, Parliamentary Assembly of the Council of Europe. 2014, April 10. The protection of minors against excesses of sects. *Assembly CoE Int.* Retrieved from https://assembly.coe.int/nw/xml/XRef/Xref-DocDetails-EN.asp?FileID=20 889&lang=EN on 20 November 2019.

Perseguidos Absueltos. 2001. *El Pais.* Editorial. Edition Madrid, 7 December.

Regina v. Secretary of State for Education and Employment and others (Respondents) ex parte Williamson (Appellant) and others. House of Lords. Decided 2005. Retrieved from https://publications.parliament.uk/pa/ld200405/ldjudgmt/ jd050224/will-1.htm on 26 January 2020.

Regional Court of Frankfurt. Judgment 2/4 0 471/88. Decided 1989.

R (on the application of Hodkin and another) (Appellants) v Registrar General of Births, Deaths and Marriages (Respondent). UK Supreme Court. Decided 2013.

R v. Registrar General, Ex parte Segerdal. Court of Appeal of England and Wales. Decided 1970.

Salles R. 2014, March 17. The protection of minors against excesses of sects. *Assembly CoE Int*. Retrieved from https://assembly.coe.int/nw/xml/XRef/Xref-XML2HTML-en.asp?fileid=20544&lang=en

Scientology v. Federal Prosecutor. Court of First Instance of Brussels. Decided 2016.

Scientology v. Ministry of Justice. Audiencia Nacional. Decided 2007. Retrieved from www.poderjudicial.es/search/doAction?action=contentpdf&databasematch=AN&reference=674967&links=%22EDUARDO%20MENENDEZ%20REXACH%22&optimize=20071108&publicinterface=true on January 26, 2020.

Scientology v. Interpol. Court of First Instance of Nanterre. Decided 1994.

Superior Court of Hamburg. 21st Chamber. Judgment 71 T 79/85. Decided 1988.

Tax Commission of Monza, documents D992-355 et seq. Decided 1991.

Valentin v. Prosecution. Court of first instance of Paris. Decided 1981

Veau et al. v. the General Prosecutor. Court of Appeal of Lyon. Decided 1997.

Ventura M. 2015. Expert report "Church of Scientology Belgium v. Prosecution". Sienna. Document in possession of the author

X and Church of Scientology v. Sweden. European Commission on Human Rights. Decided 1979.

5 No stranger to litigation

Court cases involving the Unification Church/Family Federation in the United States

Michael L. Mickler

Background

The Unification Church is one of numerous new religious movements (NRMs) which became prominent in the United States during the 1970s. It was founded in Korea by Moon, Sun Myung (1920–2012), hereafter Rev. Moon, and four followers in 1954. Since then, it has grown into a global organization, consisting of religious, cultural, educational, media, commercial, and industrial enterprises worldwide. The Church's first missionaries to the United States arrived in the Pacific Northwest in 1959, and its early mission extended through the decade of the 1960s until the arrival of Rev. and Mrs. Moon in 1971. While the society around the movement exploded in protest and rebellion, UC missionaries translated core theological texts into English, established important patterns of community life, and developed characteristic ways of relating to the wider culture. Nevertheless, core membership stood at not much more than 300 after more than a decade of effort (Lofland 1966; Bromley and Shupe 1979; Mickler 2000).

One missionary initiative of lasting importance formed the legal basis for the Church in America. This was the establishment of the Holy Spirit Association for the Unification of World Christianity (HSA-UWC), or Unification Church, a California corporation on 18 September 1961. Incorporation was a defining moment and had a significance for the UC that extended beyond the United States. Legal recognition of HSA-UWC in the United States preceded the legalization of the Church in either Korea or Japan and provided a model for the UC to attain legal standing in its countries of origin. It also meant that the UC was no longer entirely inspirational and charismatic. Maintenance of the Church's corporate identity required adherence to norms and legalities of its various host societies. It also afforded important legal protections and access to privileges enjoyed by other religious bodies, at least in theory.

The Church's legal standing as well as its adherence to norms and legalities were put to the test following Rev. Moon's decision to focus his work on the United States. The UC emerged as a national movement from 1972 to 1976. During this period, earlier missionary groups merged, national membership multiplied ten times to more than 3,000, and the UC attained widespread visibility. Nevertheless, a good portion of its visibility turned to notoriety as the Church's rapid growth provoked negative reactions. Increasingly, questions about the Church's religious and organizational legitimacy led to organized efforts to stop it. Rev. Moon's Asian origin, presumed connections to the Korean government, alleged lavish lifestyle, and even his name afforded grist to enemies who derided followers as 'Moonies' and the movement as a 'cult.' By 1976, a broad-based anti-cult movement (ACM) designated the Unification Church a primary target.

Their actions put the UC on the defensive, caused it to spend millions in litigation, sparked government investigations, and generated widespread public hostility. Members were subject to forcible removal and 'deprogramming' through court-sanctioned conservatorship rulings. Hundreds of local municipalities refused to grant solicitation permits to Church fundraisers or re-wrote regulations to keep the UC out. The Church was denied tax-exempt status in New York City, and its foreign members were denied the right to enter the country as missionaries on the same basis as members of other Churches. However, each of these situations was reversed between 1977 and 1985. The UC staffed a legal affairs office, but it served primarily as a liaison to legal counsel which the Church had the financial resources to retain. Although embroiled in near-constant litigation, the UC gained gradual recognition as a bona fide religion with tax-exemption privileges, public solicitation rights, and access to missionary visas. It also was able to extend constitutional protections to its members and successfully press for action against deprogrammers.

Unification Church litigation

This section highlights litigation and legal opinions that vindicated the Church's position and solidified its standing in the United States. However, despite these gains, the UC lost the one case that was the most highly publicized, costliest, and most important to it. Rev. Moon's conviction and imprisonment on tax evasion charges dominated press coverage of the Church at the time and continued to be a point of reference in accounts of the UC in the 1980s. Moreover, as a convicted felon, Rev. Moon was denied entry to Japan and eventually, most of Europe. Still, this should not overshadow the UC's gains. In 1977, the UC had a tenuous existence in the United States. By 1985, the UC existed on a solid legal footing. In this respect, it is important to distinguish Rev. Moon's case from unambiguous court affirmations of the UC's legal and religious status.

United States v. Sun Myung Moon (1982)[1]

In 1976, responding to complaints from constituents, Sen. Robert Dole (R-Kas) convened a 'Day of Affirmation and Protest' in which critics presented grievances against the UC before representatives of seven US government agencies. Dole, as ranking member of the Senate Finance Committee, also wrote a letter to the Internal Revenue Service stating that an audit of the Unification Church 'may be warranted.'[2] Within days, "a squad of IRS agents had taken up permanent offices in the Unification Church's downtown New York headquarters, while a team of field agents began round-the-clock surveillance of selected Church members and their telephones" (Sherwood 1991: 77). In 1978, after two years of investigations, the IRS was unable to find anything that compromised the Church's tax-exempt status but turned over to the New York District Attorney's Office 'certain anomalies' in Rev. Moon's tax returns for the years 1973–1975.

At issue were two sets of assets openly held in Rev. Moon's name: (1) accounts totalling $1.6 million at the Chase Manhattan Bank; and (2) $50,000 worth of stock in Tong Il Enterprises, Inc., a Church-owned company The government contended that Rev. Moon owned these assets beneficially and therefore owed taxes on the bank interest and stock value. An audit of tax returns showed a liability of $7,300, less than the $2,500 per year required by IRS guidelines for criminal prosecution. In addition, career attorneys from the Criminal Section of the US. Department of Justice's Tax Division did not deem Rev. Moon's alleged tax liability sufficient to warrant prosecution and signed off on a negative recommendation. The Office of the US Attorney for the Southern District of New York pursued the matter aggressively but, despite convening three grand juries, was having trouble getting an indictment. However, in August 1981, the New York District Attorney's Office presented new charges of perjury, conspiracy, and obstruction of justice that reopened the case and led to Rev. Moon's indictment.

Prosecutors successfully pressed criminal conspiracy charges based on back-dated documents, a 'Japanese Fund Ledger' submitted by the Church to account for those funds. The trial began on 1 April 1981 and lasted approximately six weeks. On 18 May 1981, the jury returned its verdict against Rev. Moon on all charges: one count of conspiracy to file false income tax returns and obstruction of justice and three counts of filing false tax returns for 1973, 1974, and 1975. On 16 July 1981, the court sentenced Rev. Moon to 18 months in prison and a $25,000 fine plus costs. Rev. Moon was incarcerated first, from 20 July 1984 until 4 July 1985 at Danbury Federal Correctional Institution, Connecticut, and then from 4 July 1985 until 20 August 1985 at Phoenix House Foundation, Inc., a halfway house in Brooklyn, New York. He served 13 months of his 18-month sentence, getting five months off for good behaviour.

Defence lawyers contended that Rev. Moon held the assets beneficially for the Church according to an accepted and widely practiced trustee role known as corporation sole and had no tax liability. Numerous religious bodies, including the National Council of Churches, the National Association of Evangelicals, and the Catholic League for Religious and Civil Rights as well as the American Civil Liberties Union, Spartacus League, and the states of Hawaii, Oregon, and Rhode Island, agreed and filed *amicus curiae*

Figure 5.1 Rally outside the court of Reverend Moon's trial.
Source: Courtesy of Holy Spirit Association for the Unification of World Spirituality.

briefs in support (Richardson 1984). The record also was barren of any evidence that Rev. Moon was involved in or consulted about the preparation of the tax returns or the Japanese Fund Ledger Defence. Attorneys further cited selective prosecution, refusal of Rev. Moon's request for a bench trial and improper jury instruction as sufficient cause to overturn the decision. However, despite exhausting every appeal motion available, their post-trial motions were all denied. The UC effectively parleyed public support into a series of 'Rallies for Religious Freedom' (Figure 5.1). The Church also considered pardon and *coram nobis* proceedings, though neither were formally pursued.

The UC used terms such as 'sacrifice' and 'crucifixion,' describing Rev. Moon as a victim who offered himself in a substitutionary way for America and the Church. These interpretations would not have won ready assent from the public. However, while Rev. Moon's case absorbed considerable attention, UC litigation proceeded mostly devoid of outcry or intrusion. In the same year that he was convicted, rights of the Unification Church and its members were upheld by federal and state courts in six separate decisions.

Tax exemption: HSA-UWC v. Tax Commission of New York City *(1982)*[3]

In March 1976, the UC applied to the Tax Commission of the City of New York for exemption from real property taxes for the tax year beginning 1 July 1976 on three properties it had acquired in 1975: a Church

Headquarters and a missionary residence, both in Manhattan, and a maintenance and storage facility in Queens. Following hearings, the Commission on 21 September 1977, by a vote of 4 to 3, denied the application on the grounds that the Church's theology was 'threaded with political motives.' This began a five-year legal battle in which mainstream religious bodies, including the American Jewish Congress, the Catholic League for Religion and Civil Rights, the National Association of Evangelicals, and the National Council of Churches filed friend of the court briefs in support of the UC. On 6 May 1982, the New York State Court of Appeals handed down a unanimous decision that overturned that tax commission action, describing it as "arbitrary and capricious and affected by error of law." The court stated, "'Traditional theology has always mandated religious action in social, political and economic matters. Virtually all of the recognized religions and denominations in America today address political and economic issues within their basic theology." More significantly, the court held that 'as a matter of law', the UC was a 'bona fide religion.'

Missionary visas: Unification Church, Nikkuni, et al. v. INS *(1982)*[4]

Yoko Nikkuni joined the UC in Japan in 1965 and entered the United States in 1973 on a tourist visa. She was later approved for a permanent residence visa to work as a missionary. However, in 1978, a review board denied her visa. The board was influenced by an earlier case in which 569 members of the Church were denied a change of status from tourist to non-immigrant 'trainees' (*Unification Church v. Attorney General*, 581 F.2d 870 (D.C. Cir.), cert. denied 439 US 828, 99 S. Ct. 102, 58 L. Ed. 2d 122, 1978). The regional commissioner who denied Nikkuni's application did so because "the work to be done by Nikkuni was the same as that required of all members" and because "the Unification Church was not a 'religious denomination' within the contemplation of the regulation."

On 16 September 1982, the US District Court for the District of Columbia ruled in favour of Nikkuni and two other members, ordering the Immigration and Naturalization Service to grant them religious worker visas and cancel any deportation proceedings. The Court stated that when Congress permitted an alien's status to turn upon religious considerations, it intended that the INS do no more than to determine if the religion in question is bona fide. As in the tax exemption case, the Court concluded, "the Unification Church, by any historical analogy, philosophical analysis, or judicial precedent (indeed, by INS' own criteria) must be regarded as a bona fide religion."

Solicitation rights: Larson v. Valenti *(1982)*[5]

As recalled by a former UC public relations officer, "Another problem faced by the Church was the banning of fundraising by innumerable local municipalities and cities throughout the nation." In some cases, he noted, "local governments re-wrote solicitation and licensing statutes to bar Church members. Other times, local police jailed and fined Church fund-raisers." The UC's response was to circulate strict 'Fundraising Guidelines' and challenge restrictions. According to a 10 November 1978 report, the Church filed 62 lawsuits in Federal courts across the country from September 1977 through October 1978. Of these, 52 were resolved in the Church's favour and 10 were still pending. In succeeding years, the UC won hundreds of solicitation cases, including one decided by the US Supreme Court.

In 1978, Minnesota amended its charitable solicitation law, under which religious organizations were previously exempt. It required religious groups that obtained more than 50 per cent of their revenue from non-members, "to file with the state, file financial disclosure forms, and be subject to state scrutiny." State officials notified the UC that it was required to register and threatened legal action if it failed to comply. The UC filed a lawsuit and in *Larson v. Valenti*, the US Supreme Court, in a 5-4 decision, ruled in favour of the Church. Before the Supreme Court, the state of Minnesota argued that the UC was not a religion after previously requiring it to register as a Church. Writing for the majority, Justice William Brennan declared that Minnesota's '50 per cent rule' creates an 'official denominational preference' that directly conflicts with First Amendment guarantees of religious freedom and that the provision was "drafted with the explicit intention of including particular religious denominations and excluding others."

Deprogramming cases (1982)

The most immediate existential threat faced by the UC, and other NRMs, were vigilante-style 'deprogrammings', that is, incidents in which members were abducted, confined, and pressured to leave the Church by paid 'deprogrammers' and their assistants, usually previously 'deprogrammed' ex-members (Bromley and Richardson 1983). Ted Patrick, a San Diego-based social worker nicknamed 'Black Lightning,' was the most well-known 'deprogrammer.' He contended that Unification Church recruiters practiced 'on-the-spot hypnosis' and the same brainwashing techniques as the North Koreans (Patrick 1976; see also Barker 1984). However, *In Re Helander v. Patrick* (1976)[6] established that the UC did not use "impermissible means... [or] techniques substantially different from those used by other religious organizations for purposes of converting or proselytizing." The courts clamped down on illegal kidnappings and 'deprogrammings,' and Patrick eventually served time in jail for his participation in such activities.

A new form of 'legal deprogramming' followed whereby sympathetic judges granted temporary conservatorships or guardianships, usually for 30 days, during which time parents could forcibly remove their adult children from the Church and turn them over to paid deprogrammers or 'deprogramming centers.' The Tucson, Arizona-based Freedom of Thought Foundation, which had emerged as the leading Western US deprogramming centre, escalated their efforts, preparing standardized forms and seeking multiple conservatorships at a single hearing. This precipitated a confrontation in San Francisco between five sets of parents and five UC members who retained counsel to fight their would-be conservators (*Katz v. Superior Court*).[7] Dubbed the 'faithful five,' their conservatorship hearing generated nationwide publicity and lasted several weeks. In the end, Superior Court Judge Lee Vavuris decided for the parents, explaining:

> I could see the love here of a parent for his child, and I don't... have to go beyond that.... It is never-ending.... A child is a child even though the parent may be ninety and the child is sixty.

Vavuris' decision touched off a firestorm of editorial protest. The California State Court of Appeals stayed the conservatorship order two weeks after it was rendered and six months later reversed it, propounding "stringent criteria for the granting of such petitions in the future."

Three cases adjudicated or argued in 1982 were significant in the UC's battle against deprogramming and in defending its free exercise rights. On 26 May 1982, in a member's lawsuit against a deprogrammer, Rev. Moon was ordered into a US District court and ridiculed in a hostile interrogation of his religious beliefs. Two days later, the US Court of Appeals in *In Re: HSA-UWC, Reverend Sun Myung Moon and Anthony Colombrito*[8] ordered the judge to end the trial and to strike all of Rev. Moon's testimony from the record, eliminating the threat of subpoenaed testimony on religious beliefs. The same year, in *Eden v. Reverend Sun Myung Moon, HSA-UWC et al.*,[9] the UC won a ruling against a damage suit brought by a former member on the grounds of alleged 'mind control.' The most consequential case was *Ward v. Conner*[10] in which a UC member subjected to 35 days of deprogramming brought suit against 31 people, including his family members and others hired to break his faith. The US Supreme Court declined to review a lower court decision allowing him to bring suit against deprogrammers, arguing that Unification Church adherents are entitled to the same civil rights protection which the law grants to racial minorities. This effectively ended coercive deprogramming as a threat to the Church.

Having established its identity as a bona fide religion and extended constitutional protections to members, the UC experienced a quarter-century (1985–2010) of relative stability. Litigation receded, and the UC's legal affairs office occupied itself with organizational management and development functions common to religious groups, that is, setting up subsidiaries, managing property, handling personnel matters, obtaining visas, etc.

There was still suspicion and negativity expressed towards Rev. Moon, but efforts to restrict the UC's activities or to treat it in ways that were differed from other religious organizations were lacking. At minimum, the UC was tolerated within the variegated pattern of religion in the United States.[11]

A new round of litigation began after 2010. This time, rather than battles against its host society, these have been against rogue individuals and groups. Beginning in 2011, the UC, now officially the Family Federation, pursued litigation to protect its assets and symbols against their unauthorized use. This litigation has occupied FFWPU for nearly a decade.

Family Federation litigation

In the United States, the Holy Spirit Association for the Unification of World Christianity (HSA-UWC) and the Family Federation for World Peace and Unification (FFWPU) are closely linked. HSA-UWC is the corporate and legal entity under which the UC is registered and has ownership of Church properties and Church businesses. The Family Federation is another name for the Unification Church in America as is shown on its official website (familyfed.org). In reality, the two organizations are indistinguishable and interchangeable. According to the HSA-UWC Bylaws:

> The name of the corporation shall be THE HOLY SPIRIT ASSOCIATION FOR THE UNIFICATION OF WORLD CHRISTIANITY (hereinafter referred to as the 'Church'). It shall also be known as the UNIFICATION CHURCH OF AMERICA, the UNIFICATION CHURCH, HSA-UWC FAMILY CHURCH, or FAMILY FEDERATION FOR WORLD PEACE AND UNIFICATION.
>
> (HSA-UWC 2008)

Both FFWPU and HSA-UWC are designations for the religious organization commonly called the Unification Church, founded in Korea by Sun Myung Moon in 1954.

As sociologists of religion, David Bromley and Alexa Blonner (2012: 87) correctly note in their study of the UC's development, "Throughout its history Unificationism has incorporated both church and social movement characteristics." They point out that Rev. Moon attempted "to arrest the UC's slide towards settled lives and an established church" during the 1990s by proclaiming the 'end of religion' and establishing the Family Federation for World Peace and Unification (FFWPU or the Family Federation) as a successor organization to HSA-UWC. The formation of the Family Federation brought about important changes to the UC, including "the extension of the sacramental Unificationist marriage blessing to non-Unificationist couples and a major concentration on peace initiatives.'"

These initiatives "reinstituted the religious movement orientation reminiscent of the early movement" but failed to resolve issues of emerging leadership. According to Bromley and Blonner (2012: 90):

> As Moon began approaching his eightieth birthday in 2000, he set in motion a succession process that eventually encompassed four of his children, all of whom were highly educated with professional-managerial degrees from prestigious universities. What emerged was a conflict among his children that mirrored the tension between religious movement and established church organization causing the momentum within Unificationism to switch again, and probably decisively this time, toward a more conventional church organization.

Preston (Hyun Jin) Moon, a Columbia University and Harvard Business School graduate, was the first sibling to assume a public role when he was appointed by Rev. Moon to be Vice President of FFWPU International in 1998. Preston Moon called upon the UC to "get rid of its Church-centered framework" and model "an inter-religious, international, inter-racial movement that can unite all religions, nations and NGOs within ... [a] 'One Family under God ...' peace movement" (Moon 2008). Utilizing FFWPU resources and building upon its network of contacts, he proceeded to convene multiple Global Peace Festivals (GPFs) in diverse international locales.

His younger siblings – Justin (Kook Jin) Moon, a successful entrepreneur; Sean (Hyung Jin) Moon, a Harvard Divinity School graduate who undertook pastoral duties in Korea; and Tatiana (In Jin) Moon, also a Harvard Divinity School graduate who became chairperson of the UC in the United States – openly opposed Preston Moon's initiatives, considered them a waste of resources, and worked to shore up the Church's institutional base. As Bromley and Blonner (2012: 90) explain, the three younger siblings "formed a triumvirate that moved rapidly in the direction of church-style organization." They gained the support of Rev. and Mrs. Moon and denounced their elder brother, who disaffiliated from the Family Federation in 2009. This set the stage for a major lawsuit.

The Family Federation for World Peace and Unification International, et al. v. Hyun Jin Moon (a/k/a Preston Moon), et al.[12]

On 11 May 2011, FFWPUI, The Family Federation for World Peace and Unification International ('Family Federation'), The Universal Peace Federation ('UPF'), The Holy Spirit Association for the Unification of World Christianity (Japan) and ousted Unification Church International (UCI) Board members Douglas Joo and Peter Kim filed suit against the UCI and individual defendants Preston Moon and four other members of the UCI

Board of Directors. The dispute arose out of the Defendants' alleged usurpation of UCI and its assets, valued at $3.4 billion according to later court filings.[13]

UCI is a non-profit, non-tax-exempt corporation established in 1975 in the District of Columbia to support Unification Church activities worldwide. In April 2006, Preston Moon became President and Chairman of the Board of Directors of UCI. FFWPUI's complaint stated:

> Beginning in 2009, Preston Moon orchestrated an illegal takeover of the Corporation after Reverend Sun Myung Moon, the founder of the Unification Church and father of Preston Moon, named Preston Moon's younger brother Hyung Jin ('Sean') Moon ... and not Preston, the future spiritual leader and head of the worldwide Unification Church and International President of the Family Federation.

The complaint further alleged, "the Individual Defendants diverted funds that the Japanese Church and other Unification Church entities donated to UCI away from their intended charitable use" and instead "caused donated funds to be used to support Preston Moon's personal and non-Unification Church-related projects." It further noted, "After taking control of the Board of Directors, Preston Moon and the Board amended the Corporation's Articles of Incorporation to remove all references to the Unification Church" and began selling off UCI assets (a building in Washington, D.C. for $113 million, a property in McLean, VA for $855,000 and the 417-room Sheraton National Hotel in Arlington, Virginia for an undisclosed sum).

In their motion to dismiss, UCI attorneys argued that UCI is a self-governing organization, not "subject to the control of persons and entities external to the corporation" (i.e., FFWPUI), and that its Articles of Incorporation state, "[t]he right to vote on any and all matters affecting the Corporation shall be vested exclusively in the Board of Directors of the Corporation." They claimed, "the contention that UCI is part of and subject to the control of a separate hierarchical church structure" to be "completely unsupported and implausible." However, the trial judge disagreed. She wrote that the Church's intention to establish a trust with fiduciary obligations could be evidenced "by written or spoken language or by conduct" and that "for decades UCI and its Directors operated in accordance with Reverend Moon's and the Family Federation's directives." UCI's motion to dismiss was denied and the suit went forward.

A maze of motions and counter-motions, a fight over tainted evidence, battles over continued dissipation and transfer of UCI assets, delays occasioned by the Court's calendar, expert witness reports, and depositions followed, tying the case up in court for eight years. Apart from UCI's claim to be independent, the other major item of dispute was UCI's contention that the lawsuit fundamentally pertained to religious matters and was constitutionally beyond the jurisdiction of the court. On 19 December 2013, the trial judge agreed and dismissed the case. However, on 14 December 2015, the District of Columbia Court of Appeals reinstated it. Their opinion was that Religious Abstention based on the Free Exercise Clause "does not mean … that churches are above the law or that there can never be a civil court review of a church action." Especially when a dispute over property arises, the Court of Appeals held:

> Religious organizations come before [the courts] in the same attitude as other voluntary associations for benevolent or charitable purposes, and their rights of property, or of contract, are equally under the protection of the law …
>
> There can be little doubt about the general authority of civil courts to resolve [the issue] … as [t]he State has an obvious and legitimate interest in the peaceful resolution of property disputes, and in providing a civil forum where the ownership of church property can be determined conclusively.

The District of Columbia Court of Appeals concluded that the UCI dispute "is susceptible to resolution by 'neutral principles of law' not requiring any forbidden inquiry into matters barred by the First Amendment." It remanded the case for further proceedings.

Case discovery concluded in 2018, and on 31 May, both sides filed motions for Summary Judgment. FFWPUI based its motion on the allegation that UCI Directors 'breached their fiduciary duty,' including the duty of loyalty, and engaged in acts beyond their legal authority. UCI again argued that the case was "impossible to resolve without delving into theological questions and weighing in on a doctrinal dispute … whether UCI and its directors correctly interpreted Reverend Moon's dogma." Despite the fact that Rev. Moon called on Preston Moon to give up UCI to no avail, Defendants submitted that their actions "were entirely in line with the theology of the 'Unification Movement'."

On 30 October 2018, Judge Laura Cordero issued an Omnibus Order on Motions for Summary Judgment. Agreeing with the Appeals Court, she did not accept the Religious Abstention argument. She stated that "the Defendants' actions unfolded amidst the conflict between Preston Moon and his parents" and "the conflict does not require that the Court wade into theological matters." She concluded that FFWPUI was entitled to summary judgment on the claim that "Defendants breached their fiduciary duty owed to UCI when they used their position as board members to fundamentally alter the articles of incorporation for the express purpose of making asset donations unaffiliated with the Unification Church."

FFWPUI filed a Motion for Remedies on 19 April 2019. It asked the Court to (1) remove the Defendants from the UCI Board and replace them with directors proposed by FFWPUI; (2) surcharge the Defendants in the amount of the wrongful donations; (3) impose a constructive trust on assets wrongfully donated; and (4) rescind the unlawful 2010 amendment of the Articles of Incorporation. FFWPUI proposed a surcharge of more than $3 billion to account for donations and/or asset transfers and interest on the donations made to the Global Peace Festival Foundation (later the Global Peace Foundation), and the Kingdom Investment Foundation (KIF), a secretly established Swiss foundation with no connection to the Unification Church to which the Defendants donated the most valuable assets controlled by UCI. In addition to $62 million in cash donations to GPF, FFWPUI's calculation of the market value of transferred assets to KIF included:

- Central City, a Seoul Marriott Hotel and mall complex: $922.5 million;
- Y22/Parc1, a 74 and 56 story office building and shopping complex in Seoul's financial district, $1.902 billion;
- Yong Pyong, a ski resort, $20.3 million;
- Il Sung, a construction company, $80.8 million;

FFWPUI attorneys pointed out that KIF's 'Donation Agreement' contained a provision "requiring the Swiss Foundation to indemnify UCI and its then-current officers and directors from any liabilities relating to the Agreement."

Attorneys representing the Defendants conceded that the Court should rescind amendments to the UCI Articles of Incorporation. However, they disputed the Court's authority to remove and replace Board members or exact a surcharge. They demanded an evidentiary hearing to demonstrate the Defendants acted 'in good faith,' believing that they were furthering the interests of UCI and the Unification Movement. The Defendant attorneys also challenged the surcharge total. FFWPUI attorneys claimed that the Defendants continued to act with malfeasance after summary judgment, secretly electing three new directors who conveniently voted to indemnify them. They argued that the Defendants' 'subjective intent' is irrelevant, that they 'grossly abused their position,' and the attempt to interject good faith was "an improper back-door attempt to relitigate their position."

The Court convened motion hearings in August and October 2019 followed by final briefs. As of this writing, the matter of remedies has not been decided.

Holy Spirit Association for the Unification of World Christianity [Family Federation] v. World Peace and Unification Sanctuary, Inc. *(2018)*[14]

On 30 July 2018, the HSA-UWC, also known as the Family Federation, brought a trademark infringement suit against World Peace and Unification

Sanctuary, Inc. (Sanctuary Church) based in Newfoundland, Pennsylvania. Sanctuary Church (hereafter 'Sanctuary'), led by Sean Moon, Rev. and Mrs. Moon's youngest son, split off from HSA-UWC in 2014 and espouses a 'gun-centred' theology which HSA-UWC (hereafter 'HSA') describes as 'repugnant' to central tenets of its theology. Sanctuary teaches that the 'rod of iron' discussed in the Book of Revelation is embodied by an AR-15 semi-automatic rifle and runs an outreach 'Rod of Iron Ministries.' On 28 February 2018, Sanctuary held a 'Marriage Gun Commitment Ceremony' in which congregants were instructed to bring AR-15 rifles or their equivalent. The ceremony attracted nationwide media attention, particularly in light of school shootings, notably a mass shooting that occurred in Parkland, Florida on 14 February 2018. HSA's 'Twelve Gate' logo, also referred to as the 'Tongil' or unity mark, was visible throughout the ceremony, and in multiple instances, the news coverage did little to differentiate the activities or beliefs of Sanctuary Church from that of HSA, causing what HSA described as 'confusion' in the public's mind.

In the complaint, HSA stated that it had used the logo continuously over 50 years, and it was registered with the US Patent and Trademark Office in 2009. HSA sued Sanctuary for trademark infringement, trademark dilution, false association, and unfair competition. Two years prior to the gun wedding, HSA sent a cease and desist letter to Sanctuary, putting it on notice for infringement. Counsel for Sanctuary defended its use on the ground that Sean Moon is the true heir of HSA-UWC and thus the owner of the Twelve Gate logo. HSA claimed that Sanctuary's continuing wilful and deliberate use of the logo was causing it 'irreparable harm.' It asked the court to preliminarily and permanently prohibit Sanctuary from use of the logo and award damages in an amount to be determined.

In its reply, Sanctuary asserted, "This is anything but a simple trademark dispute." It claimed that 'Tongil' is a 'universal symbol' at the core of Unification faith and cannot be 'owned' by anyone without violating their First Amendment rights. Its counterclaim stated, "One branch of a worldwide religion cannot claim to own and have the exclusive right to use a core symbol of that religion" any more than the Catholic Church could "obtain trademark registration for the cross" and prevent access to Lutherans and Methodists. Sanctuary disputed that it was a 'splinter Church' rather than "the rightful and true Church led by the rightful and true successor to Rev. Moon." It also disputed whether HSA had the right to trademark 'Cheon Il Guk,' a term coined by Rev. Moon generally equivalent to 'the Kingdom of God.' Sanctuary's alternative pleading was that should the court find that the 'Tongil' and 'Cheon Il Guk' do in fact function as trademarks, "Sean Moon be named as the rightful owner or licensee."

HSA denied that Tongil and Cheon Il Guk identified 'a general class of spiritual organizations' rather than a 'single, unique organization' and cited court decisions against splinter groups, "divorced from the charter of the primary Church," that seek to "adopt the Church's emblem." It accused

Sanctuary of draping its infringement "in the mantle of religious freedom" and "shifting the focus from trademark matters legitimately in dispute to issues of Church theology and succession – none of which are properly at issue" or can be adjudicated by a court. However, the trial judge denied HSA's motion to dismiss. Though acknowledging "a presumption in favour of a registered trademark," he determined on 22 July 2019 that the 'sharp disputes' set forth in factual assertions and legal conclusions required further discovery and argument. HSA and Sanctuary completed depositions and filed motions for Summary Judgment on 7 October 2019. As of this writing, the court has not ruled on the motions.

Moon v. Moon *(2019)*[15]

In a separate action, Hyung Jin 'Sean' Moon filed a complaint against Hak Ja Han Moon (his mother), HSA-UWC, FFWPU, and eight Church officials in the US District Court for the Southern District of New York on 22 February 2019. The suit alleged that in January 2009, Rev. Moon appointed his son, Sean Moon, as his successor and leader of the Family Federation and Unification Church by way of three public coronation ceremonies and a written proclamation, each described as 'irrevocable.' It charged that "Mrs. Moon and her co-conspirators orchestrated a malicious and illegal scheme to seize control of these organizations and to strip Sean Moon of his proper authority." Sean Moon claimed that he was suspended from his role as the International President of Family Federation for acting "as a whistleblower exposing the improper conduct of those claiming power within the Family Federation and the Unification Church." He brought the action "seeking a declaration of this Court to confirm his legal status as leader."

The Court noted deficiencies in the original filing and allowed a First Amended Complaint (FAC) on 14 June 2019. On 29 June, the Defendants filed a motion to dismiss, stating that "the Court cannot provide him [Sean Moon] the relief he seeks. The First Amendment precludes this Court from declaring him the leader of the Unification Church." Counsel for the Defendants noted, "Under the First Amendment, religious organizations have the 'power to decide for themselves, free from state interference, matters of Church government as well as those of faith and doctrine'." The motion highlighted additional technical matters related to personal jurisdiction and statute of limitations.

On 19 December 2019, the Court dismissed the lawsuit in its entirety for lack of subject matter jurisdiction. Judge Naomi Reice Buchwald found that "this Court may not, consistent with the First Amendment, intervene in" a "controversy over who should replace the late Rev. Moon as leader of the Unification Church." In her discussion, she pointed out that neither 'Deference to Ecclesiastical Authority' nor 'Neutral Principles of Law' would be of assistance because there was 'substantial controversy' over ecclesiastical authority and because there were neither governing documents nor 'accepted or honoured custom' that would assist in 'contract interpretation.' She acknowledged that the ecclesiastical abstention rule "will in certain instances leave aggrieved parties without a forum for the adjudication of their claims." Nevertheless, she cited a judicial opinion that "The First Amendment serves to prevent exactly this sort of picking winners and losers in ecclesiastical matters."

On 11 March 2020, Sean Moon filed an appeal brief to the Court of Appeals. Hak Ja Han Moon, HSA et al. filed an opposition brief on 15 April. As of this writing, the case remains under appeal.

Conclusion

In litigation over nearly a half century, the Unification Church/Family Federation exemplifies a pattern common to religious denominations in the United States and to religious development generally. Whether set in a sect-to-church, sect to denomination, sect-to-institutionalized sect, or cult to denomination framework, the pattern is that of an outsider religion subjected to social control measures gradually gaining legitimation and varying degrees of social acceptance followed by the at least marginally accepted faith also employing social control measures and the law to protect its gains. Rather than against a hostile government and society, the battle is with rogue groups and individuals from within. This is a familiar trajectory and typifies the life cycle of many religious traditions and organizations (Niebuhr 1929).

Rev. Moon was the unquestioned leader of the Unification Church for nearly six decades. For followers, he fit the classic definition of the charismatic leader. As such, he had few internal constraints in making policy or personnel decisions and in allocating organizational resources. This was a double-edged sword. In the course of a single generation, Rev. Moon's leadership fuelled UC's advance from exceedingly humble origins to become a complex, diversified, multinational organization with an imposing, even astonishing array of churches, educational and cultural foundations, and businesses. At the same time, his persona and leadership sparked opposition and efforts to hinder or even destroy the Church which the UC countered with various tactics, including litigation. Rev. Moon's leadership also raised the issue of succession. Schism and division were anathema to his vision for the 'Unification' Church. Nevertheless, that is precisely the context within which the UC/Family Federation's recent litigation has unfolded.

For most of its history, few within the UC challenged Rev. Moon's authority or sought to undermine Unification institutions (Mickler 2016). That changed during the last decade of Rev. Moon's life as Preston Moon took to lecturing his father on the 'needs of the providence,' rejected his authority, and led several breakaway organizations. After Rev. Moon's passing, Sean Moon denounced his mother, stated that she was no longer Rev. Moon's legitimate wife, and established a breakaway Church. Both of them reject HSA-UWC/FFWPU. In February 2010, the Board of Directors of the Holy Spirit Association for the Unification of World Christianity removed Preston Moon from the Board because of his "disregard for the wishes of [Reverend Sun Myung Moon] and his disregard for Church authority." In March 2015, FFWPU suspended Sean Moon from his authority and duties as International President and later replaced him for "Abuse of authority and violation of Church tenets."

Discord of this sort is far from uncommon in religious traditions. Often, challenges to authority overwhelm communities of faith, especially new ones, driving them to extinction.[16] Other times, religious traditions withstand attacks and root out opponents, stigmatizing them as heretics or schismatics and seeking recourse in the law (Lewis and Lewis 2009; Miller 1991). Although recent rulings are favourable to the UC/Family Federation, final decisions and the entire legal process have yet to play out fully. Regardless, the law as a neutral arbiter has been critical to the development of the Unification Church/Family Federation in the United States.

Notes

1 *United States v. Sun Myung Moon*, 93 F.R.D. 558 (S.D.N.Y. 1982); id., 532 F. Supp 1360 (S.D.N.Y. 1982).
2 Letter from Robert Dole, United States Senator, to Donald Alexander, Commissioner, Internal Revenue Service, January 9, 1976. Cited in Sherwood 1991, p. 55.
3 *HSA-UWC v. Tax Commission of New York City*, 59 N.Y.2d 512, 435 N.E.2d 662, 450 N.Y.S.2d 292 (1982), rev'g 81 A.D.2d 64, 438 N.Y.S. 2d 521 (1981), prior opinion remaining for plenary hearing, 62 A.D.2d. 188,404 N.Y.S.2d 93, leave to appeal denied, 45 N.Y.2d 706, N.E.2d, 408 N.Y'S.2d 1025 (1978).
4 *Unification Church, Nikkuni, et al v. INS*, 547 F. Supp. 623 (D.D.C. 1982).
5 *Larson v. Valente*, 102 S. Ct. 1673 (1982), affg 637 F.2d 562 (8th Cir. 1981).
6 *In Re Helander v. Patrick*, Superior Court, Fairfield County (Conn.) No. 195062, Sept. 8, 1976.
7 *Katz v. Superior Court (people)*. 73 Cal. App. 3d 952, 141 Cal. Rptr. 234 (1977).
8 *In Re HSA-UWC, Reverend Sun Myung Moon and Anthony Colombrito*, United States Court of Appeals for the Second Circuit, Docket No. 82-3035, M16 28, 1982.
9 *Eden v. Reverend Sun Myung Moon*, HSA-UWC et al., Michigan, Wayne County Circuit Court, No. 77-736-880 NO, Dec. 3, 1982
10 *Ward v. Connor*, 657 F.2d 45 (4th Cir. 1981), Rev'g in part 495 F. Supp. 434 (E.D.Va. 1980), cert. denied sub nom. *Mandelkorn v. Ward*, 102 S. Ct. 1253 (1983).
11 *Molko and Leal v. Unification Church*, 179 California Appeals 3rd 450 (1986) and 46 Cal. 3rd 1092, 762: 26, 46 (1988) was an exception to the pattern

of acceptance. Two former members sued the UC, claiming they were 'brain-washed' and subject to mind control prior to their decision to join. The case, which continued for a number of years, included a significant dispute among psychologists and sociologists of religion as to the admissibility of 'brainwashing' arguments. For a full treatment, see Richardson (1996).

12 *Family Federation for World Peace and Unification International et al., v. Hyun Jin Moon et al.*, Civil Action No. 2011 CAB 3721 (D.C. Super. Ct.).
13 For early discussions of UC finances, see Bromley (1985, 1988).
14 *Holy Spirit Association for the Unification of World Christianity v. World Peace and Unification Sanctuary, Inc.*, Civil No. 3:18-CV-01508 (M.D. Pa).
15 *Hyung Jin "Sean" Moon v. Hak Ja Han Moon et al.*, No. 1:19-cv-01705-NRB (S.D.N.Y.).
16 Rodney Stark (1987: 11) notes that it is 'very difficult' to study how new religions succeed, "for the fact is that virtually all new faiths rapidly fail ... nearly all the others can be rated as successes only in comparison with the absolute failures, for they too seldom become more than footnotes in the history of religions."

References

Barker, Eileen. 1984. *The Making of a Moonie: Choice or Brainwashing?* Oxford: Basil Blackwell.

Bromley, David. 1985. "Financing the Millennium: The Economic Structure of the Unificationist Movement". *Journal for the Scientific Study of Religion* 24: 253–74.

———. 1988. "Economic Structure and Charismatic Leadership in the Unificationist Movement", in: James T. Richardson (ed.), *Money and Power in the New Religions*. Lewiston: Edwin Mellen, pp. 335–64.

Bromley, David and Alexa Blonner. 2012. From the Unification Church to the Unification Movement and Back. *Novo Religio* 16(2): 86–95.

Bromley, David and Anson Shupe. 1979. *Moonies in America: Cult, Church and Crusade*. Beverly Hills, CA: Sage.

Bromley, David and James T. Richardson. 1983. *The Brainwashing/Deprogramming Controversy: Sociological, Psychological, Legal and Historical Perspectives*, Lewiston, NY: Edwin Mellen.

Holy Spirit Association for the Unification of World Christianity (HSA-UWC). 2008. *Bylaws*. As amended by resolution.

Lewis, James and Sarah Lewis. 2004. *Sacred Schisms: How Religions Divide*. Cambridge, MA: Cambridge University Press.

Lofland, John. 1966. *Doomsday Cult: A Study of Conversion, Proselytization and Maintenance of Faith*. Englewood Cliffs, NJ: Prentice-Hall.

Mickler, Michael. 2000. *40 Years in America: An Intimate History of the Unification Movement, 1959–1999*. New York: HSA-UWC.

———. 2016. "Mainstream Unificationism". *Applied Unificationism*, https://appliedunificationism.com/2016/08/29/mainstream-unificationism/. Accessed 1 February 2020.

Miller, Timothy. 1991. *When Prophets Die: The Post-Charismatic Fate of New Religious Movements*. Albany: State University of New York Press.

Moon, Preston. 2008. *Report to Parents*. www.tparents.org/Moon-Talks/HyunJin Moon/HyunJinMoon-080323.htm. Accessed 6 February 2020.

Niebuhr, H. Richard. 1929. *The Social Sources of Denominationalism.* New York: Henry Holt and Company.

Patrick, Ted. 1976. *Let Our Children Go.* New York: Ballantine.

Richardson, Herbert. 1984. *Constitutional Issues in the Case of Rev. Moon.* New York: Edwin Mellen.

Richardson, James T. 1996. Sociology and the New Religions: 'Brainwashing, 'the Courts and Religious Freedom, in: Jenkins, Pamela J. and Steve Kroll-Smith (eds), *Witnessing for Sociology: Sociologists in Court.* Westport, CN: Praeger, pp. 115–34.

Sherwood, Carleton. 1991. *Inquisition: The Persecution and Prosecution of the Reverend Sun Myung Moon.* Washington, DC: Regnery Gateway.

Stark, Rodney. 1987. How New Religions Succeed: A Theoretical Model, in: Bromley, David and Phillip Hammond (eds), *The Future of New Religious Movements.* Macon, GA: Mercer University Press, pp. 11–29.

6 Legal challenges posed to the Unification Church in Europe

Perspectives from a Unificationist advocate for religious freedom

Peter Zoehrer[1]

The entry ban against the Unification Church leaders: a personal account[2]

I joined the Unification Church (UC) in Graz, Austria, in 1972, and have been an active member ever since. I have had numerous profound experiences with Rev. Sun Myung Moon, the founder and leader of the UC, but one encounter 25 years ago definitely changed the course of my life. In November 1995, Rev. and Mrs. Moon visited Hungary, where I was serving as the UC's national leader between 1993 and 1997. As part of an international speaking tour, Rev. Moon had given a well-attended public speech in Budapest on the meaning of family values, which was published on the same day in a national newspaper. He was very happy and signed many copies for us as a token of remembrance. However, after the Moons left Hungary for Spain, things started to go terribly wrong.

On the afternoon of their departure on 9 November 1995, my organization team received a telephone call informing us that Rev. and Mrs. Moon would be on the next flight back to Hungary. We learned that they had been intercepted at Charles de Gaulle Airport in Paris *en route* to Madrid and interrogated like criminals by the French police before being sent back to Hungary. On the same day, an article published in the *Bild-Zeitung*, Germany's most popular boulevard newspaper, informed us that the German authorities had placed Rev. Moon on the Schengen Information System (SIS), a blacklist of undesirable foreign nationals, implying that he was banned from entering the entire Schengen area. At that time, the Schengen area covered 12 states including all major continental European countries.[3] This news triggered a shock-wave throughout the entire European Unification Movement (UM). Because the Moon couple – affectionally known among our members as the 'True Parents' – had departed in the early morning, we had already signed out of the hotel and thus immediately had to arrange new accommodation. We received Rev. Moon and his wife at the airport and drove them to the Hilton, where only a small group formed a welcoming party. Four of us joined them for a late lunch in their suite.

During the lunch, the massive significance and impact of this Schengen ban hit us. I felt intensely nauseated and unable to eat on contemplating the fact that Germany, and with it other Schengen countries, had chosen to treat our founders – whose only 'crime' was to spread the message of love and peace – as undesirables. I was visibly shaken. Mrs. Moon sat on her chair in a calm but serious manner, while her husband tried to comfort me. He walked to the window. It was already getting dark and the lights of the Hungarian Parliament could be seen reflected on the Danube. It was a beautiful sight. Rev. Moon looked out of the window, softly whistling and trying to raise our spirits. He asked me why I was not eating: "Eat! It's good!" Replying to my answer that I was deeply sorry for Europe's treatment of them, he said with a shrug, "Oh, I am used to this! It always happens to me!" But the more he tried to comfort me, the more serious I became until in his messianic wisdom he changed the subject to fishing. He asked, "Can you fish in the Danube or is it too polluted?" This was an excellent tactic to calm my mind because fishing happens to be a favourite topic of mine.

I remember this meeting as if it were yesterday. To me, it was a defining, life-changing experience: on that day, I decided to become a passionate human rights activist and religious freedom advocate. That afternoon, I made a promise to myself, and to God: "From now on, I will invest myself for religious freedom in Europe and the world! No matter what anyone says, I will fight until Rev. and Mrs. Moon have been vindicated and can travel freely in Europe." There and then, the internal foundation was laid for what later, in 1998, would become FOREF, the Forum for Religious Freedom–Europe, an international human rights organization.[4] Two years later, in 2000, the European UM created the 'Schengen Committee' with the help of the American branch. The committee's sole purpose was to have the ban lifted. A Schengen entry ban is normally terminated after three years. However, in the case of Rev. and Mrs. Moon, a strong European anti-cult lobby headed by the European Federation of Centres of Research and Information on Sectarianism (FECRIS) ensured that the ban was repeatedly renewed.[5]

The ban against the Moons was a serious violation of the basic right of Unificationists to practice their faith as thousands of European members were deprived of the ability to meet their religious leaders in person and have their leaders conduct religious ceremonies in their nations. This abuse of the Schengen Convention crassly violated international standards. The Schengen blacklisting of Rev. and Mrs. Moon was contested on several levels. On the one hand, UC members took legal action and fought the unjust treatment of their religious founders before the German courts. It required 12 long years before the German courts declared the entry ban against Rev. and Mrs. Moon as unconstitutional and a violation of religious freedom. Section 2 provides an overview of this process.

On the other hand, several human rights organizations, including the US-based International Coalition for Religious Freedom (Fefferman 2002), criticized the German government openly. The vanguard that protested the Schengen entry ban on the ground in Europe was the Forum for Religious Freedom – Europe, an organization I co-founded. It was a learning by doing-job and I steadily gained deeper insights into the machinery of the anti-cult lobby. Driven by indignation at their blatant attacks on fundamental rights, FOREF Europe advocated for religious freedom in Europe on a broad scale and defended the rights of numerous minority groups apart from the UC. FOREF Europe worked in particular through the annual delivery of statements at the Human Dimension Implementation Meetings of the OSCE[6] as well as through regular online reporting of anti-cult activities by state and private actors.[7] This form of advocacy for religious freedom received remarkable support from religious representatives, human rights groups, the US State Department and even the United Nations. Over time, I developed a network that was instrumental in achieving an important legal victory for the UC in Austria. Section 3 outlines the challenges the Austrian UC had to face by a repressive legal system and how it turned state-endorsed persecution including the systematic denial of any legal status into legal 'recognition' as a registered confessional community.

In my concluding remarks, I will offer some reflections on the UC's past engagement in legal battles, which were heavily influenced by a public opinion that has been essentially informed by anti-cult lobbyists and the mass media.

The Schengen Convention and the Case of Rev. and Mrs. Moon

In 1995, the Border Police of Koblenz, Germany, entered the names of the founders of the international UC, Rev. Moon (1920–2012) and his wife Mrs. Hak Ja Han Moon (b. 1943), into the SIS. The stated reason for reporting the Moons to the SIS was the German government's general concern that the activities of the leaders of the UC could pose a possible threat to "the personal development of young people" and that their public sermons could lead to "violent reactions" in Germany (Oberverwaltungsgericht Rheinland-Pfalz (OVG) 2002; cf. Brouwer 2008: 5–6).[8]

The primary purpose of the Schengen Agreement, signed by several European countries in 1985, is to achieve the gradual abolition of controls at the member states' common borders, which entails the provision of coordinated measures to counter the "risks in the fields of security and illegal immigration" (EU 1990: 36). Under the terms of the Schengen Convention of 1990 that supplemented the earlier Agreement, persons considered security risks by any member nation – that is, suspected terrorists, drug dealers, smugglers, and other international criminals – should be registered to prevent them from freely travelling within the Schengen area. Once a person is blacklisted by a single member country, he or she is banned from entering any of the other Schengen countries as well. Thus, blacklisting the founders of the UC through the SIS was tantamount to declaring them criminals without any due process of law whatsoever.

The origin of the case

The founders of the UC experienced the effects of their Schengen-wide entry ban in the same year that it was issued. In the autumn of 1995, Rev. and Mrs. Moon conducted an international speaking tour that took them to several European and African countries to deliver a speech entitled *The True Family and I* (cf. Moon 1995). Earlier that year, Rev. Moon had delivered this speech in 16 Latin American nations and 16 states of the United States. All of the events had been carried out without incident. In November 1995, Rev. Moon delivered his speech in Paris, again with no public order disturbance. The tour continued with a speech in Budapest, and the next event was to be in Madrid.

Why were the Moons less free to travel in Western Europe – considered a bastion of liberty and democracy – than in Eastern Europe, Latin America, Africa, the Middle East, Russia and China?

They were improperly blacklisted under the SIS. Young couples seeking their leader's blessing on their marriages were forced to travel overseas to participate in the UC's well-known large wedding ceremonies.[9]

The charges against the Moons

France and especially Germany were the main instigators of the ban, the imposition of which then included all Schengen countries (Brouwer 2008: 6–8). But since the ban against the Moons was an administrative action related to security issues, it was not easy to clarify the charges against them. France does not allow a listee or his attorney even to see his file or know the precise nature of the charges against him and often simple and crucial items of information were withheld from the Moons' French attorneys.

In Germany, the reasons behind the ban were more transparent. It was instigated by the German 'Federal Ministry of Family Affairs, Senior Citizens, Women and Youth' (*Bundesministerium für Familie, Senioren, Frauen und Jugend*), in short Ministry of Family Affairs; however, the actual Schengen blacklisting was executed by the Ministry of the Interior.[10] The Ministry of Family Affairs appeared to be acting on information supplied by 'anti-cult' activists and church-affiliated 'sect-watchers' connected to the Lutheran and Catholic churches, that is, the Institute for

Research on Religious and Ideological Issues (*Evangelische Zentralstelle für Weltanschauungsfragen*)[11] or the Department for Ideological Issues of the Archdiocese Munich and Freising (*Erzdiözese München und Freising Fachbereich Weltanschauungsfragen*),[12] respectively. Other factors, such as a worldwide climate of anti-cult hysteria generated by the Solar Temple suicides in 1995 as well as the particular German reaction against other new religious movements, especially the Church of Scientology, undoubtedly played a major role in shaping the UC's public image as a 'cult' (*Sekte*).

The response of the UC to the charges

The UC initiated a number of legal and administrative actions to challenge the ban, including court actions in France and Germany. The substance of the legal defence of the UC rested on several facts. First, the charge of totalitarianism and working for a world government under Korean dominance is patently ridiculous because the foundational doctrine of the UC, the Exposition of the Divine Principle, explicitly endorses representative democracy as the ideal form of government and opposes all forms of totalitarianism (HSA-UWC 2006: 357–61). Second, concerning the charges of brainwashing young people and breaking up families, the record is similarly clear. Already in the 1970s and early 1980s, an elaborate sociological analysis conducted among British Unificationists debunked the widespread media myth that the UC was employing sinister methods of 'brainwashing' (Barker 1984). Moreover, contrary to the claims of uniformed critics, the family ideal and the cultivation of sincere and loving relationships are a crucial element of Unificationist basic teachings (HSA-UWC 2006: 34). Third, the UC has been recognized as a *bona fide* religion in many countries. The Constitutional Court of Spain, for example, had overturned two lower courts in ordering that the UC must be allowed to register officially as a religious organization (Constitutional Court of Spain (CCS) 2001).

When the Schengen Ban is considered in the context of international law, it is very clear that the blacklisting of Rev. and Mrs. Moon was a gross abuse of the agreement, in violation of fundamental human rights, which the Schengen countries themselves are legally bound to uphold. All members of the Schengen System are also members of the United Nations and thus adherents of the UN's Universal Declaration on Human Rights (UDHR) of 1948, which states in Article 18:

> Everyone has the right to freedom of thought, conscience and religion; this right includes freedom to change his religion or belief, and freedom, alone or in community with others, and, in public or private, to manifest his religion or belief in teaching, practice, worship and observance.[13]

In its General Comment 22, the Human Rights Committee clarified that religious freedom is "not limited in its application to traditional religions or to religions and beliefs with institutional characteristics or practices analogous to those of traditional religions" (Human Rights Committee (HRC) 1993). Therefore, the Committee: 'views with concern any tendency to discriminate against any religion or belief for any reasons, including the fact that they are newly established, or represent religious minorities that may be the subject of hostility by a predominant religious community'. Thus, as a new religious movement, the UC has the right to enjoy the same fundamental freedoms as any other religion – traditional or non-traditional. However, the action of Germany and France to ban Rev. and Mrs. Moon violated international standards of human rights, including section 32 of the Vienna Concluding Document of the OSCE (1989), which requires signatory states to allow believers, religious faiths and their representatives, in groups or on an individual basis, to establish and maintain direct personal contacts and communication with each other, in their own and other countries, inter alia, through travel, pilgrimages and participation in assemblies and other religious events.

, The German branch of the UC filed a number of lawsuits against the Federal Republic of Germany as will be discussed in more detail in Section 3. UC lawyers lobbied for the repeal of the entry ban in the United Kingdom, which was no formal member of the Schengen area. Additional support for the Moons and the UC came from United States officials. Prominent current and former government officials of the United States at that time expressed concern to the Government of Germany regarding Rev. Moon's treatment. In December 2001, the US State Department issued a formal *demarche* to the Ministry of the Interior stating the opinion of the United States that the German government should allow the ban against the Moons to lapse.

Final victory in the Schengen case: higher administrative Court rules entry ban not justified

Between 1998 and 2007, the German UC filed a total of seven lawsuits in their fight for justice. The response of Interior Ministry Otto Schily of Germany to these developments was to harden his stance and hire an outside attorney.[14] However, after 12 long years of legal wrangling, the German courts finally confirmed that the Schengen ban was indeed a serious violation of the religious freedom of Rev. and Mrs. Moon and the members of their church. On 24 October 2006, the German UC succeeded with their complaint against the entry ban for Rev. and Mrs. Moon at the Federal Constitutional Court. The Court recognized that the former claim of the Higher Administrative Court that a visit of the founders would have "no particular meaning for the communal worship" of UC members has clearly violated Article 4 of the Basic Law for the Federal Republic of Germany, that is, the fundamental right to religious freedom (*Unification Church vs.*

Germany, BVerfG 2006). According to the verdict of the Federal Constitutional Court, it is not the UC that was violating the Constitution, as some sect-experts of the mainstream Churches have repeatedly suggested to the federal authorities. It was rather the Federal Government which acted against the Constitution, when in 1995, it surrendered to the persuasive push of the men of the cloth by listing the founders of the UC on the Schengen list.

On the basis of this decision, the Higher Administrative Court of Rhineland-Palatinate ultimately acknowledged on 19 April 2007 that the entry ban commissioned by the Interior Ministry in 1995 was not justified. In the court's opinion:

> the level of supposed danger, justifying a listing leading to an entry ban, is not explained, all the more, since over the past 10 years there was not a single case of a member of the Unification Church being prosecuted, let alone the Church as an institution.
>
> (OVG 2007)

The final verdict thus stated explicitly that:

> because of the outstanding weight of the protection of the plaintiff's religious freedom, the alleged reasons stated by the defendant unambiguously recede as the fundamental right of freedom of religion need not yield to vaguely argued fears in the manner invoked by the defendant.[15]

In other words, the Schengen ban against Rev. and Mrs. Moon was finally lifted to the great relief of the European UC. In a press release from 4 May 2007, Fritz Piepenburg, spokesperson of the UC Germany, announced this victory quoting the verdict of the Upper Administrative Court of Rhineland-Palatinate:

> The listing of the Moon couple for the purpose of prohibiting entry is unlawful and violates the rights of the plaintiff, being a religious community. The listing violates the basic right for religious freedom as spelled out in the German Basic Law Art. 4 § 1 and § 2.
>
> (Vereinigungskirche e. V. 2007a)

A press release in German language was followed on 20 June, reporting that the Interior Ministry sent an official letter the UC Germany (dated June 14), which confirmed that directorate of the federal police in Koblenz had deleted the names of the founders from the SIS (Vereinigungskirche e. V. 2007b). Mr. Piepenburg explained that the Federal Government has made a political decision that was long overdue. Indeed, it should have been executed immediately after the Judgement of the Higher Administrative Court on 19 April 2007, when the judges found that the SIS listing of the founders, which had subsequently led to the entry ban into Germany as well as the other Schengen countries, was unlawful. Despite the good news, Mr. Piepenburg also gave a realistic assessment of the post-Schengen-ban scenario of the UC in relation to the German public that is still fairly accurate today:

> Even though the entry-ban against our founders is now history and Rev. and Mrs. Moon can enter Germany and the Schengen countries any time they want, the unspeakable damage to the public image of the Unification Church and its founders remain. Members of the Church will be forced to think carefully before they identify themselves [as UC members] in public or in their workplace. Understandably they live in fear of severe discrimination or even of losing their job. Children and youth from UC families who attend religious education in schools and colleges still face defamation, bullying and stigmatization from their peers and sometimes even from their teachers.

This ominous scenario is re-enforced, whenever the imperative 'anti-sect lessons' are being given as an intrinsic part of the religious education curriculum. Pupils who are members of new religious movements have to face this year after year. They report that their parents' religious belief is being portrayed as inhuman, dangerous, corrupt and unlawful.

Mr. Piepenburg further reported that the notorious 'Office 522' still exists, which it does until this day. This institution – along with 63 other anti-sect offices throughout the country[16] – is the political arm of the German anti-cult movement and it is acting under the auspices of the Federal Family Ministry. The official title of the office is 'So-called Sects and Psycho Groups' [sic]. This is the very office which created the political will to violate the Constitution by issuing the Schengen ban. To the hundreds of families whose fundamental right to practice their religion in freedom has been denied for so many years and whose image has been damaged, it is deeply irritating that no one will ever be held to account for the psychological pain and considerable financial loss that has been caused by various public officials and anti-cult clergy to the members of the UC. Mr. Piepenburg, who was acting as the spokesperson of the German UC for many years, had the impression that the director of 'Office 522' perceived that his primary duty was to denounce religious minority groups and make them into social outcasts.[17]

From persecuted Underground Church to legal 'recognition': the special case of the Austrian UC

The UC in Austria was effectively legally interdicted from 1974 onwards. However, after a long legal struggle,[18] the UC in Austria was officially recognized as a confessional community by the government of the Federal

Figure 6.1 The Reverend and Mrs. Sun Myung Moon. (Photograph courtesy of the Family Federation for World Peace and Unification)

Republic of Austria in June 2015[19] (Figure 6.1). Austria's amended legislation on religion, in effect since 1998, allows for three ways in which religious communities may be constituted: (1) religious associations (*religiöse Vereine*); (2) registered confessional communities (*staatlich eingetragene religiöse Bekenntnisgemeinschaften*) and (3) legally recognized churches and religious communities (*Religionsgesellschaften*).[20] A confidential source confided to me that he once asked an official of the Office of Religious Affairs why the Law on Confessional Communities was introduced in 1998, and whether the motive was to prevent the Jehovah's Witnesses from obtaining state recognition. He replied that the major motive for the new law as to prevent the recognition of two groups: Scientology and the 'Moon-sect'.

A brief timeline will highlight the most crucial steps taken by the UC towards recognition as a confessional community. On 16 May 1966, the association "Society for the Unification of World Christianity" (*Gesellschaft zur Vereinigung des Weltchristentums*, in short GVW) was founded by the German-American missionary Rev. Paul Werner in Vienna (Werner had first arrived in Austria one year earlier). In June 1970, the first negative media coverage of the UC in Austria marked the beginning of a nationwide wave of public persecution. For many decades, apologists from the mainstream churches and the leftist media had been publishing disparaging depictions of new religious movements. In the 1970s, our movement was regarded as one of the most dangerous cults.

In early 1974, the legal status of the GVW was suspended through action by the Security Agency (*Sicherheitsdirektion*) of Vienna due to 'formal reasons' regarding the name, which was allegedly misleading as it indicated ecumenical activities. The Security Agency informed the GVW that its missionary activities would contradict its stated objective of "encouraging people to consider religious questions" (Höfinger 1976: 19). Furthermore, the Security Agency insisted that the name 'Unification of World Christianity' starkly contradicts the activities of the GVW, which were deemed not to advance Christian ecumenism (ibid.).[21]

Shortly after the abrogation of the GVW, a renewed registration as an association under the name 'Association for the promotion of the Unification Church' was prohibited. A face-to-face visit of UC representatives with the then Federal President Kirchschlaeger in April 1975 was fruitless. In 1997, the Austrian branch of the Family Federation for World Peace and Unification – the religious core community of the UM – was registered as a legal association without any administrative obstacles. Numerous discussions took place among leaders and members on whether or not we should apply for the status of a confessional community. In November 2011, the decision to go ahead with the application was finally made, based on a clear consensus among the majority of the leaders and members. Furthermore, Prof. Christian Bruenner, honorary president of FOREF Europe, gave his encouragement and promised his support in our application process.

On 26 August 2014, Prof. Bruenner and Mrs. Goach, an attorney at law, sent in the petition together with a theological self-description, and Peter Zoehrer (UC national leader, 2000–2017) submitted 306 signatures to the government's Office of Religious Affairs (*Kultusamt*). One week before the deadline of 26 February 2015, Mr. Henhapel, director of the Office of Religious Affairs, asked us to make amendments in the statutes and to provide more details on our theology, social structure and ritual practice. Mr. Henhapl was especially interested in the structure of our Sunday Service, our textbooks, the Seonghwa-ceremony, the contents of our Holy Days and our calendar. Although supplementary documents were submitted immediately, a final decision by the Office of Religious Affairs was repeatedly delayed. After two meetings between Mr. Henhapl and UC representatives, the UC received notification that it has been officially recognized as a confessional community by the Office of Religious Affairs on 15 June 2015.[22]

The status as a confessional community signifies social recognition without any further material privileges, for example, regarding school law (state-funded teachers), military law, tax exemption, etc. Groups that apply to be registered as a confessional community are required to prove the existence of 300 members, submit their bylaws and provide a detailed description of their religious teachings, ethical practice and rituals. Upon application, the Office of Religious Affairs investigates to ensure that no threat to public security or order, health, morality and security or freedom of the individual is posed by the religious group in question.

Attaining this status changes the public perception of a group as it is tantamount to a 'hallmark of quality' granted by the government and constitutes a significant step towards a full legal recognition as a 'religious body' (under the auspices of the Ministry of Education, Arts and Culture). Full recognition as a legally recognized church 'religious society' (*Religionsgesellschaft*) can be obtained if the community can prove that it has a membership of 16,000 on a federal level. Recognized Churches are rewarded with important privileges, including financial benefits.

Several advantages are connected with the UC's newly gained status as a confessional community. First of all, the UC will be seen as a stable and enduring community. As a matter of consent, a verifiable number of 300 members living in Austria guarantee the lasting maintenance of a religious community, which ideally implies the abolition of the 'cult' or 'sect'-image. Elementary and high-school students who are members of a confessional community are entitled to receive religious education organized by their Church. Unificationist pupils and high-school students, being members of a confessional community, are less likely to be discriminated against by their teachers on grounds of their religious affiliation. Until now, the religious affiliation of Unificationist pupils/students has been labelled as 'O.B.' ('Ohne Bekenntnis' – without confession) in official school documents. Now they can proudly declare themselves as members of the 'Unification Church of Austria'.

There have been no harsh media attacks since the announcement of our legal recognition and not one agency labelled us as a 'cult' in its headlines. Instead, they call us the 'Moon-movement' or 'Unification Church'. The national broadcasting station, the Catholic Press Agency (which had been writing negative articles about the UC ever since 1970) and a few national level newspapers reported immediately on the UC's recognition after we published a press release.[23]

The registration of the UC as a confessional community in itself is an important achievement for restoring the Church's public image and being recognized as part of the mainstream religious landscape in Austria. However, this status is not yet a full recognition with all privileges (tax exemption, paid religious teachers and military pastoral care, voting power in national television, etc.). The current legislation on religion in Austria is in fact still very discriminatory: only a few of the recognized Churches actually fulfil the official standards for recognition. Although 16,000 members are necessary for full legal recognition, most of the recognized religions in Austria, including the Church of Jesus Christ of Latter-day Saints, Oriental-Orthodox Churches, Methodists, etc., do not fulfil this criterion. At the same time, most groups formally enjoying the public status as a fully recognized religion do not claim the full spectrum of privileges granted to the Roman Catholic or Protestant Church.

Understanding of the clearly discriminatory nature of the Austrian law on religion is important because the Austrian system serves as a model for various Eastern European governments, in particular those administrating former Habsburg territories. Therefore, a reform of Austria's legal framework on religious matters will hopefully have a corresponding impact on other countries.

Conclusion and outlook

In the mid-1990s, the German anti-cult lobby managed to have the German authorities consider the Moons as *persona non grata*. Entering their names into the SIS has effectively prevented them from travelling to most European countries between 1995 and 2007, even though there was no evidence of any wrongdoing whatsoever on their part. Neither in Germany nor in any other Schengen country had the UC violated any law although the German government assumed that a visit of the UC founders to Europe could pose a serious threat to public order despite the acute lack of any evidence. Its 'preventive' measure to block Rev. and Mrs. Moon's activities in Europe amounted to a *de facto* abuse of the Schengen System. On the positive side, the UC's victory in having the ban repealed demonstrated that the rule of law and the European commitment to human rights have ultimately prevailed.

The role of the media has been – and in certain respects still is – especially destructive when it comes to reporting about new religious movements. Throughout the last 50 years, the media has played a key role in spreading the blatant lies of the anti-cult lobby to the public. In the historical records of the German UC, there are thousands of press cuttings containing defamatory and false allegations against the Church and its founders. It seems that many journalists have been willing helpers of a new inquisition, without making serious efforts to do their own research.[24] Although it may be difficult to gauge its impact in quantitative terms, the confessionally independent religious freedom advocacy and monitoring done by FOREF Europe have certainly contributed to changing the atmosphere in Europe with regards to religious minorities, including mainstream media coverage. Roman Catholic Church-run offices on ideological issues (*Weltanschauungsreferate*) have taken down the word 'cult' or 'sect' in connection with their names. State-run offices, such as the Federal Office on Sect Issues of the Austrian government, have taken a more careful and passive role. Information campaigns directed at misrepresenting religious minorities in school programmes had to be revoked. Persons who have been imprisoned for their faith in countries such as Moldova or Kazakhstan have received justice.[25] Cases of systematic kidnapping and deprogramming in Japan have been exposed. The funding, ideological motives and questionable methods of FECRIS have been made public. In recent years, FOREF

Europe has closely followed and monitored the severe persecution and torture of Chinese Christians. In short, the irresponsible style of stereotype-dependent reporting by state, church or media representatives has become increasingly risky.

Furthermore, in the light of actual and much more urgent security threats such as terrorism or political Islam, anti-cult lobbies are steadily being defunded by national governments. According to reports of the human rights organization HRWF (2019) as well as the Protestant Office on Ideological Issues EZW (2019), MIVILUDES, a French government agency and major supporter of FECRIS, has already been dissolved.[26] Accordingly, the message control regarding the narrative about good and bad religions is gradually disintegrating. While the influence and interpretational sovereignty of mainline Churches in politics and society is declining, alliances of religious groups willing to uphold human dignity, freedom and the rule of law may receive more political weight in the future.

Perhaps, it is already safe to claim that the classical "youth sects" (*Jugendsekten*) of the 1970s and 1980s have grown up and that new religious movements such as the UC are not that new anymore. The approach of the UC's members (some already elderly) in dealing with accusations from the media and anti-cult lobbyists has matured, and there is an impetus to professionalize its media relations on European and international levels. To achieve its declared long-term goal – nothing less than a world of peace and unity – and keep up the millenarian enthusiasm of its members, the UC and its affiliated NGOs will have to define their place not only within international (i.e., as associations) but also within local legal frameworks. Following the teachings of their founders, the majority of Unificationists do not intend to create 'just another religion', and they still prefer to call the Family Federation for World Peace and Unification (FFWPU)[27] and related organizations as 'the movement'. However, wherever legally possible and if only for practical reasons, local UC chapters might benefit from adjusting their legal bodies to the state regulations regarding religious entities. Thus, in countries where official registration as a religious community is feasible and obtained, the group's new social status may elevate it above the level of public 'cult'-defamations. The legal registration process of the Austrian UC, which at least formally rehabilitated a once persecuted underground Church, has been a case in point.

Notes

1 Peter Zoehrer is by profession a journalist and human rights advocate. In 1982, he received the marriage blessing with his wife Gabriele by Rev. and Mrs. Moon in Madison Square Garden, New York.
2 This story was also shared by the author at the annual INFORM conference in London, King's College, June 2019.

3 Cf. Article 96 of the Convention Implementing the Schengen Agreement (CISA), EU 1990. The United Kingdom was not part of the Schengen area but uses the Schengen Information System. While Articles 70–91 of the Schengen Convention deal in detail with firearms, narcotics and the smuggling of these items, nothing in the document mentions sects, cults, mind control, psycho groups, brainwashing, breaking up families or the spreading of controversial religious or political teachings (EU 1990).

4 FOREF Europe is an independent civil society structure to monitor threats to religious freedom and advocate for respect for international human rights standards and obligations. FOREF Europe was formally registered as an association in December 2005 with Prof. Christian Bruenner serving as its first president. Prof. Bruenner, a former Austrian MP and Dean of Law at Graz University, is an international authority on the freedom of religion.

5 Founded in 1994, FECRIS is a France-based non-profit but state funded association that serves as an umbrella organisation for several anti-cult organisations in Europe and Russia (see fecris.org).

6 See, for example, https://www.osce.org/secretariat/42404?download=true.

7 See https://foref-europe.org/.

8 The German appeals court summarized the government's rationale as follows:

> In the opinion of the German government, the Moon movement is one of the so-called youth sects and psycho groups whose activities could represent possible risks for the social relations and personality development of young people. In addition to this, the aim of all activities of the Moon movement was to establish a world governed by Korea under the leadership of the 'Moon Family'. A public appearance of Mr. and Mrs. Moon would encourage the spread of this movement and lead to strong public reaction. It would therefore be detrimental to public order and national security and to significant interests of the Federal Republic of Germany, thus providing sufficient reason to order refusal of entry pursuant to Article 96 § 2 of the Schengen Convention.
>
> (*Unification Church vs. Federal Republic of Germany*, OVG 2002)

One of the most comprehensive analyses of the Moons' ban from the Schengen area between 1995 and 2007 was compiled by Brouwer (2008).

9 The Unification Church traditionally holds large marriage blessing ceremonies presided over jointly by Rev. and Mrs. Moon. Participation in the marriage blessing, officiated by the Moons, is considered an essential element of a Unification believer's life of faith. Thus, to prevent the Moons, access to their European followers is not only a violation of the Moons' right to travel for religious purposes but also creates a serious spiritual and financial hardship on their followers.

10 See the court rulings in the case *Unification Church vs. Federal Republic of Germany*, OVG 2001, BVerfG 2006.

11 See https://www.ezw-berlin.de/html/index.php [accessed: 26.01.2020].
    Under the German system of church–state relations, the government collects taxes on behalf of the Catholic and Evangelical (Lutheran) churches, who in turn maintain 'sect-watchers'. Some, though not all, of these sect-watchers maintain contacts in the German Congress *(Bundestag)* and the Family Ministry and actively campaign against new religious movements.

12 See https://www.weltanschauungsfragen.de/ueber-uns [accessed: 26.01.2020].

13 Similar language has been incorporated in the European Convention on Human Rights, which has also been signed by every Schengen nation.

14 Manfred Kanther (b. 1939) and Otto Schily (b. 1932) served as Interior Ministers between 1993 and 1998, and 1998 and 2005, respectively.

15 Original text:

> Wegen des hervorragenden Gewichts des Schutzes der Religionsfreiheit des Klägers müssen die von der Beklagten geltend gemachten Gründe eindeutig zurücktreten, weil das Grundrecht der Religionsfreiheit nicht nur vage geltend gemachten Befürchtungen in der von der Beklagten angeführten Art weichen muss.
>
> (OVG 2007)

16 Even to this day, the proliferation of anti-sect offices in Germany is unbelievably strong. They can be broadly divided among church-run and state-run sect-observatory offices. The Protestant Church (*Evangelisch-Lutherische Kirche in Deutschland*) administrates one central (www.ezw-berlin.de) and 22 branch offices, the Roman Catholic Church has about 22 offices. Sixteen anti-cult offices are run by the federal and state governments, e.g. Bundesverwaltungsamt – Sekten und Psychogruppen (www.bva.bund.de); Leitstelle für Sektenfragen – Senatsverwaltung für Bildung, Jugend und Wissenschaft (www.berlin.de./den/jugend/familie-und-kinder/leitstelle-fuer-sektenfragen); Berliner Familienportal – Sogenannte Sekten und Psychogruppen (www.berlin.de/familie); Bayern Familie und Soziales/Bayrisches Landesjugendamt (www.blja.bayern.de).

17 In 2006, Peter Streichan led the 'Office 522' and worked under the supervising department "Children and Youth" headed by Dr. Peter Fricke, which again is subordinate to the Ministry for Family Affairs.

18 Höfinger, Gertraud. 1976. Weisung von Oben. Religionsfreiheit in Österreich dargestellt am Beispiel der Vereinigungskirche. Wien: R. Heinrich.

19 See official media reports, e.g. ORF: Moon-Bewegung als Bekenntnisgemeinschaft anerkannt. URL: http://orf.at/stories/2284358/ [accessed: 2015-06-16].

20 Rechtsinformationssystem des Bundes. Gesamte Rechtsvorschrift für Rechtspersönlichkeit von religiösen Bekenntnisgemeinschaften. URL: https://www.ris.bka.gv.at/GeltendeFassung.wxe?Abfrage=Bundesnormen&Gesetzesnummer=10010098 (accessed: 31.12.2019).

21 Höfinger, Gertraud. 1976. Weisung von Oben. Religionsfreiheit in Österreich dargestellt am Beispiel der Vereinigungskirche. Wien: R. Heinrich.

22 Other confessional communities in Austria (among others) are the Baha'i community, the Hindu Society, the Islamic Shiites and the Seventh-day Adventists. These are all respectable religious groups in Austria. The official websites of confessional communities are listed on the official government citizens service website: https://www.oesterreich.gv.at/themen/leben_in_oesterreich/kirchenein__austritt_und_religionen/3/Seite.820016.html [accessed: 27.01.2020].

23 Press Release via APA-Austrian Press Agency: https://www.ots.at/presseaussendung/OTS_20150616_OTS0008/vereinigungskirche-als-religioese-bekenntnisgemeinschaft-anerkannt.

24 See also Michael Breen's critical comment in *The Korean Times* 2012.

25 See for this and the following examples the respective reports on the website of FOREF Europe: https://foref-europe.org/.

26 See HRWF: https://hrwf.eu/wp-content/uploads/2019/10/From-Warsaw-to-Paris-MIVILUDES-will-cease-to-exist-on-1-January-2020.pdf. See EZW: http://ezw.kjm6.de/nlgen/tmp/1574327205.html.

27 FFWPU is the official name of the UC since 1996 and constitutes the communal backbone of the broader UM.

Bibliography

Primary Sources

Bundesverfassungsgericht. 2006. *Unification Church vs. Federal Republic of Germany*, Beschluss der 2. Kammer des Zweiten Senats des Bundesverfassungsgerichts vom 24.10.2006, Aktenzeichen: 2 BvR 1908/03, Rn. (1–30). [Decision of the Federal Constitutional Court.] Available at: www.bverfg.de/e/rk20061024_2bvr190803.html [accessed: 26.01.2020].

Bundesverwaltungsgericht. 2001. *Unification Church vs. Federal Republic of Germany*, Urteil vom 10.07.2001; Aktenzeichen: BVerwG 1 C 35.00 [Judgement of the Federal Administrative Court].

Constitutional Court of Spain. 2001. *Unification Church vs. Spain*, ruling of the Constitutional Court in the appeal for legal protection no. 3083/96, 15.02.2001. Available at: www.cesnur.org/2001/moon_march01_en.htm [accessed. 26.01.2020].

Department for Ideological Issues of the Archdiocese Munich and Freising (*Erzdiözese München und Freising Fachbereich Weltanschauungsfragen*), respectively. Available at www.weltanschauungsfragen.de/ueber-uns [accessed: 26.01.2020].

Deutscher Bundestag. 1998. Endbericht der Enquete-Kommission "Sogenannte Sekten und Psychogruppen". Drucksache 13/10950. Available at: https://dip21.bundestag.de/dip21/btd/13/109/1310950.pdf [accessed: 27.01.2020].

European Union. 1990. *Convention Implementing the Schengen Agreement of 14 June 1985 between the Governments of the States of the Benelux Economic Union, the Federal Republic of Germany and the French Republic, on the Gradual Abolition of Checks at their Common Borders ("Schengen Implementation Agreement")*. 19 June 1990. Available at: www.refworld.org/docid/3ae6b38a20.html [accessed 26 January 2020]

Family Federation for World Peace and Unification Germany. 2007. Milestones in the German and European Battle to lift the Entry Ban for Dr. and Mrs. Sun Myung Moon and remove their names from the Schengen Information System. Available at www.familyfed.de/vk-archiv/einreise/english/reassessment/entry-ban-chronic.doc [accessed: 27.01.2020].

Family Federation for World Peace Austria (Österreichische Familienföderation für Weltfrieden – official website): www.famfed.org/. [accessed: 27.01.2020].

Family Federation for World Peace USA. 2015. Austrian Government Grants Unification Church Legal Status. URL: http://familyfed.org/news-story/austrian-government-grants-unification-church-legal-status-15511/ [accessed: 27.01.2020].

Fefferman, Dan. 2002. *ICRF White Paper. The Schengen Treaty and the Case of Rev. and Mrs. Sun Myung Moon*. Updated 27 August 2002. Available at: www.familyfed.de/vk-archiv/einreise/english/reassessment/schengen-white-paper.pdf [accessed 26.01.2020].

Human Rights Committee. 1993. *Compilation of General Comments and General Recommendations Adopted by Human Rights Treaty Bodies*, General Comment 22, Article 18 (Forty-eighth session, 1993). File number: U.N. Doc. HRI/GEN/1/Rev.1 at 35 (1994).

Institute for Research on Religious and Ideological Issues (*Evangelische Zentralstelle für Weltanschauungsfragen*). Available at www.ezw-berlin.de/html/index.php [accessed: 26.01.2020].

Moon, Sun Myung. 1995. *The True Family and I*. Available at: http://unification.net/1995/950625.html (accessed: 26.01.2020).

Oberverwaltungsgericht Rheinland-Pfalz 11. Senat. 2000. *Unification Church vs. Federal Republic of Germany*, Urteil vom 13.09.2000. Aktenzeichen: 11 A 10349/99; 3 K 938/98.KO. [Decision of the Higher Administrative Court of Rhineland-Palatinate.] English translation available at: www.cesnur.org/testi/moon_02.htm [accessed: 26.01.2020].

Oberverwaltungsgericht Rheinland-Pfalz 12. Senat. 2002. *Unification Church vs. Federal Republic of Germany*, Urteil vom 07.06.2002. Aktenzeichen: 12 A 10349/99. [Decision of the Higher Administrative Court of Rhineland-Palatinate.] Available at: www.landesrecht.rlp.de/jportal/portal/t/7qe/page/bsrl pprod.psml?pid=Dokumentanzeige&showdoccase=1&doc.id=MWRE10676 0200&doc.part=L [accessed: 26.01.2020].

Oberverwaltungsgericht Rheinland-Pfalz 7. Senat. 2007. *Unification Church vs. Federal Republic of Germany*, Urteil vom 19.04.2007. Aktenzeichen: 7 A 11437/06. [Decision of the Higher Administrative Court of Rhineland-Palatinate.] Available at: www.landesrecht.rlp.de/jportal/portal/t/7qe/page/bsrl pprod.psml?pid=Dokumentanzeige&showdoccase=1&doc.id=MWRE07000 3344&doc.part=L [accessed: 26.01.2020].

OSCE. 1989. Concluding Document of the Vienna Meeting 1986 of Representatives of the Participating States of the OSCE. Available at: www.osce.org/mc/40881?download=true [accessed: 07.02.2020].

Piepenburg, Fritz. 2002. Berlin Rally Against True Parents Entry Ban. Available at www.tparents.org/UNews/Unws0209/berlin_demo.htm [accessed: 27.01.2002].

The Holy Spirit Association for the Unification of World Christianity (HAS-UWC). 2006. *Exposition of the Divine Principle*. New York: The Holy Spirit Association for the Unification of Christianity (first printing 1996).

Breen Michael. 2012. How society handled Moon Sun-myung, *The Korea Times* 9 March.

UN General Assembly. 1948. Universal declaration of human rights, 217 [III] A. Paris.

US Department of State. 2001. International Religious Freedom Report 2001. Germany. Available at https://2009-2017.state.gov/j/drl/rls/irf/2001/5650.htm [accessed: 27.01.2020].

Vereinigungskirche e. V. 2007a. Founding Couple Rev. and Mrs. Moon are allowed to enter Germany. Date: 04.05.2007. Available at www.familyfed.de/vk-archiv/einreise/english/pressrelease/uc-pressrel040507.doc [accessed: 27.01.2020].

———. 2007b. Pressemitteilung: Bundesregierung löscht die Namen von Dr. Sun Myung Moon und Ehefrau Dr. Hak Ja Han aus dem Schengener Informationssystem. Datum: 20.06.2007. Available at www.familyfed.de/vk-archiv/einreise/deutsch/presseerkl/vk-presseerkl200607.pdf [accessed: 27.01.2020].

Vereinigungskirche Österreich [Unification Church in Austria]. Website: https://vereinigungskirche.at [accessed: 27.01.2020].

Secondary Sources

Barker, Eileen. 1984. *The Making of a Moonie: Brainwashing or Choice?* Oxford: Basil Blackwell.

Brouwer, Evelien Renate. 2008. *The Other Side of Moon. The Schengen Information System and Human Rights: A Task for National Courts*. CEPS

Working Document No. 288, April. Available at: www.ceps.eu/download/publication/?id=5903&pdf=1642.pdf [accessed: 26.01.2020].

Höfinger, Gertrud. 1976. *Weisung von Oben.* [Analysis of the administrative liquidation of the UC in 1974]. Vienna.

Pokorny, Lukas and Steinbeiß, Simon. 2012. 'To Restore This Nation'. The Unification Movement in Austria. Background and Early Years 1965–1966, in: Gerald Hödl and Lukas Pokorny (eds.), *Religion in Austria*. Volume 1. Vienna: praesens, pp. 161-192

———. 2014. 'Pioneers of the Heavenly Kingdom': The Austrian Unification Movement, 1966–1969, in: Gerald Hödl and Lukas Pokorny (eds.), *Religion in Austria*. Volume 2. Vienna: praesens, 181-216

7 The "Doukhobor Problem" in Canada

How a Russian mystical sect responded to law enforcement in British Columbia, 1903–2013

Susan Palmer and Shane Dussault[1]

Introduction

This chapter explores 50 years of conflict between the provincial government of British Columbia and a Russian immigrant Christian sect known as the Doukhobors, focusing on the fate of a radical splinter group within the Doukhobor community; the *Svobodniki* or "Sons of Freedom" ('Freedomites' for short). This conflict began in 1903 and reached a peak in the mid-1950s, when the Royal Canadian Mounted Police (RCMP) conducted a series of raids on the Freedomite villages. Around 200 children were seized and bussed to a residential school in New Denver, B.C. where they were forcibly confined between 1952 and 1959 (Androsoff 2013; Janzen 1990; McLaren 2002; Tarasoff 2002; Woodcock and Avakumovic 1977).

In 2001, exactly 100 years after the Doukhobors had arrived in Canada, these former school children formed the 'New Denver Survivors Collective' (NDSC). They launched a class action suit against the B.C. government, claiming that their identity and heritage had been 'stolen' due to the government's policy of 'cultural genocide'.

Their claims had been supported by the Ombudsman of British Columbia. Dulcie MacCallum, in her 1999 *Public Report No. 38*, "Righting the Wrong: The Confinement of the Sons of Freedom Doukhobor Children". She had interviewed many of the former children of New Denver, and her report contained ample evidence of abuse (psychological, physical and sexual). She concluded her Report by making five recommendations to the B.C. government for response and action. By 2001, the government had not yet responded to her recommendations.

In the interim, these 'stolen children' (by now in their 50s) had formed a group called the NDSC. In 2001, 49 of them filed a lawsuit against the B.C. government. Their complaint was of negligence, unlawful confinement and forcible removal from their parents' homes. They demanded a full apology, free counselling services and financial compensation (Alphonso 2001; Nesteroff 2012a). This lawsuit marked a turning point in the Doukhobors' 100-year history of dramatic dissent and violent confrontations with the provincial governments of Saskatchewan and British Columbia.

The New Denver Survivors were descendants of the Russian Christian anarchists who, since 1903, had been flouting Canada's laws with defiance. The Freedomites' resistance strategies involved arson, bombings and nude demonstrations which resulted in notoriety and prison sentences. But, today, we find that their living descendants have become fully integrated and law-abiding citizens of Canada. In their quarrel with the government, they chose to resort to legal means, hoping to resolve the painful legacy of their anarchist parents' conflicts with the law.

The aim of this study

This chapter will focus on this recent *denouement* in a century-long struggle. Many excellent studies of the Doukhobors' colourful history in Canada already exist. The 'Doukhobor problem' has fascinated journalists and academics (Janzen 1990; McLaren 2002; Woodcock and Avakumovic 1977) and has been chronicled by Doukhobor historians (Maloff 1957; Tarasoff 1977) and documentary film-makers (Hamm 2004). But the New Denver Survivors' quest for an apology has not yet, to our knowledge, been the subject of academic study. To accomplish this task, we follow five steps:

1   A brief overview of the Doukhobors' complex history from its origins in Russia to the settlements in Saskatchewan and British Columbia.
2   An account of the ideology and issues that fuelled conflicts with the government: military exemption, land ownership, public nudity, arson and bombings and truancy from public schools.
3   An account of the escalating conflict between the Sons of Freedom Doukhobors and British Columbia, culminating in the RCMP raids on the Sons of Freedom children in the 1950s and their placement in the New Denver residential school.
4   An account of the New Denver Collective's demand for an apology from the B.C. government.
5   A discussion of why these descendants of the Sons of Freedom have received no apology or compensation for the neglect and abuse they clearly suffered at the New Denver residential school.

Methodology

This chapter is partially based on archival research and partially on data collected by the authors during a field trip to the Kootenays region of B.C. in July and August 2019. There, we interviewed 16 descendants of the Sons of Freedom and other members of the larger Doukhobor community, including the current leader, J. J. Verigin. Most of our informants had been active parties in the New Denver Survivors project. Archival materials were supplied by Doukhobor family historians or accessed through the Doukhobor Museum in Castlegar. We also travelled in June 2018 to Ottawa to interview Canada's leading Doukhobor historian, Koozma Tarasoff. This research was funded by the Social Sciences and the Humanities Research Council of Canada for the four-year project, *Children in Sectarian Religions and State Control* (www.spiritualchildhoods.ca).

A brief history of the Doukhobors in Canada

The Doukhobors might be described as a Christian mystical sect that dates back to the 1700s in Russia where it spread among the peasant class in the Transcaucasia region. The label 'Doukhobor' was first used as a term of derision in 1885 by Russian Orthodox Archbishop Amvrosii Serebrennikov. It originally meant 'Spirit Wrestlers,' meaning those who fought *against* the Holy Ghost. But the Doukhobors adopted the name, claiming that they were fighting *with* the Spirit of God, who they believe dwells within each man and woman (Woodcock and Avakumovic 1977).

The Doukhobors were radical Christian anarchists who refused to pledge allegiance to any secular government. They rejected the sacraments of the Russian Orthodox Church, the priesthood, 'idolatry' and the written Bible to embrace 'Toil and a Peaceful Life', attributes reflected in their simple way of life based on communal living and hard work. Their radical non-violence and pacifism led to conflict with the Tsars. As a result, they were shunted around different parts of the Russian Empire, settling wherever their farming skills were needed. The Doukhobors were persecuted under Tsar Alexander III and Tsar Nicholas II, who were demanding an oath of allegiance. The Doukhobors' charismatic leader, Peter Vasilievitch Verigin ('Peter the Lordly'), had been exiled to Siberia as the result of an internal schism, but through letters sent by courier, he instructed his people to burn their weapons (Woodcock and Avakumovic 1977: 24–25). Thus, in 1885, at midnight on St Peter and Paul's Day, his followers burned their firearms in three districts of the Caucasus. The Tsar then ordered his Cossacks to drive 4,000 Doukhobors from their homes (Hamm 2004).

In 1899, after weathering intense persecution in Russia, the first 1,000-odd Doukhobors emigrated to Canada, settling in Saskatchewan. The Canadian government paid for half their transportation costs and promised to exempt them from military service (Tarasoff 2002: 5–6). Peter 'the Lordly' Verigin, once released from his Siberian prison, joined them in 1902. By 1911, around 7,500 Doukhobors had emigrated to Canada while 12,000 Doukhobors remained in Russia (Tarasoff 1977: 380).

The five issues of contention

The Doukhobors proved to be uncooperative as Canadian citizens. They refused to pledge an oath of allegiance to the Crown to register marriages, births or deaths. They also refused to register ownership of land under the names of private individuals. A study of Peter the Lordly's writings elucidates the religious motives behind Doukhobor behaviour.

While in exile in Siberia, Peter V. Verigin had kept a diary, and these cryptic writings were sent out to his followers by secret couriers. While some Doukhobors interpreted them as ruminations or ideals to be contemplated, others understood them as imperative precepts to be followed. Five themes in Verigin's writings influenced those Doukhobors who went on to challenge Canada's laws: pacifism, land ownership, truancy, nudity and arson.

Pacifism/nonviolence

Verigin advised his flock not to bear arms and to abstain from eating meat (Janzen 1990: 37). While the federal and provincial governments would honour their initial promise of military exemption, the Doukhobors' refusal to fight in World Wars I and II elicited resentment from land-hungry Canadian veterans and sparked public intolerance towards this strange Russian communal (or 'communist') sect in their rural midst.

Land ownership

Verigin advised his followers to return to 'the ancient Doukhobor traditions of Christian communism' (Janzen 1990: 37). This sparked "a new spiritual revival where a third of the Doukhobors in Russia reorganized their properties into the communal system of former times" ("Doukhobor History"). The Doukhobors' conviction that private ownership of land was against God's will would lead them to conflict with the governments of Saskatchewan and British Columbia.

Truancy

In the early 1800s, the Russian Doukhobors, who were mainly illiterate peasants, renounced the written Bible, following the advice of their current leader, Kolesnikov. They replaced the Bible with the "Living Book" – the daily life of peace and virtue cultivated in their charismatic communities, led by the promptings of the Holy Spirit within. Christ's teachings became enshrined within an oral tradition, notably in their 200 memorized psalms and polyphonic choral works (Woodcock and Avakumovic 1977: 22). Verigin supported Kolesnivok's hostile stance towards literacy in his 1896 diary, and Doukhobors continued to speak Russian inside their communities in British Columbia.

Nudity

Verigin wrote in his 1896 diary that Doukhobors must seek "primitive conditions... and a spiritual stature lost by Adam and Eve," and that "the sons of God shall never be the slaves of corruption". He wrote, "I propose that people would gradually get used to physical nakedness – spiritual nakedness is much more sad" (Soukeroff 1959). The Sons of Freedom regarded human skin as God's creation, thus more perfect than clothing, the imperfect work of human hands (Mealing 1976). For them, public nudity was not erotic, but rather a way of identifying with Adam, Eve and the animal kingdom before the Fall and a way of protesting against materialism and 'corruption' (Makarova 2013: 137, 41–2).

Arson and bombing

According to Androsoff (2011), the Freedomites' ritual practice of setting fire to buildings, clothing and vehicles originated in the 1885 burning of arms in the Caucasus, Russia. Hamm's documentary (2004) suggests they adopted the Russian peasants' 'scorched earth' strategies from the Napoleonic wars in 1812.

The sons of freedom – first conflicts

Soon after Peter Verigin's arrival in Canada in 1902, the radical movement of the Sons of Freedom was formed. Their members freed their farm animals, adopted a vegetarian diet and organized public demonstrations in the nude (Tarasoff 2002: 6–12). Tarasoff describes "a frenzied back-to-nature trek by 1,700 Doukhobors…on the prairie motivated by government pressure to take out land individually, and their misinterpretation of [Peter Verigin's] anarchistic letters" (Tarasoff 1977: 380).

Saskatchewan authorities had given the Doukhobors free land, but in 1907, around 300,000 acres reverted to the Crown, due to the Doukhobors' insistence on collective ownership. There was government pressure on the Doukhobors to become naturalized citizens (i.e., British subjects) and to swear an Oath of Allegiance to the Crown. This situation led to a three-way schism in the Doukhobor community.

The 'Independent Doukhobors' (*edinolichniki*) decided to cooperate with the secular state by assenting to the signing of contracts. In 1907, they constituted around 10 per cent of Doukhobors in Canada.

Community Doukhobors continued to follow the teachings of Peter V. Verigin. They became known as the Christian Community of Universal Brotherhood (CCUB), later known as the Union of Spiritual Communities of Christ (USCC). In 1908 and 1912, Peter Verigin purchased large tracts of land in British Columbia where he and around 8,000 Orthodox/Community Doukhobors relocated. There, they established farms and planted fruit trees. Because it was a private transaction, an oath of allegiance to the Crown was not required (Tarasoff 2002: 9).

The Sons of Freedom formed the third schism. They were disappointed by their leader Peter V. Verigin's moderate approach and willingness to negotiate with the Canadian government. Outbreaks of arson ensued, which escalated with the burning down of 11 schools between 1921 and 1922. Some Freedomites set fire to their own houses and clothing.

Peter the Lordly was assassinated in 1924 in a train bombing. Three years later, his son, Peter Verigin, Chistiakov ('Peter the Purger') arrived from Russia to assume the mantle of Doukhobor leadership. He sought to reconcile the Community Doukhobors with the Independents. He commended the Freedomites as the very soul, the 'bell ringers' of the Doukhobors. However, the Freedomites were confused by his mixed messages. In public, he would deplore the depredations of 'the nudes' (as he called them) and beg them to stop the violence, but they believed that he actually meant the opposite and was speaking in code. According to their view, Peter the Lordly had been killed for encouraging his people to resist government control, so perhaps his son Peter the Purger dared not speak openly?

By 1932, more than 700 Doukhobors were incarcerated behind 20-foot barbed-wire fences on the otherwise-deserted Piers Island off the coast of B.C. The government also revised the law against nudity in order to target Doukhobors. Until 1931, public nudity had not been a crime in Canada, although it could be punished under 'public indecency'. But since the Freedomite demonstrations, section 205A was added to the criminal code which made it a crime to 'parade' in the nude. Six months had been the maximum sentence for public indecency, but after 1931, the punishment for nudity entailed a three-year prison sentence (Tarantino 2007: 92–3). The imprisoned Freedomites' 365 children became wards of the provincial government, and many were placed in orphanages or industrial schools.[2]

In 1929, British Columbia legislation barred Doukhobors and other conscientious objectors from voting in provincial elections. In 1934, Doukhobors were barred from voting in federal elections also, as confirmed in 1938 Dominion Elections Act (Tarasoff 2015).

In 1943, the Brilliant Jam Factory (estimated value $300,000) was bombed. By 1950, bombings, dynamite and arson had resulted in millions of dollars of property damage. These events coincided with the Cold War era of patriotism, with its fear-mongering and McCarthyism. Since Doukhobors were Russians who lived communally, they were easily be misconstrued as 'communists'. In 1940, the National Registration Act required registration births, deaths and marriages of all Canadians.

In 1949, the B.C. government made efforts to resolve the Doukhobor problem and to accommodate their culture (Woodcock and Avakumovic 1977: 335). The Doukhobor Research Committee was appointed to study Doukhobors from 1950 to 1952, and it brought forth some 40 proposals, calculated to accommodate the Doukhobors' needs and to support their culture (Tarasoff 1977: 368). Sullivan's Royal Commission, after investigating arson and bombing attacks in British Columbia, recommended a number of measures to help integrate the Doukhobors into Canadian society. But these efforts were short-lived. In 1952, the Social Credit Party came to power under W. A. C. Bennett, who adopted a hard-line ('tough on Douks') policy and rejected the recommendations of the Doukhobor Research Committee (Woodcock and Avakumovic 1977: 340).

'Operation Snatch' in Krestova

In 1953, Bennet's new government announced that every Doukhobor child must be placed in public school, and any parents who refused would have their children taken away to be placed in a residential school in New Denver, a village 99 kilometres north of Krestova. That same year, a rumour circulated among the Sons of Freedom that the RCMP had been setting off bombs and burnings in an effort to frame their community. This sparked a new wave of bombings, arson attacks on public buildings and nudist marches.

Between 1953 and 1955, the RCMP conducted what was called the 'Operation Snatch'; a series of ongoing raids on the Sons of Freedom homes, mainly in the village of Krestova, where they apprehended between 150 and 200 children, supposedly of school age (7–14). But since the Sons of Freedom refused to register births, often children as young as four and five were seized. The children were loaded on buses accompanied by social workers and were incarcerated in a former tuberculosis sanatorium in New Denver (Woodcock and Avakumovic 1977: 341). Androsoff offers an eloquent description of life in New Denver:

> The children had left a family-centred communal environment to a cold, unfriendly, punitive English-speaking environment. The children's relatives were permitted to visit every second Sunday: a privilege taken away if a child was deemed to misbehave. Parents often drove over one hundred miles to see their children in vain. Sons of Freedom parents and children spent Sunday visits divided by a chain link fence. Parents kissed the children through metal links, and passed them picnic baskets and blankets...over the fence (Figure 7.1).
>
> (Androsoff 2011: 333)

In 1959, the Sons of Freedom parents finally agreed to send their children to public school and signed a contract with the government. Their children returned home and were welcomed with much rejoicing, and the residential school in New Denver was closed down the same year.

Figure 7.1 For many Sons of Freedom children, this was their first winter in New Denver. Peter Savinkoff (left, wearing the bunny rabbit jacket) was around 7 years old when this photo was taken in the winter of 1956/57. The fence that separated the children from their families during their monthly visit and moleniye – or prayer service – had only gone up the summer before. (Credit: Savinkoff family collection, courtesy Lunya Savinkoff-Foyle).

The New Denver survivors: the quest for an apology

In 1999, the B. C. Ombudsman's report stated, "the actions...of the government caused irreplaceable loss to the children of New Denver" (MacCallum 1999: 69). Many violations of civil liberties were noted, including rights to language, religion and culture. This report galvanized 100 former residents of New Denver (now in their fifties) to form the NDSC. In 2001, 49 of them filed a lawsuit against the B.C. government, complaining of negligence, unlawful confinement and forcible removal from their family homes in the 1950s.

On 31 March 2001, the NDSC contacted all the former child residents of New Denver to fill out a survey on their reactions to the 1999 Ombudsman's report. On 15 August 2001, the NDSC sent "A Brief on behalf of the New Denver Survivors" to Geoff Plant, B.C.'s Attorney General, announcing results of the survey; the response rate was 60 per cent; and the tabulated results showed an overwhelming majority consensus for the full implementation of the Ombudsman's recommendations. The Brief concludes:

> We also hope that your Ministry...will not be distracted by other issues in regard to the historical tensions between the Sons of Freedom... and Governmental authorities...We are simply stating that, as children, we were innocent of any wrongdoing and did not deserve to be punished... Since the New Denver episode that caused our suffering

was the direct result of Governmental policy and action, we believe it is the Government which must offer an apology and provide some type of restitution.

In 2002, the Ombudsman published a second report to see if progress had been made (Kushner 2002). In this, Ombudsman Howard Kushner noted that only the fifth recommendation in the 1999 Report had been respected, but the 'full apology' had not yet been implemented ("Kushner found the government has not yet apologized", *B.C. Provincial*, 23 April 2002). Law professor John McLaren described the B.C. governmental policy as 'forced assimilation'. He claimed many human rights, as defined by the United Nations, had been violated as a direct result of the 1950s raids (McLaren 2002).

In 2004, the NDSC sent out a storm of letters in which they quoted McLaren's statement. In a letter sent to a fellow Doukhobor, the NDSC noted, "We have sent over 100 petitions to the Attorney General...to issue a clear, unconditional and public apology in the Legislative Assembly". In August 2004, the NDSC sent an "Open Letter to the Right Honourable Prime Minister of Canada" (Paul Martin). This was copied to the Mayor of New Denver and to 14 leading politicians in Canada, including the Attorney General, Geoff Plant.

The 'Open Letter' refers to how in the 1950s, "approximately 200 Doukhobor children were apprehended and confined in New Denver in a prison-like environment by the B.C. Government and the RCMP/ Federal Government". It cites the two Ombudsmen reports and Professor John McLaren's research in which he condemned the Government's policy of 'forced assimilation'. The letter concludes: "After having researched the United Nations Human Rights violations, there is sufficient historical evidence to file a complaint before the United Nations against the B.C. Government and the RCMP/Federal Government." The Open Letter referred to receiving support from the Canadian Race Relations Committee, the Affiliation of Multicultural Services Agencies and the Law Commission of Canada that produced the 'Restoring Dignity' report in March 2000.

This Open Letter elicited a prompt response from the Attorney General. In a letter dated 30 September 2004, Geoff Plant asserts (rather vaguely): "We have striven to achieve as many of the Ombudsman's recommendations as possible: balancing the interest of former residents with the larger community as a whole". He promises to make "this important statement in the legislature later this fall". But in a private letter to Walter Swetlishoff and his wife, Marlene, he promised far more: "We will be proceeding with an apology in the Legislature as discussed, on October 4, 2004". However, when the October 4 meeting rolled round, no apology was forthcoming. Instead, the Attorney General made a 'Statement of Regret':

> On behalf of the government of British Columbia, I extend my sincere, complete and deep regret for the pain and suffering you experienced

during the prolonged separation from your families. We recognize...
that you were deprived of the day-to-day contact with your parents....
We...regret the anguish that this must have caused. We will continue
to offer counselling to former residents and to your relatives...who
wish to access this service. We hope that this acknowledgement will
enable you to work with us toward continued reconciliation and
healing.

The very next day, on October 5, Geoff Plant was interviewed on the CBC
Radio show "Daybreak" by host Marian Barschel. She asked him, "So
what's the difference between a Statement of Regret and an Apology?"
Plant explained:

Usually an apology involves an admission on the part of the person
making the apology that they did something wrong...it becomes an
admission of wrongdoing. There's a couple of reasons why that's problematic here. One is that we're still having to face litigation as a government...and secondly (and this is the harder part) ...what we do know is
that when government began to change its policy about half a century
ago, the long wave of terrorism finally and gradually came to an end.

Barschel objected, "But the Ombudsman called for an *Apology*". Plant
responded:

I would argue that a Statement of Regret is a pretty profound thing. I
mean we are sorry for the harm done to the children, but we did not
accept – and I don't accept – the Ombudsman's recommendation that a
government acknowledge it did something wrong.

Plant elaborated on why such an admission was not expedient:

We have worked with a group of about one hundred and forty of these
people over the last number of years, and there is a wide range of opinions... Some people...want the government to pay compensation. Well,
we're in the courts arguing about that thing, unfortunately, and we're
going to have to continue to do that.

Walter Swetlishoff, spokesperson for the NDSC, explained to the BBC why
an apology was essential for him and other NDSC members:

The apology is important because the children were living in real isolation, as if they'd done something wrong. Their life always consisted
of thinking that it was their fault. To me, myself and the Doukhobor
children were taken away not [for] education, but [because the authori-
ties] felt that the parents were difficult because they had this religion...
so it was more like a punishment for the parents. I suspect the reason

the government is not giving an apology is because [their action] was drastic and criminal... to accept that is just too much liability.

(Anon 2004)

The controversy over the New Denver memorial project

One of the most controversial issues, fiercely debated between 2001 and 2013, was the New Denver 'historic site' project. In 2001, the government had appointed a committee to work on a monument in New Denver. The committee had acquired a plot of land on which to construct two picnic tables with a plaque commemorating the children of the Sons of Freedom. This was meant as a conciliatory gesture towards the New Denver Survivors. However, there had been no prior consultation, and when the New Denver Survivors found out, they protested vigorously, saying that the project was akin to 'idolatry' (Makortoff 2012).

In the fall of 2004, the NDSC sent an "Open Letter to the Right Honourable Prime Minister of Canada" (Paul Martin) expressing their objections to this project. The Open Letter accused the Government of "only paying lip service to...the 1999 report [while] inflicting another wave of suffering on the New Denver Survivors by secretly building a symbolic emblem that romanticizes the site of our prison where great suffering and abuse took place".

NDSC Spokesperson, Walter Swetlishoff, complained to the *Nelson Star* that "they were trying to build a monument or form of commemoration, but it was done unilaterally" (Nesteroff 2012a). In a letter dated 24 September 2003, Geoff Plant wrote to the NDSC complaining, "We have spent considerable time and resources developing a comprehensive plan for an historic site...in New Denver". But, he announced, "at your request we have put that project on indefinite hold [since] you have advised us that an apology in the Legislature is crucial to many before healing can commence". He concluded, "as for personal [meaning financial] compensation, the appropriate process...is through the courts".

The 2012 Human Rights Tribunal hearing

In 2004, the New Denver Survivors adopted a new strategy. They filed for an appeal before the British Columbia Human Rights Tribunal. Eight years later, the Hearing was set for January 2012. Walter Swetlishoff explained to a journalist that the Human Rights case was not directly related to the raids and incarceration in New Denver in the 1950s. Rather, it was about how the New Denver Survivors "were victims of discrimination by the Attorney General and ministry responsible for multiculturalism" during the negotiations in the wake of the 1999 Ombudsman's report (Nesteroff 2012a).

On 15 January 2012, the opening day of the Hearing, the New Denver Survivors suffered a serious setback. Their lawyer suddenly quit. This was somehow left unexplained. The Tribunal advised Walter Swetlishoff to obtain new counsel, but Swetlishoff explained that he would go ahead because "This case has been going on for eight years... It's got to be resolved. It's taking a toll on us. We can't delay it any longer" (Nesteroff 2012b).

When the Tribunal resumed, Walter Swetlishoff agreed to conduct the case himself, but he declined to make an opening statement. Rob Horricks, his opponent, outlined the government's position in his opening statement. Horricks claimed that the government had 'legitimate concerns' about the Ombudsman's report, which was based exclusively on interviews with the former children. The report did not include interviews with adults who had worked at New Denver school (Swetlishoff v. B.C. (Ministry of Attorney General) (No. 2), 2013: 106).

In February 2012, members of the NDSC stood before the B.C. Human Rights Tribunal to argue that the government had unjustly refused to apologize to them. They referred to cases involving other minority groups whose children had been abused in residential schools and had received 'hefty compensation packages'. The NDSC argued that the schooling issue had been a deliberate strategy to forcibly assimilate the Sons of Freedom into Canadian society; that, between 1953 and 1959, the children were the victims of a long-standing cultural battle between the Freedomites and the province. Like thousands of Indian Residential School survivors, they had experienced psychological, physical and sexual abuse in New Denver. They were punished for speaking their own language. Visits from parents were strictly limited. Traditional Russian dress had been banned, and cultural and religious ceremonies were forcibly relinquished (Makortoff 2012).

The final ruling was announced on 29 April 2013. Enid Marion, the Tribunal member, wrote a 76-page ruling which stated that there was no evidence the government had discriminated against the New Denver Survivors in its response to the 1999 Ombudsman's report. Marion wrote, "I cannot conclude, based on the limited evidence before me, that the Survivors' race, ancestry or religion was a factor in the Ministry's refusal to implement any of the report's recommendations" (Swetlishoff v. B.C.: 29). She added:

> I also appreciate that the Survivors felt deeply hurt and offended by the Ministry's refusal to formally apologize to them, despite their consistent expression of need for a real and sincere apology in order to truly heal. The value of a sincere apology cannot be underestimated.
>
> (ibid.: 75)

Government response to the 'Doukhobor Problem' and Canada's post-war patriotism

One way to understand the government response to the "Doukhobor problem" is to analyse it within the framework of Canadian social history after World Wars I and II and the Canadian patriotic effort to rebuild the

Nation. Historian Strong-Boag, in her chapter, "Intruders in the Nursery", brings our attention to post-war attempts to reshape early childhood in Canada, using the example of the Ontario government's micromanagement of the Dionne quintuplets:

> Babies were a boom industry after WWI, when many Canadians agreed that by age six some children had already been damaged by improper parental management. Doctors, social workers, psychologists and teachers across English Canada enlarged their mandate to include... younger siblings who were also in jeopardy. These modern experts in childhood led a peacetime campaign to reshape the critical pre-school years...in cribs and nurseries they sought the power to fashion a better future.... In the post-war era, Canadian babies were born into an environment that increasingly subjected them and their parents to the rigors of so-called expert scrutiny.
>
> (Strong-Boag 1982: 160)

An eloquent example of this patriotic attitude is found in a statement made by the British Columbia Teachers' Federation in a 1956 article in the *Nelson Daily News*:

> The guiding principle of those in charge [of the children] should be to make their lives as happy as possible, to show that there is love...in Canadian hearts and that the Canadian way of life gives a fuller opportunity for happiness than the narrow bigoted existence of their parents. If the future should bring a better life for these unfortunate children, the money will have been well spent.
>
> (Anon. 1956)

Why no apology?

The refusal of the B.C. Government to apologize to the Freedomites' children is surprising, considering that Canada has quite an impressive history of government apologies. There have been no systematic studies, to our knowledge, of the legal or administrative processes or of the political conditions that are necessary before a government can issue a public apology and admit wrongdoing without losing face. There have, however, been examples of apologies tendered by top international politicians.

In Australia, one finds the dramatic apology of the newly elected Labour Prime Minister, Kevin Rudd. On 13 February 2008, at the opening session of Parliament, Rudd issued an apology to Australia's 'Stolen Generation'. This event occurred after 12 years of a conservative administration said to be "hostile to indigenous rights and [to] its own Aboriginal populations" (Anon. 2008).

Canada has an impressive record of apologizing for past wrongs. Journalist Daphne Braham, in her 2017 *Vancouver Sun* article, 'Learning from the Past is as Important as Governments Saying Sorry' notes, "Ottawa has apologized frequently and compensated First Nations children who were forced into residential schools". She offers other examples of apologies. In 1988, Prime Minister Brian Mulroney apologized to the Japanese-Canadians who were rounded up and sent to internment camps or back to Japan during World War II. In November 2017, Justin Trudeau apologized to the LGTBQ community for decades of "state-sponsored, systematic oppression and rejection" of "two-spirit Canadians" (Bramham 2017).

The B.C. government also has a record of public apologies. It apologized to the residents of Vancouver's Jericho School for the Deaf, also to Woodlands Schools for the mentally disabled in New Westminster, B.C. In 2014, B.C.'s Liberal Premier, Christy Clark, apologized to Chinese Canadians for "historical wrong" (Bramham 2017). So why, demands Braham, did the B.C. government "balk at apologizing to the 200 or so Sons of Freedom Doukhobor kids who were seized from their parents and sent to a residential school in New Denver?" (Bramham 2017).

This is not an easy question. On the one hand, it is painfully clear that the Freedomite children were wronged and deserve an apology. On the other hand, Geoff Plant was quite transparent in stating why an apology was not politically expedient at that time. While the NDSC appears to have been united in an effective strategy in terms of their public relations (in sending out letters to politicians and the Press), in hindsight, it is clear that their legal strategy was flawed. If they had filed a case before the Tribunal of Human Rights that their rights as children had been violated, most probably they would have won. If they had sued the B.C. government for forcibly confining them to a residential school that was inadequately equipped and understaffed with no counselling services, they might have won. There is ample evidence that the dormitory was overcrowded, understaffed, dirty and disorganized. The food was of poor quality and not for vegetarians. The failure to extract an apology from the B.C. government might have been due to internal divisions among the Doukhobor community.

Internal divisions among the Doukhobors

Certainly, if all the Doukhobors in Canada had supported the 100-odd New Denver Survivors, it would have added more weight to their plea. According to the Canadian Census, there were 13,175 'self-identified' Doukhobors in Canada in 1951. The mystery and confusion surrounding the bombings and arson attacks had widened the rifts between the different Doukhobor factions, since it was often unclear who had initiated the violence. Many Sons of Freedom suspected that they were being 'framed' by CCUB or by government agents fabricating pretexts to send the Freedomites to prison and seize their land. The Community Doukhobors (CCUB) resented the media for often failing to distinguish between the CCUB and the Freedomites, from whom they sought to distance themselves.

Peter Maloff points to these internal divisions in his book *In Quest of a Solution: Three Reports on the Doukhobor Problem* (1957). The son of an Independent Doukhobor, Maloff became the first Doukhobor lawyer in Canada. As a spiritual seeker involved with the Peace Movement in California, Maloff empathizes with the Sons of Freedom. He analyses the faulty understandings and moral failures of the four different parties involve in their struggle. He finds that each of the three Doukhobor factions (the Sons of Freedom, the CCUB, the Independent Doukhobors) and the Government of Canada share the blame (Maloff 1957: 9–11).

The Freedomites, Maloff argues, were not 'criminals' (as widely portrayed), but rather 'spiritual anarchists and rebels'. Maloff commends their spiritual worldview and uncompromising stance on pacifism, but condemns their hypocritical daily habits such as smoking, drinking and eating meat, and their damage of property, which he considers a "violation of the moral law" (Maloff 1957: 9).

He next finds fault with the CCUB whose "moral cowardice... [is]a betrayal of the Doukhobor cause" (Maloff 1957: 9). He notes that they are "pointing an accusing finger at the Freedomites for the same work they themselves started and maintained over many years". For Maloff, this "shifting back and forth in regard to Doukhobor ideology has had a profound influence of the Sons of Freedom movement because, by such shifting, they either give substantial support to the Freedomites or prompt them to the extremes". He concludes that the CCUB could "contribute much to solving the Doukhobor problem by sharing the guilt with Sons of Freedom in the general struggle" (Maloff 1957:10). He also criticizes his own community, the Independent Doukhobors:

> ... their contribution to the extremities of Sons of Freedom is immense, though it is of a negative character. They were the first to violate the fundamental issues of Doukhobor ideology and prompted the Sons of Freedom to a most vigorous protest in the hope... [of] warning others not to follow violators.
>
> (Maloff 1957: 10)

Maloff argues that the Independent Doukhobors should "confess their guilt in the general Doukhobor downfall, for they were the first to furnish motives for the Sons of Freedom activities" (Maloff 1957: 10). Finally, Maloff castigates "certain provinces [that] have contributed tremendously to this Doukhobor-Canada knot" by failing to recognize the Doukhobors for who they were from the outset. Instead, the government tried to force them to become 'normal' Canadians (Maloff 1957: 10). As Maloff sagely points out:

> The Doukhobors came to Canada with firmly established ideologies and principles which they considered to be infallible and they had

no intention to abandon. It was the ultimate meaning of their life. The Canadian government was well aware, or should have been well aware, of these facts and the kind of people it was accepting into the country. The Government of Canada failed to take into consideration these factors and treated the Doukhobors as ordinary immigrants. It proceeded to subjugate the Doukhobors under its control.... As years went by, the Government pursued its relentless onslaught upon the Doukhobors, so that many bitter conflicts have taken place since. For many years the Doukhobors were on the defensive and suffered tremendous losses, both of property and of lives.

(Maloff 1957: 10)

Maloff lists the atrocities perpetrated by the government: The torture to death of several Doukhobor prisoners [between 1903 and 1916]; the confiscation of Doukhobor land and property in 1907 and 1948, valued at several million dollars; the imprisonment of nearly 1,000 persons including 365 children in 1932, when 20 adult prisoners died as well as four nursing-age babies, malnutrition and neglect (Maloff 1957: 10). He concludes, "All these persecutions and oppressions were presumably committed with the intention of assimilating Doukhobors into the Canadian way of life" (Maloff 1957: 10).

Maloff suggests that the New Denver episode may have reinforced a lifelong mistrust of and hostility towards Government:

[T]he latest development, primarily on education background, particularly taking the children away from a whole group of people with the alleged purpose of educating them... only deepens the crisis... The memory of a forcible separation from their parents alone may instil in these children a life-long feeling of insult and hatred towards the authorities which no amount of education can eradicate.

(Maloff 1957: 19)

How this religious minority responded to the law

In this study of how a religious minority responded to the law, we find within one generation a dramatic change or *volte face*. Whereas their Russian parents and grandparents were anarchists who defied the law, these Freedomite children were forcibly "Canadianized" and raised to become well-behaved citizens. In taking up their quarrel with the government in 2001, the New Denver Survivors resorted to socially acceptable legal strategies, eschewing the terrorist antics of their progenitors.

The Doukhobors had initially responded to legal pressures in Canada by forming schisms which led to internal conflict, but today, the different factions tend to overlook their differences in their common purpose to preserve Doukhobor culture and identity. Most of the descendants of the Freedomites we interviewed have relationships with Community and Independent Doukhobors, while some attend Sunday prayer meetings at the Community with the traditional altar set with bread, water and salt. They sing the psalms in Russian as part of the church choir and encourage their grandchildren to participate in the Doukhobor youth festival (Kryak 2018b).

The NDSC have recently requested an apology from B.C.'s current Attorney General, David Eby. In 2018, David Eby responded to their request by announcing that: "Government is considering the issue of a formal apology to the New Denver survivors" (Kryak 2018b).

While David Eby's office declined to elaborate on what options the government is considering, some of the surviving members of the NDSC remain hopeful. For many, however, this hope is overshadowed by the fact that they are still waiting for an apology for something that happened over 60 years ago. Regardless of what happens with the request for an apology, a cynical view of government is likely to persist. Although all minorities struggle to maintain their identity in North America, the government's past actions and ongoing inaction lead many of them to blame the government for grim predictions that, by 2030, no one will identify as Doukhobor (Kryak 2018a). A pervasive attitude of suspicion and anger towards government has taken hold. There is nonetheless a strong sense that, even if the identity gets lost in name, Doukhobor values of pacifism and community activism continue to live on in the region's broader culture. That view has also been confirmed by a study of the history and legacy of these values in the West Kootenays (Rodgers and Ingram 2014: 113). This was explained to us in mystical terms by two community leaders with different views about the Freedomite case. They appealed to the perennial nature of the Doukhobor spirit, which renews itself when the surrounding culture calls for it.

Notes

1 The authors would like to thank the Hon. Barry Strayer for his helpful response to an earlier draft of the chapter.
2 Industrial schools were used for teaching juvenile vagrants and orphans one or more branches of industry; they were trade or vocational school where children were trained to work in factories.

References

Alphonso, Caroline. 2001. Doukhobors Detained in 1950s Seek Redress. *The Globe and Mail.* Retrieved 28 November 2020 (www.theglobeandmail.com/news/national/doukhobors-detained-in-1950s-seek-redress/article4146027/).
Androsoff, Ashleigh. 2013. Pacifist "Terrorists" in the "Peaceable Kingdom": Cultural Conflict in Twentieth-Century Canada. *Journal for the Study of Radicalism* 7(1): 1–35.

Androsoff, Ashleigh Brienne. 2011. *Spirit Wrestling: Identity Conflict and the Canadian "Doukhobor Problem," 1899–1999.* Toronto: University of Toronto. Retrieved https://tspace.library.utoronto.ca/bitstream/1807/29660/1/Androsoff_Ashleigh_B_201106_PhD_thesis.pdf

Anon. 1956. The Sons of Freedom. *Nelson Daily News*, 3 May.

———. 2004. "Stolen Children" Demand Canada Apology. *BBC*. Retrieved 28 November 2020 (http://news.bbc.co.uk/2/hi/americas/3946115.stm).

———. 2008. Australia Apologizes to Aborigines for Stolen Generations. *Cultural Survival Quarterly Magazine*, March.

Bramham, Daphne. 2017. Learning from the Past Is as Important as Governments Saying Sorry. *Vancouver Sun*. Retrieved 28 November 2020 (https://vancouversun.com/opinion/columnists/daphne-bramham-learning-from-the-past-is-as-important-as-governments-saying-sorry).

Hamm, Jim. 2004. *The Spirit Wrestlers.* Canada: Moving Images Distribution, Jim Hamm Productions Ltd., History Television.

Janzen, William. 1990. *Limits on Liberty: The Experience of Mennonite, Hutterite, and Doukhobor Communities in Canada.* Toronto, ON: University of Toronto Press.

Kryak, Violetta. 2018a. Are Doukhobors Dying Out? *Globe and Mail.* 9 September (www.theglobeandmail.com/canada/british-columbia/article-are-doukhobors-dying/).

Kryak, Violetta. 2018b. B.C. Government Reconsiders Apology for Doukhobor Children Taken from Their Families in 1950s. *Globe and Mail.* Retrieved 28 November 2020 (www.theglobeandmail.com/canada/british-columbia/article-bc-government-reconsiders-apology-for-doukhobor-children-taken-from/).

Kushner, Howard. 2002. Righting the Wrong: A Progress Report. *Public Report No. 43 to the Legislative Assembly of British Columbia.*

MacCallum, Dulcie. 1999. Righting the Wrong: The Confinement of the Sons of Freedom Doukhobor Children. *Public Report No. 38 to the Legislative Assembly of British Columbia.*

Makarova, Veronika. 2013. Doukhobor "Freedom Seeker" Nudism: Exploring the Sociocultural Roots. *Culture and Religion* 14(2): 131–45.

Makortoff, Kalyeena. 2012. Doukhobors Want Apology from B.C. Government. *The Globe and Mail.* Retrieved 28 November 2020 (www.theglobeandmail.com/news/british-columbia/doukhobors-want-apology-from-bc-government/article4198163/).

Maloff, Peter. 1957. *In Quest of a Solution: Three Reports on Doukhobor Problem.* Doukhobor Archives, The University of British Columbia Library.

McLaren, John. 2002. The State, Child Snatching, and the Law: The Seizure and Indoctrination of Sons of Freedom Children in British Columbia, 1950–60 , in: J. McLaren, R. Menzies, and D. E. Chunn (eds) *Regulating Lives: Historical Essays on the State, Society, the Individual, and the Law.* Vancouver: UBC Press. pp. 259–93.

Mealing, F. M. 1976. Sons of Freedom Songs in English. *Canadian Journal for Traditional Music.* Retrieved 28 November 2020 (http://cjtm.icaap.org/content/4/v4art4.html).

Nesteroff, Greg. 2012a. Hearing Set for "New Denver Survivors". *Nelson Star.* Retrieved 28 November 2020 (www.nelsonstar.com/news/hearing-set-for-new-denver-survivors/).

————. 2012b. Tribunal Adjourns as Lawyer Quits. *Nelson Star.* Retrieved 28 November 2020 (www.nelsonstar.com/news/tribunal-adjourns-as-lawyer-quits/).

Rodgers, Kathleen and Darcy Ingram. 2014. Ideological Migration and War Resistance in British Columbia's West Kootenays: An Analysis of Counterculture Politics and Community Networks among Doukhobor, Quaker, and American Migrants during the Vietnam War Era. *American Review of Canadian Studies* 44(1): 96–117.

Soukeroff, William A. 1959. The Origin of the Freedomite Movement. *Doukhobor Geneology Website.* Retrieved 28 November 2020 (www.doukhobor.org/Soukeroff.html).

Strong-Boag, Veronica. 1982. Intruders in the Nursery: Childcare Professionals Reshape the Years One to Five, 1920–1940, in: J. Parr (ed.) *Childhood and Family History in Canada.* Toronto: McLelland & Stewart, pp. 160–78.

Swetlishoff v. B.C. (Ministry of Attorney General) (No. 2). 2013. BCHRT 106 www.bchrt.bc.ca/shareddocs/decisions/2013/apr/106_Swetlishoff_v_BC_Ministry_of_Attorney_General_No_2_2013_BCHRT_106.pdf IN THE MATTER OF THE HUMAN RIGHTS CODE R.S.B.C. 1996, c. 210 (as amended) AND IN THE MATTER of a complaint before the British Columbia Human Rights Tribunal.

Tarantino, Bob. 2007. *Under Arrest: Canadian Laws You Won't Believe.* Toronto, ON: Dundurn Press.

Tarasoff, Koozma J. 1977. *Traditional Doukhobor Folkways: An Ethnographic and Biographic Record of Prescribed Behaviour.* Revised. Ottawa, ON: University of Ottawa Press.

————. 2002. *Spirit Wrestlers: Doukhobor Pioneers' Strategies for Living.* Ottawa, ON: Spirit Wrestlers Publishing.

————. 2015. 'Canadian Doukhobors and Voting'. *The Spirit Wrestlers.* Retrieved 28 November 2020 (www.spirit-wrestlers.com).

Woodcock, George and Ivan Avakumovic. 1977. *The Doukhobors.* Toronto, ON: McLelland and Stewart.

8 Making sense of the institutional demarcation

Tenrikyō's response to legal environments in France[1]

Masato Kato

Introduction

Religious groups of foreign origin almost inevitably face different legal environments when they expand into a new host society. The move to a new legal environment may entail a more relaxed environment or more strict regulations concerning religious organisations. The changes encountered leads in many cases to a process of renegotiating the place of the religious organisation in the wider host society. One way in which such a process can be observed is when a group moves into a legal environment that strictly demarcates institutional spaces for religious and other types of organisations. The present chapter contributes to the discussion on minority religions' reactions to legal environments by focusing on a Japanese 'new religion'[2] known as Tenrikyō[3] as it operates in France. It will highlight the distinctive ways Tenrikyō, as a minority religion in this socio-cultural context, responded to the French legal environment concerning religious organisations.

At an early stage of its organisational expansion to France, Tenrikyō established two legally separate institutions involving a religious association and a cultural association as per the relevant legal regulations. The cultural association, whose core activity is a Japanese language school, was opened at a time when the demand and interest in the Japanese language and culture was growing in the country. This institutional demarcation has in effect meant that Tenrikyō as a religious organisation opted for a low-profile, indirect method of public relations in France, bringing the promotion of cultural activities to the fore in its outreach to the general public. This chapter will explore the implications of this two-tier institutional arrangement, which led to some unintended consequences. I will focus on how the reaction to the new legal environment has led to the emergence of distinctive discourses concerning the place of 'culture' and the roles of 'cultural activities' in Tenrikyō's teachings and propagation amongst those who have been involved in Tenrikyō's mission in France.

Tenrikyō's expansion to France in the post-World War II period[4]

Tenrikyō is a religious organisation that originated from a religious movement born in mid-nineteenth century Japan. The religious movement centred on the teachings and practices proclaimed by a woman named Nakayama Miki[5] and subsequently developed into an institutionalised organisation after the passing[6] of the foundress in 1887 (Inoue et al. 1990: 755–6). The religious organisation grew rapidly in subsequent decades and, after going through a shifting membership, claimed 941,315 followers as of 2016, most of whom resided in Japan (Tenrikyō Omote Tōryōshitsu Chōsa Jōhōka 2017: 4, 12). The headquarters of the religious organisation—that is, Tenrikyo Church Headquarters—is located in Tenri, Nara Prefecture, and is built around a place called Jiba, which is considered to be the site of original human conception in Tenrikyō's doctrine (Inoue et al. 1990: 755–6).[7]

Tenrikyō's expansion to France took place against the background of the movement of Japanese religions to overseas contexts in the post-World War II period. From around the 1960s, religions of Japanese origin had begun to expand beyond areas marked by a large number of Japanese immigrant communities such as in North and South America, on the one hand, and Japan's former colonial territories, including South Korea and Taiwan, on the other (Shimazono 2006 [1992]: 185–7). European countries including France fall into this new frontier, with most of the potential converts expected to be people of non-Japanese national origin with no or little connection with Japan's pre-war colonial empire. As a religious organisation with an active engagement in overseas propagation since the pre-war period, Tenrikyō was no exception to this trend. In 1961, Nakayama Shōzen, the leader of Tenrikyo Church Headquarters, announced the revitalisation of Tenrikyō's overseas missionary efforts, which had been hampered due to Japan's defeats in World War II and ensuing surrender in 1945. This action, which was primarily informed by the leader's interpretation of the foundress's sacred words regarding the propagation of Tenrikyō worldwide, served as one of the precursors to the religious group's expansion to France in subsequent years. An interview with a former head of what would later become Tenrikyō's religious centre suggests that the Church Headquarters had a rough idea about launching a Tenrikyō centre in Europe as early as in 1961, although the specific country was yet to be named (Interview 11 November 2014). This plan overlapped with a different Tenrikyō church's plan, which had been in preparation since 1960, to send someone to France. In 1964, two followers were posted to France as students with a scholarship from the Tenrikyo Ichiretsukai Foundation as a first step to assess the possibility of promoting Tenrikyō's teachings in Europe.

Around 1968, a concrete plan to establish a centre in Paris began to take form at the Overseas Mission Department of Tenrikyo Church Headquarters. The decision to establish the centre in Paris as opposed to other major capitals in Europe such as London reflects two particular circumstances. On the one hand, Paris served as an important transit point for Tenrikyō vis-à-vis its missionary activity in Brazzaville, the Republic of Congo, where the number of Tenrikyō followers had been steadily rising. On the other hand, there was recognition amongst Tenrikyō officials who were involved in this initiative that Paris was a major cultural capital and transportation hub of Europe. The two students were then delegated the task of gathering information to find a suitable property for the centre. It was then that different initiatives within Tenrikyō's organisations and communities led to a plan to establish a centre in Paris as a gateway to wider European countries.

It is important to note, however, that Tenrikyō's officials were not planning to launch two separate institutions at this point. Towards the end of the year, the two students received a letter from the section chief of Tenrikyo Overseas Mission Department in charge of this matter. The letter provided a detailed proposal of the facility, including information regarding the preferred location of the facility, the layout inside the property, the procedure to purchase a property, the function of the property as a facility for missionaries from Japan, and the proposed budget to purchase land and a property. Worth mentioning here is that the proposed layout of the facility included the functions of both *religious* and *cultural* centres (Personal letter 15 December 1968). This implies that there was already a vague idea to conduct some kind of cultural activities at the Tenrikyō centre to be established in France and that there was probably an assumption amongst the parties involved that these two things could be done in one institution. This dual purpose can be indeed identified in one of the two students' accounts. He recalls that although Tenrikyō's officials purchased land and a property in November 1969 in Antony, which is a Paris suburb, there were various ideas as to what kinds of activities should be conducted (Figure 8.1):

> We have thus purchased land and a property. At this point, however, the only thing we knew was that we were going to open a centre; nothing was decided as to what kinds of specific activities we were going to conduct. We came up with many ideas such as running a nursery, holding tea ceremony and/or flower arrangement classes, or running a Japanese language school.
>
> (Kamada 2013; author's translation)

It was later decided that most activities would be conducted in central Paris rather than at Tenrikyō's newly opened centre, which was located at a suburban area, and was not conveniently accessible for holding activities intended for the general public (Kamada 2013). Out of various options for activities, the language school was finally chosen as the core activity to be

Figure 8.1 Tenrikyo Europe Centre.
(Photograph courtesy of Masato Kato, 10 July 2015.)

conducted in Paris. In choosing the Japanese language school as the core activity, the two students reportedly received guidance from Suzuki Atsuya, who was an official in charge of cultural matters at the Japanese Embassy in France as well as having a close connection with Tenrikyō through his acquaintance with Nakayama Shōzen (Kamada 2013). The discussions between the Tenrikyō staff in Paris and the Japanese government official covered a wide range of information relating to procedures for obtaining a property, legal requirements for establishing an association, and specific activities to be conducted. The idea of launching a Japanese language school was then communicated to the relevant section of the Overseas Mission Department and became official in September 1970 (Interview 11 November 2014; Kamada 2013; Personal letter 19 September 1970) (Figure 8.2).

The selection of a Japanese language school as the core activity for Tenrikyō's public relations reflects the social circumstances pertaining to the supply and demand for Japanese language tuition in France in the late 1960s through the early 1970s. On the one hand, there was an increasing demand for Japanese language tuition against the background of Japan's post-war economic growth. This is indeed attested in part by the increasing number of Japanese language institutes and students in France in the decades after the 1970s. For instance, records indicate that there were 560 students enrolled in a Japanese language programme at the National Institute of Oriental Languages and Civilisations (*Institut National des Langues et Civilisations Orientales*, aka. INALCO), in the academic year 1970–1971. The number of students had indeed more than doubled

Figure 8.2 Association Culturelle Franco-Japonaise de Tenri.
(Photograph courtesy of Masato Kato, 8 July 2015.)

from 240 students in 1967–1968 and would reach over 800 by 1974–1975 (Hosokawa 1987: 70). Another record shows that the number of Japanese language school students in all of France reached 1,935 in the academic year 1974–1975, which is nearly four times the 575 in West Germany, the country with the second highest number of Japanese language students in Europe at that time (Kokusai Kōryū Kikin 1975). On the other hand, there were only seven language institutes offering Japanese language courses in France in 1970, including INALCO, mentioned above (Shuppan Bunka Kokusai Kōryūkai 1970).[8] Tenrikyō's Japanese language school, which was to be founded to cater to the needs of working adults wishing to learn the language, was thus established at a time there was a lacunae of Japanese language institutes in the host society.

One important implication of the historical sketch of Tenrikyō's development in France is that the legal conditions and social climate surrounding religious and other institutions in France were not the main consideration in choosing France as a gateway for Tenrikyō's propagation in Europe. Such considerations also did not determine the types of activities that were to be used for reaching out to the public. The selection of France as a place to establish Tenrikyō's centre was linked with various factors, including the recognition of Paris as the transit point to the Republic of Congo and other parts of Europe. Moreover, Tenrikyō's officials initially assumed that religious and cultural activities could be conducted in one centre, as evidenced by the initial proposal for establishing a Tenrikyō centre. Furthermore, the idea of opening a Japanese language school indicates a response to a *cultural* rather than a religious interest that was growing in France. Most importantly, it can be inferred from available sources that Tenrikyō's officials came up with the idea to launch a separate institution for a Japanese language school, not because they were aware of the legal requirements but primarily because of the inconvenience of the location. These arrangements had an important implication for the institutional demarcation with which Tenrikyō would subsequently need to deal in France.

French laws and institutional separation of Tenrikyō's organisations

Opening Tenrikyō's centre in Antony and a Japanese language school in central Paris inevitably meant that there should be a legal basis for lawfully organising these activities. In France, religious and other non-profit organisations fall into the broad category of 'association' (*association*), which is regulated by what is commonly known as the Law of Association (*loi relative au contrat d'association*). First promulgated on 1 July 1901, this law allows two or more people to establish a 'non-profit organisation' (*association culturelle*) without making any declaration or obtaining permission beforehand, and the established organisation can obtain a legal status by making a declaration at a prefectural government office. A non-profit organisation can also engage in the practice of a religious faith according to the 1901 law. However, it can also be declared as an 'association of worship' (*association cultuelle*) by complying with legal requirements stipulated by the Law of the Separation of Churches and the State (*loi concernant la séparation des Églises et de l'État*), which was passed on 9 December 1905 (cf. Beckford 2004: 31; Bunkachō 2008: 106–15).

The establishment of an association of worship basically follows the same legal procedures for other non-profit organisations as indicated in Article 5 of the 1901 law, but there are two important differences that make the establishment of this type of association more regulated than ordinary associations. First, Article 19 of the 1905 law stipulates that an association of worship "shall be exclusively for the purpose of worship (author's translation)", indicating that these associations cannot engage in any other activities including charitable, educational, or commercial ones. Second, the same article states that a minimum number of members

are required for the establishment of an association of worship, depending on the population of the local municipalities—for example, at least
seven members are required in a municipality of fewer than 1,000 residents. These additional rules, amongst others, indicate that an association
of worship is more closely scrutinised by the government authority at the
time of establishment than an ordinary association. In return for more
strict regulations, an association of worship can receive certain benefits
including the permission to receive donation for the activities of the association (Bunkachō 2008: 113–5).

One important implication that the two sets of laws had for Tenrikyō's
initiatives was that the religious centre and the cultural association needed
to be clearly separated on the basis of French law, with the religious centre
devoted exclusively to Tenrikyō's religious activities. In compliance with the
1901 and 1905 laws, Tenrikyō's religious centre made a legal declaration as
an association of worship under the name Tenrikyo Mission Centre à Paris
(*Tenrikyō Pari Shutchōsho*) on 6 October 1975. Article 1 of the statutes
submitted at the time of the association's declaration states as follows:

> TENRIKYO PARIS SHUCHO-SHO, which was organized in July
> 1970 like independent churches of the French state in compliance with
> the laws of July 1st, 1901 and December 9th, 1905, is constituted in as
> an association for the practice of the Tenrikyō faith according to the
> prescriptions of the said law.
>
> (Author's translation)

Also submitted along with the statutes was a list of 43 members, including
four directors (i.e., president, vice president, secretary, and treasurer). In
the meantime, Tenrikyō's officials made a declaration for another non-
profit organisation called Association Culturelle Franco-Japonaise de
Tenri (*Tenri Nichi-Futsu Bunka Kyōkai*) on 16 February 1971, which
hosts various kinds of cultural activities including the language school.
The goal of the association written in the statutes state that this association "aims to develop friendship and mutual understanding between
French and Japanese people in the area of culture (author's translation)".
The Japanese language school, which was to be operated as part of the
cultural association's activities, was established as a private educational
institute under the name Cours de Japonaise de Tenri (*Tenri Nihongo Ga-
kkō*). In this way, Tenrikyō's leaders established two different non-profit
organisations in France that can lawfully conduct religious and cultural
activities, respectively (Figures 8.1 and 8.2).

The institutional separation, however, ineluctably meant that institutional spaces in which religious and cultural activities were to be conducted needed to be legally demarcated. It may be recalled that Tenrikyō's
officials initially had an idea of using Tenrikyō's centre for both religious
and cultural activities, which later came to be seen as impractical mainly

due to the size and the location of the centre. At that time, cultural activities were probably intended to be more directly connected with Tenrikyō's propagation efforts in France. However, the idea of holding two types of activities in one centre became impossible at the time of establishing two organisations as per the 1901 and 1905 laws. This meant that cultural activities conducted at the cultural association could only be used to indirectly aid Tenrikyō's propagation in France.

The selection of the Japanese language school as a main activity of Tenrikyō's cultural association reflects this idea. The official narrative appearing in the centre's historical document and in an interview with a former president of the cultural association points to three reasons that specifically show how Japanese language tuition can be a useful resource for Tenrikyō's propagation. First, a Japanese language school can appeal to a wide range of people who are keen to have contact with Japan. Second, it can contribute to establishing a long-term relationship with the students, given that it normally takes years to master a language. Third, teachers can earn trust and respect from students without necessarily having a high social status (Interview 11 November 2014; Kamada 2013). One of the two students posted to Paris in the 1960s also noted in an interview that the Japanese language school started as a way to help spread Tenrikyō's teachings in France (Interview 11 November 2014). It can be said that Japanese language tuition was seen as an effective way of reaching out to the general public without violating the legal regulation prohibiting the formal activity of proselytisation in a non-religious association.

It may not be unusual for a religious group in any given context to establish two legally separate institutions for different purposes, but the relatively strict regulations on religious organisations in France make the case of the institutional separation of Tenrikyō's organisations in the country rather distinctive. This can be most usefully illustrated by comparing the case of Tenrikyō in France with its counterpart in New York, an area in which Tenrikyō also established religious and cultural centres—namely Tenrikyo Mission New York Center and Tenri Cultural Institute—in 1976 and 1991, respectively.[9] Tenrikyo Mission New York Center's website states that Tenri Cultural Institute is a "division" of the religious centre, which seems to reflect the legal status of the relationship between the two organisations. The minutes of the Board of Trustees' meeting dated 26 September 1989, a copy of which was obtained from a former president of Tenri Cultural Institute, states:

> It is hereby resolved that Tenrikyo Mission, New York Center, Inc. shall appoint an Executive Committee to oversee and implement the stated intentions of providing a Japanese Language School and Cultural Institute in New York City. *Such operation shall be wholly a division of Tenrikyo Mission, New York Center, Inc. and any and all profits derived by such an operation and any other activities conducted on*

those premises shall be donated and become the sole property of Tenri-kyo Mission, New York Center, Inc. in accordance with the non-profit exemption accorded under section 501 (c)(3) of the Internal Revenue Service code.

(Emphasis added)

Together with other accounts obtained from the former president (Personal email 14 November 2019), this document confirms that the cultural institute is operated as an activity of Tenrikyo Mission New York Center, which is recognised as a religious organisation within the US legal framework, and thus has a completely different legal status than the cultural association in France.

The institutional demarcation of Tenrikyō's organisations in France, which can be in some ways seen as an unintended consequence of launching the cultural centre, has had a significant impact on the way Tenrikyō's officials and other followers promote the religious teachings in France. For one thing, the cultural association and its activities, which were originally intended to be a method of public relations for Tenrikyō, could not be directly linked with Tenrikyō's religious activities and propagation. This can be first and foremost attested by the name of the institution, that is, Association Culturelle Franco-Japonaise de Tenri, which does not bear the name "Tenrikyō" per se. When the author visited the cultural association in July 2015, there was very little that could be linked with the religious tradition or its religious symbols in the association's building. Among the very few exceptions were several books on Tenrikyō, which were shelved together with books on other faith traditions in a small corner of the association's library under the category "Religion". Other examples involve Tenrikyō's doctrinal phrases written by successive leaders of Tenrikyō in Japanese calligraphy format, which were posted on the association's walls. The current president of the cultural association noted that they were presented as works of Japanese calligraphy and therefore had not caused any serious issues (Fieldnotes 8 July 2015). These can be seen as conscious efforts to present the cultural association as having no direct link with the activities of the religious counterpart. This more subtle approach may have been informed by what had happened in the past; one of the former presidents noted, for instance, that the association had once received complaints from students of the Japanese language school about Tenrikyō pamphlets placed in the association's building (Interview 11 November 2014).

This kind of strict separation again comes in stark contrast to the relatively flexible legal framework concerning Tenrikyō's organisations in New York. A staff member of the cultural association in Paris who had visited Tenri Cultural Institute in New York to serve as an instructor noted that there was a marked difference between the two cultural centres. For instance, he saw a poster on the wall of the Cultural Institute advertising a pilgrimage trip to Jiba, which is an important religious practice in the faith of Tenrikyō and can thus be considered as a religious activity. He noted that the cultural institute even hosted a briefing session for the trip, indicating that prospective participants in the religious activity attended an event hosted in an institutional space of the cultural centre. The staff member from the cultural association in Paris also had an opportunity to observe a workshop on Tenrikyō's teachings held in the institute's building. Moreover, he saw Tenrikyō followers working at the Cultural Institute wearing Tenrikyō's religious costume when going in and out of the building of the institute and also learnt that these staff members were even allowed to go out to spread the teachings in the street during their working hours (Interview 10 July 2015). These examples show the different extent to which the teachings and symbols and other characteristics associated with Tenrikyō can be more freely expressed at the Cultural Institute in New York.

This is not to suggest, however, that legal restrictions as required by the 1901 and 1905 French laws meant that there was no way these two institutions could be in contact with one another. In fact, Tenrikyō's officials made various kinds of efforts to bridge the gap as they sought to promote the religious teachings a tendency that is identified particularly in the period between the 1980s and early 1990s. For instance, between 1979 and 1983, the cultural association published a quarterly magazine called *Le Japon*, which featured current news of Japanese society as well as various other topics, including economy, history, politics, and culture in Japan in both French and Japanese (Interview 11 November 2014; Tenrikyō Yōroppa Shutchōsho 1992: 114). The contents of this self-printed magazine are in principle of no religious character, but at the end of each volume, there is a short article entitled "*Tenri yūgen*" (A keyword of Tenrikyo), which introduces a selected doctrinal concept of Tenrikyō without any explicit messages of proselytisation or sectarian interests. In addition to this short essay on Tenrikyō's doctrinal concepts, some of the volumes also have Tenrikyō-related photos or illustrations on the front cover without explicitly stating the name Tenrikyō (e.g., no. 11 [January–March 1982]; nos. 12–13 [October–December 1982 and January–March 1983]; cf. Kato 2021).

In addition to conveying doctrinal concepts and visual representations of the religious tradition through a publication, the Tenrikyo Mission Centre in Paris hosted a pilgrimage tour to Tenri in a way that could accommodate non-Tenrikyō followers. Held annually from 1981 to 1987, the pilgrimage tour involved not only a visit to Tenri for participating in Tenrikyō-related events and activities but also sightseeing and various kinds of cultural activities, including flower arrangement, a tea ceremony, a calligraphy workshop, judo practice, and Japanese language lessons (Tenrikyō Yōroppa Shutchōsho 1992: 147–9). Striking in this regard is that this event was presented as more of a trip to *Japan* rather than as a religious pilgrimage to Tenri in both the religious centre's newsletters and *Le Japon*, the latter using an image of Tenrikyo Church Headquarters as a representation of

Japan on its advertisement for the trip (e.g., no. 9 [April–June 1981]). A former president of the cultural association, who was a key member of staff dealing with this magazine, notes that the cultural association, as the publisher of the magazine, was able to post advertisements for the Japanese language school and the trip to Japan without additional cost (Interview 11 November 2014; cf. Kato 2021). In recent years, Tenrikyō's religious centre, now under the name of Tenrikyo Europe Centre (*Tenrikyō Yōroppa Shutchōsho*), also conducts social outreach programmes. These include a Hot Meal activity, in which Tenrikyō members and other participants provide a hot meal to rough sleepers in Paris during the cold season. Also, a charity bazaar is sponsored. This is an annual, open-to-public event in which the Tenrikyō centre raises funds to donate to other charitable organisations by selling items collected through various networks as well as hosting attractions intended for the participants.

Making sense of the institutional demarcation

The examples mentioned above show that Tenrikyō's officials have in one way or another tried to bridge the institutional gap in a lawful manner, with a certain degree of success. For instance, a former president of the cultural association noted that some of the students of the Japanese language school did indeed attend the pilgrimage tour (Interview 11 November 2014). Conversations with the current president of the cultural association and the head of Tenrikyo Europe Centre also suggest that some of the students from the Japanese language school have attended these events. It is not clear, however, to what extent these initiatives have yielded the intended results. In my observations during my fieldwork conducted in 2015, there were not many followers at the Tenrikyō centre who had been introduced to the religious teachings primarily through the activities of the cultural association. There were about 30–40 full-time and part-time staff members working at the cultural association, but the followers of Tenrikyō only constituted about 10–15 people (Interview 10 July 2015). This small proportion makes it difficult to claim this endeavour aids Tenrikyō's mission, raising a question about how Tenrikyō's officials and followers who have engaged in propagation in France see the role of cultural activities conducted at the cultural association. Do they think that it is an effective method of propagation or not? How do they make sense of the legal framework that requires strict institutional separation between a religious association and other types of associations?

Some of the ways in which Tenrikyō followers have negotiated this legal restriction are reflected in the meanings that they ascribed to the role of cultural activities. One of the most common views expressed by followers who have an experience of engaging in propagation in France is that cultural activities are a method of propagation that may help disseminate a positive image of the name 'Tenri' by making a contribution to French society in response to public interest in Japanese culture in particular and cultural activities in general (Interview 11 November 2014; Interview 22 April 2015; Interview 24 April 2015; Interview 22 August 2015). In this view, cultural activities are not seen to be a direct method of propagation, but rather as a means of public relations. For instance, one of the former presidents of the association noted that he always explained to Japanese government officials and French people that the Japanese language school was intended not only to benefit Tenrikyō but was also a way of making a contribution to French society. He notes that he also told them that even if Japanese language tuition did not lead to a quick result of gaining more members like other religious groups do, it would hopefully help Tenrikyō in France to grow in number in 100 or 200 years' time (Interview 11 November 2014).

With regards to how cultural activities can be useful in making a contribution to French society, some former and current officials expressed a view that France is a country that is more receptive of art and cultural activities in general compared to other countries (Interview 11 November 2014; Interview 22 April 2015; Interview 22 August 2015). This can be illustrated by a comment from one of the former presidents of the cultural association:

> France is a country where you need to show interest in arts and cultures especially when you have a certain status in the society. After all, art is something quite valuable for human beings, and once you have established a certain status in this society, you need to be able to appreciate art.
>
> (Interview 22 April 2015; author's translation)

In another related view, it is emphasised by some of the current and former Tenrikyo officials and other followers who have engaged in mission in France that it is normal for religions in general to promote cultural activities as a way to reach out to society (Interview 22 April 2015; Interview 24 April 2015; Interview 8 July 2015). In this view, Tenrikyō's cultural activities are understood as part of the way to earn respect from the countries into which they go, and therefore the efforts are deemed an important part of a religion's propagation efforts. This view is most succinctly expressed in one of the former heads of Tenrikyo Europe Centre. In writing about the role of cultural activities in his autobiography, he states:

> Is it appropriate for a religion just to remain in its most natural state, that is to say, only engaging in propagation and faith practices? I would rather suggest that *people pay respect to religions that contribute to cultural activities in society*. [...] I would presume for the same reason that Christianity has developed and preserved paintings and music, just as Buddhist temples have provided education for children.

Not only Tenrikyō, but any religion should, in a concrete manner, contribute to the happiness of the people in the countries which they enter. In Japan, for example, there are Christian-related universities and hospitals as well as facilities for physically challenged people.

(Nagao 2014: 58; emphasis added; author's translation)

In this way, the idea of 'contribution to society' is brought to the fore in Tenrikyō's officials and other followers' discourses concerning the role of cultural activities. It can be said that the purpose of cultural activities is understood in a slightly different manner than originally intended, which was to establish a relationship with the students in the hope of sharing the teachings through an interpersonal communication with them. This is not to say that Tenrikyō's officials and followers have completely shifted the focus from attracting potential members. In one way or another, it can be seen that they are making sense of the role of the cultural association in relation to the propagation of Tenrikyō in France in ways that reflect the actual roles it has been—or is seen to have been—playing over the decades. Apart from the legal environments, it could also be said to reflect the kind of social climate Tenrikyō has gone through in relation to the place of minority religions in France. As has been well documented, many minority religions have invited criticism from the general public in what is referred to as a 'cult controversy' (Beckford 1985), which became prominent from about the 1980s in France.[10] At the height of the controversy in the mid-1990s, Tenrikyō became the target of a local newspaper, which reported that Tenrikyō was allegedly recruiting members to a religious centre through its cultural association as a sort of a front organisation (Kato 2021). This may have affected those officials and other followers who worked at the cultural association at that time in terms of the way they saw the roles of the cultural association.

Apart from the postulation of cultural activities as a 'contribution to society', there also developed the notion of culture as an inherent part of the religious teachings. This view, which does not appear in Tenrikyō's official teachings, was expressed by one of the officials who had experience of working both at the religious centre and the cultural association. When asked about the role that cultural activities can play in the French and European contexts, he expressed his opinion as follows:

In Japan, Tenrikyō has spread through saving people suffering from illnesses. But in Europe, it may be possible to spread the teachings by 'saving people through culture' (*bunka tasuke*). It is about cultivating the qualities of human nature in a sense of enhancing the potential to pursue happiness. We would like to be able to show that Tenrikyō can provide a means to cultivate such qualities.

(Interview 22 August 2015; author's translation)

In this statement, the official coins a phrase 'saving people through culture' (*bunka tasuke*), which combines the notion of 'culture' (*bunka*) with the general idea of 'salvation' (*tasuke*) in Tenrikyō's doctrinal discourse. Notable in this personal view is that the operation of cultural activities itself is seen to be part of the *religious* practice of Tenrikyō. Although it is not entirely clear whether this idea is a response to the legal restrictions, it is indicative how cultural activities are seen as part of the faith practice of Tenrikyō. Put differently, the operation of cultural activities is considered to be a *means* and *end* at the same time, which is very different from the originally intended idea of using activities at the cultural association as a gateway to become familiar with Tenrikyō. Elsewhere in the interview, this official commented that Tenrikyō followers should also become able to 'embody' culture during the course of their life of faith. In this way, the operation of cultural activities is imbued with a spiritual meaning in such a way that it allows Tenrikyō followers to demonstrate the teachings without speaking about Tenrikyō.

The view that cultural activities can contribute to the propagation of Tenrikyō in France in one way or another indeed reflects the belief of the majority of followers with whom I have spoken. This may be largely informed by an official narrative, which, according to a staff member I interviewed, is shared amongst Tenrikyō followers at a meeting that is annually held on the day of the founding of the cultural association (Interview 10 July 2015). In one rare exception, however, a follower who has worked at the cultural association noted that he felt a 'huge dilemma' during his experience of volunteering as a Japanese language teacher. Before being posted to France as a Japanese language teacher as part of Tenrikyo Young Men's Association's programme, he was told that he was going to spread the teachings in France. He then faced a completely different reality in Paris:

> When I came to France, I was told that I could not spread the teachings at the cultural association. It was a dilemma that I had to wrestle with. I felt lost as to why I had come to France. I did not really enjoy teaching Japanese. [...] I did not really feel passionate about teaching Japanese. So I had a huge struggle. I was just doing what I did not really want to do.
>
> (Interview 21 August 2015; author's translation)

He further notes that it was challenging for him to think that he was spreading the teachings of Tenrikyō through teaching Japanese:

> I was trying to convince myself that I was spreading the teachings of Tenrikyō through teaching Japanese. This was a very hard thing to do. But that is how I was taught about what I was doing—we were spreading the teachings through teaching Japanese. I am not too sure if

teaching Japanese really helps spread the teachings. It may help, but that is not what I felt about what I was doing.

(Interview 21 August 2015; author's translation)

This shows that not all Tenrikyō followers who have worked at the cultural association were fully convinced of the role of Japanese language tuition as an indirect way of promoting Tenrikyō in France. Evident in the view expressed above is that the institutional demarcation of Tenrikyō's organisations has had a huge impact on the way in which the former Japanese language teacher sees the role of the cultural association. He does not deny the possibility that cultural activities can help spread the teachings of Tenrikyō, but personally thinks that there is too much energy and resources used for the cultural association and that more energy needs to be spent on religious association's activities (Interview 21 August 2015). Seen in this light, the relatively strict demarcation of religious and other types of associations in France can be seen as a hindrance for those members of Tenrikyō who prefer more direct ways of religious proselytisation.

Conclusion

In expanding into the new socio-cultural context of France in the decades after the 1960s, Tenrikyō faced a new legal environment that required relatively strict institutional demarcation between religious and other types of non-profit organisations. Tenrikyō's way of reaching out to the general public through cultural activities was inevitably affected by this legal framework, leading to the establishment of two legally separate institutions that conduct religious and cultural activities, respectively. Whilst complying with the regulations stipulated by the legal framework, the officials and other followers of Tenrikyō in France made various efforts to connect them at the levels of representations and discourses. These efforts led to distinctive ways of articulating the roles of the cultural association and its cultural activities in relation to the propagation of Tenrikyō in France. In this sense, the case of Tenrikyō is indicative of how a minority religion's response to a particular legal framework that defines a lawfully compliant institutional arrangement for religious organisations can reflexively have an impact on the ways in which an activity of the religious group is understood and negotiated in relation to the teachings of the religious tradition. The interaction between legal regulations and internal discourses within a minority religion may be further explored by looking at branches of a religious organisation in different legal contexts, as demonstrated, albeit in a cursory manner, by the comparison between Tenrikyō's cultural centres in Paris and New York. The case of Tenrikyō in France may thus provide some insights into the ways in which legal conditions come to interact with practices and discourses of a minority religion as religious actors embark on propagation in a new social context.

Notes

1 I wish to thank Rin Ushiyama for the useful comments he gave me at an early stage of drafting this article. I would also like to express my gratitude to Tenrikyo Overseas Department, Tenrikyo Europe Centre, and Association Culturelle Franco-Japonaise de Tenri, for allowing me to use their archival resources as well as current and former officials and other members of these organisations with whom I conducted personal interviews. My thanks also go to the former president of Tenri Cultural Institute, who has shared with me valuable information about the organisation.

2 It must be noted that the term 'new religion' as a translation of the Japanese term *'shinshūkyō'* has a distinctive history of usage and connotations in the study of Japanese religions. It generally refers to religious movements and groups that have emerged since around the outset of Japan's modern period in the nineteenth century. The 'newness' of Japanese new religions does not refer to chronological newness in a general sense of the term but rather concerns these groups' "historical development in conjunction with the continuing processes of modernity", "public perception as 'alternative' and 'outsider' movements", and "contradistinction to established mainstream traditions" (Reader 2005: 93). See Astley (2006) and Reader (2005) for more comprehensive discussions.

3 In this chapter, I follow the convention of using diacritical marks for Japanese words including names of religions, except where the religious organisations concerned use unmarked ones as English proper nouns.

4 Unless otherwise stated, the general information about the development of Tenrikyō in France and Europe in this section is based on Tenrikyō Yōroppa Shutchōsho (1992, 2000, 2010) as well as internal archival resources obtained from Tenrikyō's organisations.

5 In this chapter, Japanese names are written in the traditional Japanese order of the surname preceding the given name.

6 In Tenrikyō's doctrine, the foundress's death is referred to as her 'withdrawal from physical life' as it is believed that she is ever-living and continues to work for world salvation.

7 For more details about Tenrikyō, see Ambros and Smith (2018) and Kato (2017).

8 For a more comprehensive overview, see the survey reports on Japanese language education abroad complied by the Japan Foundation: www.jpf.go.jp/e/project/japanese/survey/result.

9 There is also another Tenrikyō-related cultural centre in Singapore. See Hamrin (2000) for more details.

10 For more details about the cult controversy, see, for example, Altglas (2008, 2010), Beckford (2004), Beckford and Levasseur (1986), and Luca (2004).

References

Altglas, Véronique. 2008. French cult controversy at the turn of the new millennium: Escalation, dissensions and new forms of mobilisations across the battlefield, in: Eileen Barker (ed.), *The Centrality of Religion in Social Life: Essays in Honour of James A. Beckford*. Hampshire: Ashgate, pp. 55–68.

———. 2010. *Laïcité* is what *laïcité* does: Rethinking the French cult controversy. *Current Sociology* 58(3): 489–510.

Ambros, Barbara R. and Timothy Smith. 2018. Tenrikyō, in: Lukas Pokorny and Franz Winter (eds,), *Handbook of East Asian New Religious Movements*. Leiden: Brill, pp. 33–51.

Astley, Trevor. 2006. New religions, in: Paul L. Swanson and Clark Chilson (eds.), *Nanzan Guide to Japanese Religions*. Honolulu: University of Hawai'i Press, pp. 91–114.

Beckford, James A. 1985. *Cult Controversies: The Societal Response to New Religious Movements*. London: Tavistock Publications.

———. 2004. 'Laïcité,' 'Dystopia,' and the reaction to new religious movements in France, in: James T. Richardson (ed.), *Regulating Religion: Case Studies from around the Globe*. New York: Kluwer Academic/Plenum Publishers, pp. 27–40.

Beckford, James A. and Martine Levasseur. 1986. New religious movements in Western Europe, in: James A. Beckford (ed.), *New Religious Movements and Rapid Social Change*. London: Sage Publications, pp. 29–54.

Bunkachō [Japan's Agency for Cultural Affairs] (ed.). 2008. *Kaigai no shūkyō jijō ni kansuru chōsa hōkokusho* [Survey Report on Religions Abroad]. Tokyo: Bunkachō.

Hamrin, Tina. 2000. Tenrikyo in Singapore: Representing the Japanese presence, in: Eyal Ben-Ari and John Clammer (eds.), *Japan in Singapore: Cultural Occurrences and Cultural Flows*. Surrey: Curzon Press, pp. 194–215.

Hosokawa, Hideo. 1987. *Pari no Nihongo kyōshitsu kara* [My Observation of Japanese Language Schools in Paris]. Tokyo: Sanseidō.

Inoue, Nobutaka et al. (eds.). 1990. *Shinshūkyō jiten* [Encyclopaedia of New Religions] (1st edition). Tokyo: Kōbundō.

Kato, Masato. 2017. Tenrikyō. *World Religions and Spirituality Project*. Accessed on 29 November 2019, https://wrldrels.org/2015/03/22/tenrikyo/

———. 2021. Legitimating a religion through culture: Revisiting Peter Clarke's discussion on the globalisation of Japanese new religions. *Journal of Contemporary Religion* 36(1).

Kokusai Kōryū Kikin (ed.). 1975. *Kaigai Nihongo kyōiku kikan ichiran* [List of Japanese Language Educational Institutions Abroad]. Tokyo: Kokusai Kōryū Kikin.

Luca, Nathalie. 2004. Is there a unique French policy of cults? A European perspective, in: James T. Richardson (ed.), *Regulating Religion: Case Studies from around the Globe*. New York: Kluwer Academic/Plenum Publishers, pp. 53–72.

Reader, Ian. 2005. Chronologies, commonalities and alternative status in Japanese new religious movements. *Nova Religio: The Journal of Alternative and Emergent Religions* 9(2): 84–96.

Shimazono, Susumu. 2006. *Gendai kyūsai shūkyō ron* [Salvation Religions in Contemporary World]. Tokyo: Seikyūsha (Orig. pub. 1992).

Shuppan Bunka Kokusai Kōryūkai (ed.). 1970. *Sekai no Nihongo kyōiku kikan ichiran* [List of Japanese Language Educational Institutions Worldwide]. Tokyo: Shuppan Bunka Kokusai Kōryūkai.

Works by Tenrikyō

Kamada, Chikayoshi. 2013. Tenri Nichi-Futsu Bunka Kyōkai sōsetsu no keii [History behind the Founding of Association Culturelle Franco-Japonaise de Tenri]. Unpublished manuscript of a speech delivered at Tenri Nichi-Futsu Bunka Kyōkai kankeisha no tsudoi [Gathering of Former and Current Staff Members of Association Culturelle Franco-Japonaise de Tenri]. 25 October.

Nagao, Noriaki. 2014. *Zaiō 25 nen* [Living in Europe for 25 years]. Tenri: Tenri Daigaku Shuppanbu.

Tenrikyō Omote Tōryōshitsu Chōsa Jōhōka (ed.). 2017. *Dai 9 kai kyōsei chōsa hōkoku* [The Ninth Statistical Review of Tenrikyo]. Tenri: Tenrikyō Kyōkai Honbu.

Tenrikyō Yōroppa Shutchōsho (ed.). 1992. *Tenrikyō Pari Shutchōsho 20 nen shi* [Twenty-Year History of Tenrikyo Mission Centre in Paris]. Paris: Tenrikyō Yōroppa Shutchōsho.

Tenrikyō Yōroppa Shutchōsho (ed.). 2000. *Ashiato: Tenrikyō Yōroppa Shutchōsho kaisetsu 30 shūnen kinen* [Footsteps: In Commemoration of the 30th Anniversary of Tenrikyo Europe Centre]. Paris: Tenrikyō Yōroppa Shutchōsho.

Tenrikyō Yōroppa Shutchōsho (ed.). 2010. *Ashiato: Tenrikyō Yōroppa Shutchōsho kaisetsu yonjusshūnen kinenshi* [Footsteps: Commemorative Book for the 40th Anniversary of Tenrikyo Europe Centre]. Paris: Tenrikyō Yōroppa Shutchōsho.

Website

Tenrikyo Mission New York Center. Accessed on 29 November 2019, https://nycenter.tenri.org/en/index.php

9 Strategies in context

The Essenes in France and Canada

Marie-Ève Melanson and Jennifer Guyver

Introduction

In 2008, the Christian Essene Church, a new religious movement that originated in France in the early 1990s, established its second religious commune in Quebec, Canada, which they called the 'Maple Village.' The community had experienced discrimination from French authorities in the wake of the Order of the Solar Temple massacre, which resulted in a government-sponsored 'war on sects' (Palmer 2011). The establishment of a new commune came at the request of their religious leader, Olivier Manitara (1964–2020).[1] However, shortly after the Maple Village was inaugurated, the community once again found themselves at odds with the state over property taxes and their violation of municipal zoning by-laws. Despite having always been guided by the same leader and the long-term retention of group members, the Essenes' responded quite differently to their legal issues in Canada than they had in France. In France, their responses to state authority were primarily passive – they kept to themselves and limited their engagement with the state, while refusing to comply with the law. In contrast, the Essenes in Canada have been assertive with the state – outwardly defending their practices – while demonstrating a willingness to comply with Canadian law and interest in using the court system to defend their rights.

This chapter compares the Essenes responses in France and in Canada. We argue that both context and collective history matter when trying to make sense of a religious minority's attitudes towards the law and the strategies they adopt to deal with the state's regulation of religion. Based on interviews with individual members conducted in 2018–2019, we reconstruct a case history of the Essenes' legal issues in the two countries, analysed through an original typology that classifies the responses of NRMs to the state and its laws into four distinct categories. In the first section of the paper, we introduce this typology and explain how it can be applied to better clarify different NRMs' responses. Drawing on this typology, we then describe and analyse how the Essenes reacted to the state and its laws, which reveals that past experiences and current perceptions of the state jointly inform the decision-making process of NRMs.

Framing reactions to the law: a typology

The extreme and violent actions of some NRMs in response to government intervention – such as the Branch Davidians, the Order of the Solar
Temple, and the Peoples Temple – received a substantial amount of media
attention and have shaped popular perception of NRMs, such that they
are often characterized as holding hostile, aggressive, and defiant attitudes
towards public policy (Beckford 1999; Bromley 2002). As a result, many
experienced considerable prejudice in their interactions with public officials
(Palmer 2011). This perception, however, does not adequately reflect the
range of responses and strategies that most NRMs, including the Essenes,
have adopted to deal with the law.

Susan Palmer (2011) identifies five self-defensive strategies employed by
NRMs in France in response to anti-cult pressure, none of which involves
the use of violence. These strategies include establishing interfaith resistance groups to advocate on their behalf; writing letters to the media; filing
legal challenges against the state; appealing to other religious leaders and
heads of state to support their legitimation; and withdrawing from public life altogether. Palmer's research demonstrates that while some groups
refuse to follow the law or cooperate with public officials, many aim to
conform to the law and may use legal means to defend their practices and
acquire legitimacy in the eyes of the state.

Palmer's findings support those of David Bromley (2002) who, in his
review of NRM-society disputes in the United States, finds that radical or
violent responses to conflict are the exception rather than the norm. Even
during periods of intensified conflict, he notes that groups often choose
accommodative strategies. Bromley identifies three response patterns in
the disputes between NRMs and society, which he terms 'contestive',
'accommodative', and 'retreatist' (2002: 12). These patterns describe the
reactions of all parties involved in the dispute. As a result, differences
between NRM responses and societal responses can be difficult to distinguish, such that, when one seeks accommodation and the other con-
testation, the overall pattern will appear contestive. For instance, when
groups are treated unfairly by the courts and use the legal system to defend their way of life, they are not necessarily contesting societal norms,
nor are they averse to following the law; rather, they may be seeking to
defend themselves against discrimination or bias embedded in the legal
system.[2]

In order to better understand NRM responses to the law and attitudes
towards the state, we propose a new typology that delineates the responses
of NRMs into four different categories based on two distinctions: *compliant* versus *non-compliant* attitudes towards law and public policy and
passive versus *assertive* reactions to state interventions.[3] The combination
of these two distinctions results in four categories of responses: 'adaptive',
'defensive', 'avoidant', and 'confrontational' (Table 9.1).

Table 9.1 Types of categories

	Passive	Assertive
Compliant	Adaptive	Defensive
Non-compliant	Avoidant	Confrontational

While both adaptive and avoidant responses are distinguished by their passive engagement with the state, these reactions are not easily confused because they result in widely different outcomes. Adaptive responses refer to when a group conforms to the laws and regulations of the state through passive means either by instituting internal reforms or by engaging in dialogue and negotiation with state authorities to mediate solutions. Such responses usually have a net-positive outcome for both the religious movements and the state and are unlikely to be reported on in the media. Avoidant responses, on the other hand, characterize when groups resist complying or cooperating with government officials yet remain passive in their outward behaviour. Examples include relocating to a new country to avoid prosecution or state intervention, withholding information from public officials, or disbanding. These responses are more likely to attract public attention and elicit negative reactions from state officials than adaptive responses, but might also pass unnoticed.

Defensive and confrontational responses, on the other hand, are often easily conflated due to their characteristic assertiveness. However, these responses are quite different. Defensive responses characterize situations where groups seek to comply with the law, while outwardly defending their own interests against challenges from the state. Examples include using the courts to contest legal decisions or state policies that impinge on their rights or appealing for recognition as a legitimate religious community to relevant government bodies. Confrontational responses, on the other hand, refer to situations where an NRM assertively manifests their unwillingness to comply with the law or recognize the legitimacy of state authority. Confrontational responses can involve obfuscating the work of state officials by denying them access to property or individual members, physically resisting interventions from public officials, or in extreme cases, engaging in public acts of violence.

We propose that the attitudes of NRMs towards the law and government intervention are not strictly determined by group ideology, nor are they fixed. Multiple factors – such as the political context, collective history, religious ideology, and access to resources, among others – impact on how a group chooses to respond. Moreover, these categories characterize the behavioural or attitudinal responses of NRMs and not the groups themselves. A particular NRM may employ a combination of adaptive, defensive, or avoidant strategies at the same time. For instance, an NRM may adapt to some regulations, while resisting others. Furthermore, their reactions may change overtime – for instance, a group may shift back and forth between adaptive and confrontational attitudes. More precisely, we argue that both context and collective history matter when trying to make sense of a religious minorities' attitudes and strategies towards the state and the law. In proposing this typology, we hope to better clarify NRMs' responses to the law within their socio-historical context.

Emerging within the 'War on Sects': avoidant responses

With regards to freedom of religion and the regulation of NRMs, France is a unique case. The country's habits of dealing with new religious groups are defined by scholars of religion as "more offensive and generalized than those of other Western Europe countries" (Luca 2004: 70), as "revealing of [a] one-track thinking" that attests of an "incapacity to accept non-conformity"[4] (Dericquebourg 1998: 9), and even as "an instance of State-sponsored protectionism in the field of religion" (Beckford 2004: 35).

The context of the late 1990s and early 2000s in which the Essene religion emerged and developed most of its fundamental tenets constitutes a peak in the history of the French 'war on sects.' Following the tragedy of the Order of the Solar Temple, French authorities began to actively persecute cults. They established anti-cult organizations, such as MILS, then MILUVIDES, which aimed to combat cults and prevent their potential excesses.[5] These publicly funded organizations wielded great power, which, according to Wright and Palmer, led to "[institutionalized] intolerant attitudes towards minority faiths" (2016: 177). Most notably, lists of *sectes* were produced and made public, and the French Parliament adopted laws against intentional or unintentional 'abuse of weakness' – a concept akin to that of 'brainwashing' – and 'mental manipulation' (Palmer 2011). Beckford observes that agents of the state were from that moment placed in "the unquestionably paternalistic position of deciding who needs protection from abusive cults and what counts as abuse" (2004: 35) before a complaint from an individual member was ever formulated. Beckford summarizes what makes France an interesting case study as follows:

> First, the degree to which agencies of the French State are actively involved in monitoring, warning against, and combating NRMs is exceptionally high. Second, the virtually unanimous consensus at the highest levels of the French political system about the 'evils' of NRMs and about the necessity to suppress them has no parallel in other countries. And, third, French public opinion appears to be strongly opposed to the activities of NRMs and equally in support of the French State's robust attitude towards them.
>
> (2004: 39)

When describing the context in which their tradition emerged, the Essenes describe a picture of France strikingly similar to the image portrayed by Beckford. This period had a strong influence on the development of their religious identity. French members often attribute their current determination to uphold their beliefs and practices to their experiences in France.

Tensions between the Essenes and the state began in 1997, shortly after the Order of the Solar Temple tragedy in France. Original French members state that their community was placed under thorough surveillance by government authorities. For instance, members maintain that their phone lines were tapped, and they observed state officials recording the registration numbers of cars in their village's parking lot. The owners of the cars were later contacted by police who tried to dissuade them from patronizing the group. The Essenes did not attempt to stop the surveillance. Although they found the government's behaviour irritating, they believed that the authorities would eventually realize that they were not dangerous and would leave them alone. However, their situation only worsened over time. According to members, the attention they attracted from government authorities led to tensions with their neighbours and local businesses. The community initially responded by trying to adapt to societal norms – they attempted to make themselves appear less religious, less spiritual, and therefore more conventional in the eyes of French people.

Today, the Essenes look back at this period with a critical eye. They see it as a time when they undertook unnecessary efforts to fit into mainstream society. However, despite the excessive monitoring of government officials and the suspicion of their neighbours, they maintained their activities and way of life.

The situation changed dramatically in November 2000 when their village, Terranova, was brutally raided by 60 agents of the French National Gendarmerie Intervention Group (GIGN) in the middle of the night. Members who witnessed this event recount that the GIGN agents arrived heavily armed, accompanied by two helicopters, and proceeded to break down their doors and windows. Manitara and his wife, who was pregnant at the time, were arrested and taken to the police station along with eight other members. To this day, the Essenes are unsure why they were targeted.[6] However, from that moment on, they recognized the state and its laws posed a threat to their community. This event constituted a turning point in the Essenes' relationship with the state in France, as they lost all hope of receiving fair treatment from the state.

After the raid, those arrested were held for interrogation regarding their activities in Terranova. Their relatives were also contacted by police, who questioned them about the group's behaviour. One French member recounts that her mother was invited to the police station only to be asked if she 'ever saw her daughter use candles or incense.' The French Essenes claim that these interviews were intended to create suspicion among their relatives with the hope that they would encourage them to disassociate from the community.

According to Beckford (2004), the French state routinely framed NRMs as dystopias by recasting otherwise familiar and common practices as irrational and corrupt, and, according to (Duvert 2004), accused the groups of mental manipulation. Although there is nothing inherently wrong with lighting candles or incense, when brought into question by the state, these practices were made to seem abnormal and potentially dangerous.[7]

Ultimately, the GIGN found nothing to incriminate the Essenes in Terranova.[8] Nonetheless, Manitara was charged on 22 counts most alleging the mismanaging the financial affairs of the group, while the other members were given the choice to plead either as 'victims of a *secte*' or 'the *gourou*'s accomplices' (Wright & Palmer 2016: 209). It took until 2003 for the Essenes to be sentenced. In the meantime, a series of crucial events happened to the community that solidified their identity as a distinct religion. In 2002, Manitara claims to have had his first encounter with an Archangel, a figure central to the Essene religion today. The Archangel Michael informed him that he had been designated the messenger of the divine world. From this moment on, the Essenes maintain that an alliance was formed between the divine and earthly worlds, which they were tasked with protecting for the sake of all humanity (Melanson 2020).[9]

Responses in France

The revelations received by Manitara clarified the movement's spiritual beliefs, which enabled them to better determine which disputes were worth fighting in the courts and motivated them to resist complying with the law. Manitara was found guilty of misuse of company assets[10] and received a conditional sentence of eight months imprisonment provided he did not speak in public or communicate verbally or in writing with his followers. Yet his role as an intermediary between the divine and earthly worlds made it difficult for his followers to accept his sentence. This led the community to implement a whole range of passive – that is, avoidant – strategies to disobey the law and maintain their mission. For instance, with the help of his followers, Manitara continued publishing his writings in the community's journal under a fake name while confined to his home. Manitara also continued giving conferences at Terranova. To accomplish this endeavour, his followers would monitor the entrance to the village, equipped with walkie-talkies. A conference room was set up to appear as if someone else was giving the talk, and a member was designated as the 'false speaker' in the event that a stranger or government official would visit. Some members who accepted a plea as 'victims' were ordered to stay away from Manitara and the Terranova village for a set period of time. One French member – who was in his early twenties when he was arrested – recounts that, given his young age, the judge determined that he was clearly a 'victim' of Manitara and could still be 'saved' from his influence if kept away. He was ordered to stay away from the village and return to live with his parents for a year; however, he broke this order on two occasions, returning to Terranova hidden in the trunk of a car.

In the years that followed, the French Essenes gradually overcame their passive attitudes and adopted more defensive strategies in response to the law. With the aim of promoting the Essenes' spiritual beliefs and denouncing the injustice of the state, some Essenes got in touch with *L'Initiation*,[11] a journal covering topics on spirituality and advocating for the rights of minority religions in France. In another case, two mothers who were living at Terranova were notified by the state that their 'communal lifestyle' no longer qualified them for child support payments, and they were now required to repay several thousand euros at the state. The women contested the case against them, and the state withdrew its claim, though it did not reinstate their support payments. Evidently, the raid on Terranova and subsequent events motivated the Essenes to find creative ways to circumvent state regulations restricting their religious practices.

Underlying factors of the responses in the French context

Reflecting on confrontations between governments and religious movements, Stuart Wright suggests that the "threat to charismatic authority by the state ... invites some level of confrontation and sets in motion the dynamics of polarization" (2002: 106). Drawing on Bromley (2002), he continues saying:

> Where accommodation is absent or ineffective, polarization increases in direct proportion to the degree that the opposing parties believe that the conditions for preserving their core identity and collective existence are being subverted and that these conditions are intolerable.

As Wright highlights, group polarization can be diverted in many ways. The Essenes' experience in France in the early 2000s illustrates how a lack of accommodation can result in polarization – not only did they become more dedicated to their religious beliefs but they also became more assertive with regards to their identity as a religious movement. Yet, the avoidant strategies they employed – maintaining their activities in secret and defying court orders to stop members from associating with the group – enabled them to secure the conditions necessary for preserving their existence. The avoidant strategy also prevented greater polarization, which could have resulted in a stronger confrontational response. This example demonstrates that avoidant – that is, passive and non-compliant – strategies can be effective at diverting polarization when accommodation is absent.

A striking feature of the French context is the degree to which the state and public bodies are able to exert control over NRMs. From the perspective of religious minorities, the state, the law, and the public were jointly mobilized to oppose NRMs, which left very little space for these groups to flourish. In the case of the Essenes, the extent to which government agents pursued legal action against them, despite their having violated no significant laws, was deeply troubling as it suggested that the legal system in France was not a tool they could use to defend themselves from the state. Rather, they perceived the legal system as an arm of the French state – something which they do not feel is the case in Canada. Their distrust in the mechanisms for legal recourse available to them in France resulted in an inward turn; they became avoidant of unnecessary interactions with French society and directed their attention to the development and safeguarding of their unique tradition.

These events nevertheless had a strong destabilizing impact on the community, which led it to establish a second commune in Quebec, Canada. In 2008, Manitara immigrated to Canada with his family and a few followers.[12] There they joined Canadian members and began constructing a new village. This time, however, when legal problems with the state arose, the Essenes were not only more experienced with the law, but they also had more faith in the capacity of the Canadian legal system to protect their religion.

The next section describes Essenes' legal challenges in Canada and analyses the factors that motivated their responses to the law.

Faith in freedom: defensive responses

The treatment of religious minorities in Canada is very different from that of France, where the law is perceived as an arm of the state. Pauline Côté points out that "[i]n Canadian public rhetoric ... toleration ... stands as a civic virtue, a distinctively Canadian achievement. Among the Western polities, Canada takes pride in being temperate, moderate, and, most of all, accommodative to pluralism" (2004: 420). This virtue of tolerance for pluralism is also reflected in judicial decisions on religious freedom. In 2004, the Supreme Court of Canada ruled that religion was above all a subjective phenomenon, meaning that any claim regarding the protection of a belief or practice should be taken seriously if an individual can demonstrate that "he or she sincerely believes or is sincerely undertaking [a practice or harbouring a belief] in order to connect with the divine or as a function of his or her spiritual faith" (*Syndicat Northcrest v. Amselm*, 2004 CSC 47, para. 46).

This understanding of religion recognizes the multiple ways that individuals live their faith in contemporary Canada (Kislowicz 2012); however, this does not mean that sincerely held religious beliefs and practices are always protected. Lori Beaman notes that "frequently new religious movements and other religious minorities are placed on the outside of the boundaries of protection" (2006: 115). Nonetheless, this general way of thinking about the Canadian legal system as tolerant and accommodating towards religious minorities influences how religious minorities in Canada respond to state limitations of their religious beliefs or practices.

In 2007, the Essenes established their second commune, the Maple Village, on the site of a former hunting lodge in the Quebec municipality of Cookshire-Eaton. Most of the land they had purchased was zoned for agricultural purposes, where construction of non-agricultural buildings was prohibited, while a small portion was zoned for recreational and tourist purposes. While this was mentioned in the deed of sale, the community claims that it was not aware of the zoning limitations at the time of purchase. From 2008 to 2010, the Essenes claim that, on the basis of verbal agreements with the mayor of Cookshire-Eaton,[13] the community constructed its village without official permits.

Their legal problems began in 2010 following the election of a new mayor, after which municipal inspectors began making regular visits to the Maple Village. The municipality insisted that their buildings must conform to municipal regulations. According to the Essenes, they were able to obtain building permits for five of their temples, which were constructed in the recreational and tourist zone. However, the municipal inspector required that their temples must be registered as 'cabins', which was the only legitimate structure that could be built on the land. Eventually, the inspector was instructed to stop issuing permits altogether, as the land was not zoned for the practice of religion. In May 2011, the city council held a meeting where they unanimously adopted a resolution to request the demolition of unpermitted buildings. The resolution further stated that permitted buildings should "not be used in the exercise of public worship either as an episcopal palace, or as a presbytery or for purposes of a religious nature, the latter uses being prohibited by the municipal regulation in zone RU-12" (*Fondation Essenia*, 2013, para. 7). To the Essenes, this resolution brought into question the municipality's true intentions; were they motivated by a concern for the land or a discomfort with religion?

In addition to contesting their use of the land, the municipality of Cookshire-Eaton also challenged their property tax status. Registered religious organizations are exempt from paying property taxes in Quebec on the basis that "like other charities, they provide socially desirable benefits that would otherwise have to be provided by governments directly" (Jukier & Woehrling 2010: 196). In 2014, the Essenes received a notice that the municipality was re-evaluating their tax exemption. Prior to this, the community had not paid property taxes on any of its land as it was purchased and held by the Essene Church, a registered religious organization. According to the Essenes, the mayor objected to the fact that the entire land, including all residential structures, was granted a tax exemption due to the fact that the Essenes define all members that reside in the village as priests and further consider the entire land a monastery. In media reports, the mayor implied that, for the property to be considered entirely exempt from taxes, it would have to contain 'twelve presbyteries' (Vachon, *La Tribune*, 12 April 2017). He further suggested that the Essenes simply 'did not want' (Teisceira-Lessard, *LaPresse*, 3 October 2014) to pay property taxes.

Responses in Canada

The Essenes responded more assertively to the challenges they experienced in Canada than they had in France. When the zoning by-law issue was first raised, the Essenes attempted to secure an exemption for their structures from the municipality on religious grounds. However, the local government proved unwilling to accommodate them and ceased providing further permits. Confident that they were well within their rights as a religious organization to develop the land, the community continued to expand their village and built more structures. Eventually, in 2015, the Essenes received a notice from the provincial Commission for the Protection of Agricultural Land (CPTAQ), ordering the demolishing of 33 non-permitted buildings – many of which were intended for worship – within 30 days. An official notice of demolition was issued a year later in 2016 (*Église Essénienne Chrétienne c Québec (Commission de protection du territoire agricole)*, 2018). In response, the Essenes filed a request with the court to amend the zoning by-laws to include the practice of worship on the list of permitted development activities on land zoned for agricultural use. Their case is expected to be heard at the Superior Court of Quebec in 2021.

With regard to the zoning by-laws issue, the Essenes believed that the best way to protect the integrity of their village and practices was to seek recourse through the Canadian legal system. They are highly confident that their case will be successful for three reasons. First, Canadian law is strongly supportive of freedom of religion, and the Essenes believe that they can effectively demonstrate that their worship practices can only be conducted in a wild, rural area. Moreover, the Essenes maintain that the Archangels instructed them to construct their village on this particular tract of land.[14] Should the courts uphold the restrictions of the current by-laws, the Essenes would be unable to effectively practice their religion. Given these factors, many Essenes find it unimaginable that the courts would not protect their village (Melanson 2020). Second, the Essenes maintain that their use of the land is compatible with the CPTAQ's objective to protect agricultural lands. Due to their profound belief in the sacredness of nature, through which humanity's connection to the divine world is mediated, the Essenes support environmentally friendly practices, such as organic farming, vegetarian diets, and reduced energy consumption. Moreover, they believe that they have a profound duty and responsibility, which surpasses that of the state, to care for the physical and spiritual needs of nature. Finally, given that the municipality had accepted the request of prior owners to rezone a part of the land for non-agricultural use, the Essenes believe that it would be hypocritical of the municipality to deny their request to rezone the land for religious use, especially in light of the fact that the Essenes have made efforts to restore neglected areas and tear down barriers that prevented animals from roaming freely (Figure 9.1).

In response to the property tax challenge, several Canadian Essenes were interested in finding a compromise. They recognized that the municipality did provide some essential services to the property, such as running water, sanitation services, and access to the fire department, and they were willing to pay a percentage of what the municipality alleged they owed. French members who had witnessed the raid in Terranova, however, disagreed. They maintained that the community was in perfect compliance with existing municipal tax laws. Therefore, the community should not submit to municipal pressure and financially disadvantage the community simply to prove its good faith.

In the end, the defensive strategy suggested by the French Essenes was favoured over the more adaptive one proposed by the Canadian Essenes. The French Essenes persuaded their Canadian counterparts that it was important to demonstrate to the municipality that the community would not be passive when it came to defending their rights. Moreover, they argued that adapting to outside pressures after having persevered against harsher discrimination in France would constitute a step backwards. From the perspective of the Essenes, the only way forward was to act assertively to prove their compliance with the law and defend their rights. The community thus

Figure 9.1 Maple Village in Cookshire-Eaton, QC, Canada. (Photograph courtesy of Marie-Ève Melanson)

hired a lawyer to defend its interests, and the municipality sent an expert on religion to visit the Maple Village to determine whether the land was being used for religious purposes. The Essenes were successful in demonstrating the validity of their practices and places of worship to the expert, and the municipality finally relented. Ultimately, the case was resolved before reaching the courts.

The internal discussion between French and Canadian members over property taxes illustrates how group history can influence an NRM's response to legal challenges in new contexts – its prior experiences in France motivated the community to opt for a more assertive approach in Canada, a decision that was further influenced by its perception of the Canadian judiciary. Whereas the Essenes were distrustful of the French state and its legal system – and, thus, they resisted complying – they have greater confidence in the Canadian legal system's support for religious freedom. There, they are more motivated to be in compliance with the law and inclined to use it to defend their interests. The fact that they were successful in their first dispute in Canada likely reinforced their preference for more assertive strategies. While they did manifest some avoidant tendencies in Canada – most notably, they continued to develop their land and to practice their religion despite a municipal order to stop development or worship – the Essenes did not perceive their actions as non-compliant. Rather, they firmly believed that their use of the land was legitimate and would be found legal in a Canadian court of law. Their response is thus more illustrative of their confidence in the law than suggestive of an inclination to resist conforming to public regulations.

Underlying factors of the responses in the Canadian context

What is perhaps most striking about the Canadian context, as revealed by the case of the Essenes, is the relative fragility of the state's tolerance of religion. While French members claim that they feel more at liberty to affirm their religious identity in Canada, the state has not always recognized the Essenes legitimacy as a religious community. Moreover, their legal problems appear to rest on the subjective opinions of various public officials. While some officials have been accommodative, others have responded contestively and attempted to use the legal system to impose limits on the community. These variations reveal that the Canadian virtue of tolerance is not as consistent as the popular perception of Canada would otherwise suggest.

For an NRM, using the legal system to defend its interests can be a costly strategy. A community needs to have the financial means to hire lawyers, time to prepare its case, and sufficient knowledge of local laws. Furthermore, deploying assertive strategies also requires the participation and cooperation of many group members, which may be a substantial burden for those involved. Moreover, there is no guarantee of success. Before

embarking on a legal strategy, NRMs must carefully weigh all these considerations against the backdrop of their current context. In many instances,
the timing of an NRM's defensive strategy can play an important role in
determining the outcome of their case. For example, defensive strategies
might not have had the greatest chances of success during the peak of the
French 'war on sects.' Similarly, defensive strategies might play out better
in Canada if they are put in motion sequentially. Submitting too many cases
to the courts could suggest that the group is attempting to obstruct state
authorities rather than comply with the law. For this reason, groups might
choose to implement more than one type of strategy as part of its overall
response to state intervention.

In the case of the Essenes, these are important factors that the group has
had to take into consideration when evaluating whether or not to pursue a
legal action in defence of its interests. For instance, the community established a third village in Panama in 2016, which it calls the 'Garden of the
Light.' Similar to their establishment of the Maple Village, the Essenes' decision to build a new commune was due in part to their inability to conform
to certain local regulations in Canada. The Essenes' religion prescribes particular burial rites that are difficult, perhaps even impossible, to conduct in
conformity with provincial laws and regulations in Canada.

According to the Essene faith, the deceased must be 'accompanied' by
other members over a period of three days, which is the time it takes for the
soul to leave the body. These members are also tasked with performing a
series of rituals during this period, after which the intact and unembalmed
body of the deceased is returned to the land through burial. To perform
these funeral rites at their own village – or elsewhere in Quebec – would require special permissions from the government. As they are currently await-
ing their hearing at the Superior Court of Quebec, the Essenes are hesitant
to make further requests of the state, which could result in more legal actions against them. They have determined that, for the moment, their best
strategy is to deal with this problem in a passive manner and to establish
a new commune in Panama. Doing so would allow them to maintain their
practices while avoiding a possible lengthy court challenge. Nonetheless, as
one member explained, many of those who were born and raised in Quebec
hope that they will also be able to die in Quebec.

This example illustrates the complex decision-making process that in-
forms NRMs responses to efforts of social control. The Essenes' decisions
to establish a third village was not an impulsive or rash decision. Their use
of an avoidant strategy to deal with their burial practices is motivated by
multiple factors. The first such factor is *timing* – another legal action might
disrupt their current case that is before the courts. A second factor is the
cost of contesting provincial regulations. Legal procedures require a significant investment of resources (time, money, and labour) with potentially
no benefit. With regard to the religious aspect, a crucial factor relates to
orthopraxy: without an exemption, the Essenes are unable to comply with

current burial regulations in Canada and thus have no way of conducting funerals in accordance with their faith. Finally, considering the general *mission* of the Essene Church, establishing a new village furthers the religious aspirations of the community and has clear benefits. For all these reasons, the Essenes intend to deal with this last issue at a later date. Meanwhile, they are content to employ a passive strategy as they do not wish to jeopardize their overall assertive approach that they have adopted in Canada.

Conclusion

In this chapter, we have proposed an original typology to distinguish four different types of NRMs' responses to the state regulation of religion. Our analysis of the Essenes' case history in France and Canada demonstrates that a single NRM can employ multiple strategies when dealing with various arms of the state. Moreover, these reactions are often the product of multiple factors, most notably its perception of the state's legal system and the group's history. This chapter further demonstrates how other considerations, such as timing, resources, religious beliefs/practices, and the underlying mission of the group, can further inform an NRM's decision to employ a particular strategy at a given time. In the context of Canada, Beaman (2006: 115) seems to be right when noting that "[r]eligious minorities, especially new religious movements, often invoke, and rely on, legal guarantees when the right to believe and practice the tenets of their faith are threatened." In contrast with France, where it is perhaps more difficult for NRMs to thrive, the Canadian context seems to be more unpredictable, yet more tolerant towards NRMs in general. There, the courts have become the main tool in fighting for freedom of religion, whereas in France, other, more creative solutions might have to be found.

Notes

1 Olivier Manitara died of a stroke in June 2020 at the Essene village in Panama.
2 Bromley's model ultimately does not distinguish between reactions to the law, reactions to the state, and reactions to societal norms.
3 This model was inspired by N. J. Demerath's useful typology of secularization introduced in "Secularization and Sacralization Deconstructed and Reconstructed," *The Sage Handbook of the Sociology of Religion*, 57–81, Los Angeles: Sage Publications (2007). Bromley and Palmer each propose a typology of different responses, though neither is specific to government or legal interventions.
4 All translations from French are our own.
5 The *Mission interministérielle de lutte contre les sectes* (Interministerial Commission to Combat the Cults) was founded in 1998 with the aim to "observe and find more effective tools to 'fight sectes'" (Wright & Palmer 2016: 203). Palmer observes that because it "evoked an outcry from religious minorities in France and foreign religious freedom advocates due to its draconian anticult policies" (2011: 5), it was disbanded and replaced in 2002 by MILUVIDES. This *Mission interministérielle de vigilance et de lutte contre les dérives sectaires*

Interministerial (Commission for the Vigilance and Fight against Sectarian Aberrations), established in 2002, had the aim to prevent 'cultic excesses', instead of 'fighting against cults' *tout court*. Contrarily to MILS, this commission had the primary official goal to work for the "prevention of sect-derived crimes and misdemeanours" (Luca in Palmer 2011: 20).

6 Palmer writes that "the community was raided in part because a caravan had been parked in an *interdit* area and there was an error in a claim for Assédic a French agency which collects and pays unemployment insurance" (2011: 209). However, French members interviewed in Canada claim that neighbours circulated rumours that the community was fabricating a bomb to commit collective suicide in the manner of the Order of the Solar Temple. Whether the raid was motivated by an unfounded complaint or inspired by the French authority's fight against 'sects' (Beckford 2004: 34; Palmer 2011: 19–21), both options stemmed from the idea that the expression of organized forms of spirituality is suspicious.

7 These attempts on the part of government officials to stoke fear and suspicion of NRMs among the public suggests that the charge of mental manipulation could easily apply to the state as well.

8 This was, according to one French member, highly disappointing for the authorities, as this evidence would have allowed the state to 'accomplish their fantasy' of 'dismantling a murderer-suicidal group.'

9 Manitara later started having encounters with three other Archangels: Gabriel, Raphael, and Uriel. As the only human invested with the ability to communicate with the divine realm, Manitara's duty is to act as the divine messenger. Within the community, his role in practical decision-making, however, is very small, and this task is left to his followers, who are in charge of the decisions pertaining to the earthly world while Manitara concentrates on the divine world. Some of the revelations that Manitara receives do affect the practical decisions of the community. For example, the Archangels have wished for the Essenes to erect temples or houses in their honour and to develop new Essene villages outside of France, all of which have practical consequences.

10 Many of the charges made against NRMs at the time-concerned practices of money management. This was because of the "Sects and Money Report" commissioned by the French government and published in 1999, which Palmer describes as "the opening move of a new attack on *sectes*" (2011: 18). Since the Essenes were raided in 2000 and the laws on abuse of weakness and mental manipulation were adopted only in 2001, it is not surprising that Manitara was only found guilty of this specific charge. The Essenes explain that Manitara had cashed a cheque that amounted to a few hundred French francs from a follower that was made to his name instead of the association. According to them, Manitara had already found a way to pay the money back and had cashed the cheque in the first place only because he didn't want to go through the trouble of tracking down the member to ask her to issue a new cheque. They claim that the authorities were willing to accuse Manitara of anything in order to frame him as a criminal and that this was the only technically illegal charge they could find. Members assert that this allowed local newspapers to depict Manitara as a 'convicted felon' for years, thus encouraging fear and hatred against them and NRMs in general.

11 Known today as *L'Essentiel*.

12 Shortly after Manitara immigrated, the Canadian government tried to deport him back to France on the grounds that he had committed a crime in France that would have been considered an act of 'serious criminality' in Canada. However, the attempt failed because the French tribunal was never able to determine if

Manitara's actions were deceitful or if they caused prejudice to another individual. In 2009, the Canadian government tried a second time to deport Manitara on the same basis. However, the charge of 'misuse of company assets' does not have an equivalent in Canadian law, and thus it could not be concluded that Manitara would be found guilty were he tried for this crime in Canada (Teisceira-Lessard, *LaPresse*, 4 October 2014).

13 In court documents, a representative from the municipality attests to the fact that the sitting mayor was known to have made many verbal agreements (Foundation Essenia, 2013 CanLII 103504 (QC CPTAQ), para.14). Essene members also recount that this mayor was sympathetic to religion and was pleased to see the land developed for religious purposes.

14 Manitara reports that the Archangel Raphael claimed: "It will be a land near the mountains, with great trees, at the center of which water flows, with two shores united by a bridge" (2015: 48).

References

Beaman, Lori G. 2006. Religious freedom written and lived, in: Pauline Côté and T. Jeremy Gunn (eds) *The New Religious Question: State Regulation or State Interference?* Brussels: P.I.E.-Peter Lang, pp. 115–32.

Beckford, James. 2004. 'Laïcité,' 'dystopia,' and the reaction to new religious movements in France, in: James T. Richardson (ed.) *Regulating Religion: Case Studies from around the Globe.* New York: Kluwer Academic/Plenum Publishers, pp. 27–40.

———. 1999. The mass media and new religious movements, in: Jamie Cresswell and Bryan Wilson (eds) *New Religious Movements: Challenge and Response.* London: Routledge, pp. 103–19.

Bromley, David. 2002. Dramatic denouement, in: David G. Bromley and J. Gordon Melton (eds) *Cults, Religion and Violence.* New York: Cambridge University Press, pp. 11–41.

Côté, Pauline. 2004. Public management of religious diversity in Canada: Development of technocratic pluralism, in: James T. Richardson (ed.) *Regulating Religion: Case Studies from Around the Globe.* New York: Kluwer Academic/Plenum Publishers, pp. 419–40.

Demerath III, N. J. 2007. Secularization and sacralization deconstructed and reconstructed, in: James A. Beckford and N. J. Demerath III (eds) *The Sage Handbook of the Sociology of Religion.* Los Angeles: Sage Publications, pp. 57–81.

Dericquebourg, Régis. 1998. La controverse sur les sectes en France. Retrieved from https://halshs.archives-ouvertes.fr/halshs-00087025. Accessed December 2, 2019.

Duvert, Cyrille. 2004. Anti-cultism in the French: Parliament desperate last stand or an opportune leap forward? A critical analysis of the 12 June 2001 Act, in: James T. Richardson (ed.) *Regulating Religion: Case Studies from Around the Globe.* New York: Kluwer Academic/Plenum Publishers, pp. 41–52.

Église Essénienne Chrétienne c Québec (Commission de protection du territoire agricole). 2018. CanLII 2746 (QC TAQ). Retrieved from http://canlii.ca/t/hq 2bv. Accessed December 16, 2019.

Fondation Essenia. 2013. CanLII 103504 (QC CPTAQ). Retrieved from http://canlii.ca/t/h0hwh. Accessed December 16, 2019.

Jukier, Rosalie and Woehrling, Jose. 2010. Religion and the Secular State in Canada, in: Javier Martinez-Torron and W. Cole Durham (eds.) *Religion and the Secular State: National Reports*. Provo, Utah: International Center for Law and Religious Studies, pp. 183-212. Retrieved from https://ssrn.com/abstract=2002271. Accessed December 16, 2019.

Kislowicz, Howard. 2012. Freedom of religion and Canada's commitments to multiculturalism. *National Journal of Constitutional Law* 31, 1–23.

Luca, Nathalie. 2004. Is there a unique French policy of cults? A European perspective, in: James T. Richardson (ed.) *Regulating Religion: Case Studies from around the Globe*. New York: Kluwer Academic/Plenum Publishers, pp. 53–71.

Manitara, Olivier. 2015. *Le village essénien: Une terre pour Dieu*. Cookshire-Eaton: Éditions Essénia.

Melanson, Marie-Ève. 2020. The Christian Essene Church: Freedom of religion in the "land of the maple," in: Susan J. Palmer, Paul L. Gareau and Martin Geoffroy (eds) *The Mystical Geography of Quebec: Catholic Schisms and New Religious Movements*. New York: Palgrave Macmillan, pp. 169–91.

Palmer, Susan. 2011. *The New Heretics of France: Minority Religions, la République, and the Government-Sponsored "War on Sects"*. New York: Oxford University Press.

Syndicat Northcrest v. Amselem, 2004. SCC 47 (CanLII), [2004] 2 SCR 551. Retrieved from http://canlii.ca/t/1hddh. Accessed December 16, 2019.

Teisceira-Lessard, Philippe. 2014a, October 3. Le maire de Cookshire s'en prend aux Esséniens. *LaPresse*, Actualités. Retrieved from www.lapresse.ca/actualites/201410/02/01-4805841-le-maire-de-cookshire-sen-prend-aux-esseniens.php. Accessed December 5, 2019.

———. 2014b, October 4. Ordre des Esséniens: Ottawa a tenté d'expulser le gourou. *LaPresse*, Actualités. Retrieved from: www.lapresse.ca/actualites/justice-et-affaires-criminelles/affaires-criminelles/201410/04/01-4806275-ordre-des-esseniens-ottawa-a-tente-dexpulser-le-gourou.php. Accessed December 5, 2019.

Vachon, Matthew. 2017, April 2. Le maire Landry rouvre le dialogue avec les Esséniens. *La Tribune*, Actualités. Retrieved from www.latribune.ca/actualites/le-maire-landry-rouvre-le-dialogue-avec-les-esseniens-c0767239e50d19fd08e7a3e6f8d0bad7. Accessed December 5, 2019.

Wright, Stuart. 2002. Public agency involvement in government – religious movement onfrontations, in: David G. Bromley and J. Gordon Melton (eds) *Cults, Religion and Violence*. New York: Cambridge University Press, pp. 102–22.

Wright, Stuart and Susan Palmer. 2016. *Storming Zion: Government Raids on Religious Communities*. New York: Oxford University Press.

10 Reactions to legal challenges by Aum Shinrikyō and its successor organisations

Rin Ushiyama

Introduction

On 6 July 2018, more than 23 years after the gassing of the Tokyo subway system using the deadly nerve agent sarin, news of Aum Shinrikyō ('Aum' henceforth) monopolised the Japanese media once again. That morning, the group's founder Asahara Shōkō (birth name Matsumoto Chizuo) was hanged along with six of his former adherents convicted of Aum's most violent crimes including multiple cases of murder, attempted murder, and two counts of terrorism. The number of convicts executed in one day was unprecedented in Japan's post-war legal history. Fewer than three weeks later, on 26 July, a second round of executions ended the lives of six others sentenced to death, completing all 13 death sentences relating to violent crimes and terrorist attacks committed by members of Aum Shinrikyō, commonly known in Japan as the 'Aum Affair' (*Oumu jiken*).[1]

The executions were not entirely unexpected. Since Emperor Akihito's announcement in 2016 that he intended to abdicate, there had been widespread speculation that the executions would be carried out whilst still in the *Heisei* imperial era ending in April 2019. Anticipating that executions might be carried out soon, earlier in 2018, a collective of public intellectuals and writers led by filmmaker Mori Tatsuya – a long-standing critic of societal responses to the Aum Affair – had called for a stay on Asahara's execution, arguing that Asahara was too mentally ill to be executed. Much to their dismay, their call was not heeded by state authorities.

Although the executions were not unexpected, there were some surprising reactions from civil society. In a macabre media spectacle, the national TV broadcaster *Fuji Terebi* ran a live news programme in which presenters held up boards showing photographs of the convicts' faces, placing stickers labelled 'executed' on them as the news rolled in. On the internet, anonymous posters bombarded a blog site run by Asahara's third daughter Matsumoto Rika, posting insulting comments that gloated over her father's death. At the same time as bringing a sense of closure to many, the executions laid bare the nation's deep-seated trauma of the Tokyo attack and the intense negative emotions held by much of Japan's population towards Asahara and Aum Shinrikyō.

While these executions demonstrated the Weberian definition of the exercise of state power – the monopoly of the legitimate use of violence over a given territory – in its purest form, the Japanese state has also sought to regulate Aum Shinrikyō through many other legal mechanisms, such as attempting to disband the group, and failing that, later putting it under state surveillance. Furthermore, the executions have not ended legal disputes surrounding Aum. For instance, as of 2020, there are ongoing disputes between Asahara's surviving family over who should take custody of Asahara's cremated remains.

This chapter examines how Aum Shinrikyō and its two main successor organisations – Aleph and Hikari no Wa – have responded to these legal disputes in the wake of the Tokyo subway sarin incident of March 1995. The social consequences of the Aum Affair are instructive for scholars of minority religions because Aum Shinrikyō continued to be active after the arrests of its founder and most of the leadership. The long-term changes in Aum's successor organisations highlight how minority religions evolve through interaction with external stakeholders including state authorities, public institutions, and local residents. In the past quarter-century, Aum, Aleph, and Hikari no Wa have all contended with difficult legal, political, and moral problems relating to criminal responsibility, financial obligations, public apology, and social integration. This chapter suggests that organisational change in minority religions cannot be understood either as purely 'internal' – caused by intra-group dynamics and doctrinal reforms – or 'external' – imposed by outside actors including state and non-state institutions such as law enforcement, local and national governments, anti-cult movements, and members of the public. The complex history of Aum, Aleph, and Hikari no Wa demonstrates that it is imperative to treat minority religions as active agents operating within the constraints of specific historical, cultural, and legal environments.

In contrast to existing scholarship which has focused on the history of Aum's development up to 1995 (Lifton 1999; Metraux 1999; Reader 2000a; Repp 2011; Shimazono 1995; Watanabe 1998) and responses by various state and civil society actors to the Aum Affair (Kisala and Mullins 2001; Mullin 2012; Pendleton 2009; Reader 2000b), this chapter foregrounds how Aum, Aleph, and Hikari no Wa have addressed legal challenges in the changing social and legal environment after the Tokyo attack through a chronological outline of the groups' development after 1995. In doing so, I identify two contrasting patterns in actors' uses of the law. Firstly, the state has used legal mechanisms in an attempt to disband, regulate, and monitor Aum. Secondly, Aum and its related members have used the law as a redressive mechanism to challenge decisions and policies by both state and civil actors, with mixed success. It is worth noting here that I include Asahara's direct family in the discussions, although they are not formally 'members' or 'adherents', due to the important leadership roles they have played in deciding the direction of the movements as well as the fact that they have been party to many of the legal disputes related to Aum.

Aum Shinrikyō – 1984–1995

Aum Shinrikyō is notorious for the sarin attack in Tokyo in March 1995, but it was also responsible for multiple accidental deaths, abduction, murder, and another terrorist attack in the city of Matsumoto in central Japan in 1994. Although Aum Shinrikyō's turn to violence and terrorism is unique in many ways, the group had less remarkable beginnings as a suburban yoga class. Asahara Shōkō, a former acupuncturist and a mostly self-taught yogi, founded *Aum no Kai* ('*Aum Society*') in 1984, attracting students interested in Tibetan Buddhism, yoga, and meditative techniques. In 1986, Asahara claimed to have reached enlightenment in the Himalayas and declared himself to be an omniscient guru. He introduced a system of communal living for 'renunciants' (*shukkesha/samana*) to train as ascetic monks before eventually changing the name of the group to Aum Shinrikyō (translated to 'Aum Supreme Truth') in 1987. Aum drew on an array of religious traditions including Tibetan Buddhism, Hinduism, Christianity, and New Age spiritualism that converged on the belief of Asahara as the 'Final Enlightened One' (*saishū gedatsusha*), tasked with producing other enlightened souls to prevent an impending Armageddon (*harumagedon*), predicted to occur by 1999.

Young people comprised the majority of Aum's membership: Aum appealed to teenagers, university students, and graduates disaffected by rigid hierarchies in schools and companies and the consumerist excesses of Japan's 'bubble' economy. At its height, it had around 10,000 members, around 1,100 of whom were full-time 'renunciants' living communally, 47.5 per cent of whom were in their 20s and 75.4 per cent in their 20s and 30s (Shimazono 1995: 384). Joining as a full member meant 'giving up' (that is to say, donating) all worldly possessions including property, cars, and cash to Aum. Renunciants lived an ascetic lifestyle including vegetarianism, limiting hours of sleep, sexual abstinence, taking scalding hot baths, and sustained periods of meditation. Corporal punishment for transgressions included being beaten with bamboo swords (*shinai*) and being hanged upside down by the ankles for hours in a practice known as 'cleansing karma' (*karuma otoshi*) as well as physical isolation in shipping containers. In the 1990s, the group introduced the use of hallucinogenic drugs – without the knowledge or consent of the participants – in so-called 'initiation rituals' to mimic spiritual experiences. These extreme training regimes led to multiple accidental deaths, which were covered up through the secret disposal of bodies.

As a rule, renunciants avoided contact with outsiders as spiritually contaminating, and social friction between renunciants and surrounding communities intensified as the group grew in size. Amidst the friction, Asahara developed a belief system that justified violence against dissenters and non-believers. Although Aum officially abhorred killing of any kind, Asahara made an exception for '*poa*', a 'ritual' in which a person that Asahara 'knew' to commit evil deeds in the future could be killed, thereby preventing them from accumulating 'bad' karma in this life and promising a better rebirth in the future.[2] Related concepts were also important for Aum's violence: the '*Tantra Vajrayāna*' 'vehicle' to enlightenment stated that the ends justified the means, while the concept of '*mahāmudrā*' was used to justify challenging tasks – such as killing others – as tests of faith in the guru (see also Reader 2000a; Shimazono 1995). In early 1989, Asahara put these concepts to use by murdering a dissident believer; later that year, they also used '*poa*' to justify the murder of lawyer Sakamoto Tsutsumi – who was representing Aum believers' parents – and his family. None of these murders was solved until 1995, after the arrests and confessions of the culprits.

Aum's millenarian eschatology became more pronounced in 1990 after a general election in which Asahara and 24 others stood as candidates. Asahara had envisioned winning political power through elections by 1999 to make Aum a state religion (Hayakawa and Kawamura 2005: 147–8). The plan was quickly derailed as Aum failed to win any seats, which Asahara blamed on a governmental conspiracy. He subsequently instructed a turn away from peaceful expansion through conversion ('*Mahayāna*') to the application of '*Tantra Vajrayāna*' through militarisation in anticipation of an apocalyptic war (Noda 2010: 30–1; Tsukada 2011: 323–5). Although their attempts at biological terrorism failed, they successfully created chemical weapons including phosgene, VX, and sarin. These chemicals were used to attack the group's critics, dissident members, and members of the public. In 1994, Asahara applied '*poa*' indiscriminately to civilians by spraying sarin in the city of Matsumoto, Nagano Prefecture, killing seven and injuring over 600 residents (Ushiyama 2019b). The following year, on 20 March 1995, five assailants boarded different trains of the Tokyo metro subway system with bags of sarin solution, piercing open the bags as they disembarked. The attack killed 13 and injured more than 6,000 passengers in the single worst terrorist attack in post-war Japan.

In response, the police raided Aum's headquarters two days later, finding evidence of sarin production. Aum initially denied responsibility and accused the state of religious persecution, but as evidence mounted against them, Asahara was arrested in May 1995, as were most of the leadership. While many ordinary members who did not know about the secret militarisation programme quit, others decided to stay. In a dramatic turn of events, in April 1995, the head scientist, Murai Hideo, widely understood to be Asahara's right-hand man and the architect of Aum's militarisation programme, was stabbed to death by a lone assailant while he struggled to move past media personnel into Aum's Tokyo office.

1995–1999: Uncertainty and stagnation

Although the arrests of the leadership brought an eventual end to Aum's violent conspiracies, there remained many legal problems surrounding how the state should respond to Aum Shinrikyō. Some tasks were as simple as closing legal loopholes, such as making sarin production a criminal offence. More complex problems related to state regulation of religion which touched upon fundamental constitutional values of freedom of religion and freedom of association: can a religious group that has committed terrorism continue to exist? As an initial step, the Tokyo Metropolitan Government moved to revoke Aum's 'religious corporation' status in June 1995. That legal status provides religious organisations a mark of public recognition and preferential tax rates. The decision was approved by the Tokyo District Court and upheld by the Supreme Court in 1996 despite Aum disputing the decision. Since then, Aum and its successor organisations have operated as 'voluntary association' (*nin'i dantai*) with no status as a legal person. The group was also declared bankrupt in 1996 and its assets were subsequently managed by a trustee after losing multiple class-action lawsuits (see also Mullins 2001).

Aum also faced the possibility of disbandment through the application of the Prevention of Destructive Activity Act (commonly known as *habōhō*, shortened from *hakaiteki katsudō bōshi hō* in Japanese, shortened here to PDAA). PDAA is a repressive law enacted in 1952 in the historical context of the Cold War, which was designed to curtail leftist activism. The act enables state authorities to arrest individuals and dissolve groups engaging in 'destructive activity'. A deeply political law from its inception, political organisations currently monitored under the Act include right-wing groups and the Japanese Communist Party.[3]

Public opinion strongly supported the use of PDAA to disband Aum, with 79 per cent of respondents in a newspaper poll supporting the idea.[4] However, the law was more difficult to implement in practice. Ironically, the Social Democratic Party, the ruling party in the 1994–1996 coalition government, had originally opposed the Act's enactment because it potentially violated the constitutional freedom of association, but decades later, it found itself considering applying the law to a religious organisation. In October 1995, Prime Minister Murayama Tomiichi requested the Ministry of Justice to exercise 'extra prudence' in applying the PDAA to Aum. Members of the Liberal Democratic Party, nominally the junior coalition partner, were also split over whether the application was essential given that the key culprits had already been arrested.[5]

Non-state actors were also divided in their opinion. The conservative newspaper *Yomiuri Shimbun* defended the move as necessary and urgent.[6] By contrast, *Asahi Shimbun*, historically a flag-bearer of progressive politics, opposed the PDAA arguing that the law was unconstitutional and merely handed the Public Security Intelligence Agency (PSIA) more investigative powers and funding.[7] The Japan PEN Club, the national branch of the free speech advocacy organisation PEN International, and the Japanese Federation of Bar Associations both opposed the application of the Act as unconstitutional and a breach of fundamental liberties.[8]

The cautiousness of some actors towards banning Aum outright must be understood with reference to Japan's violent past of persecuting minority religions during the militarist–fascist regime before 1945. Since the Meiji Restoration (1868), which resulted in the modern Japanese state, the enforcement of State Shinto – a religious and political ideology that places devotion to the Emperor at the core of politics – as an official religion went hand-in-hand with the denigration of Japanese Buddhism and minority religions as 'promiscuous evil cults' (*inshi jakyō*) (Dorman 2012; Hardacre 1989). Most notably, the new religion Ōmoto, a charismatic movement founded in the late nineteenth century, was persecuted and shut down by state authorities on two separate occasions in 1921 and 1935. The group was investigated on suspicion of *lèse-majesté* and for the violation of the Peace Preservation Act, a notorious law that initially targeted left activism but later expanded to suppress religious and civil activity. The Ōmoto leadership was eventually acquitted of all charges in 1942, but not before their buildings were razed, dozens were tortured to death, and its reputation slandered. Given Japan's history of state oppression of religions, then, authorities were anxious to avoid historical comparisons between historical religious repression and Aum's potential dissolution through the PDAA. Likewise, for progressives and liberals cautious of state abuses of power, the freedom of association and freedom of religion were sacred inalienable rights, even if it meant begrudgingly allowing Aum to continue to practice.

In December 1995, following several months of debate and inaction, the Prime Minister eventually gave the PSIA the go-ahead for legal proceedings of the PDAA to start.[9] Yet, the PSIA's plan to forcibly dissolve Aum did not come into fruition. In 1997, the Public Security Examination Commission, a separate body that considers PDAA applications, rejected PSIA's claims, ruling that Aum did not pose an imminent security threat.[10] As authorities sought alternative solutions to disband or regulate Aum, the group continued to practice as before, albeit under the scrutiny of law enforcement.

Parallel to the debates surrounding the PDAA, there were minor reforms made to the Religious Corporations Act (*shūkyō hōjin hō*, RCA). The reformed law brought the registration of religious corporations active in multiple prefectures under central administration by the Ministry of Culture – now the Ministry of Education, Culture, Sports, Science and Technology.[11] The new law also expanded the state's authority to investigate religious organisations and required registered organisations to file annual financial records for greater transparency (Inoue 2011: 410–2).[12] However, unlike other countries that enacted 'anti-cult' laws to regulate minority religions (Edelman and Richardson 2005; Palmer 2011), Japan did not pass equivalent laws, despite widespread public distrust towards religions as 'dangerous' (*abunai*) (Reader 2012).

As the application of the PDAA failed, the government enacted a new set of laws in 1999 to enable continuous surveillance of Aum, colloquially known as 'New Aum Laws'. The 1999 Act Relating to the Regulation of Organisations Which Have Committed Indiscriminate Mass Murder (*Musabetsu tairyō satsujin kōi o okonatta dantai no kisei ni kansuru hōritsu*, colloquially known as *dantai kisei hō*), abbreviated here as the Organisations Regulation Act (ORA), effectively acted as a diluted version of the PDAA. As the name suggests, the Act placed groups that have committed indiscriminate mass murder under state supervision for an initial period of three years, subject to renewal. Unlike the PDAA, which forcibly dissolved those organisations in question, the ORA allowed designated organisations to practice on the condition of submitting regular financial and membership reports and being subject to unannounced searches by law enforcement. The legislature also passed a corollary Act which enabled the state to recover assets belonging to organisations monitored under the ORA.[13] This ensured that Aum's successor organisations were liable for the same financial liabilities and obligations as Aum in perpetuity. Since the ORA's enactment, Aum, Aleph, and Hikari no Wa have all contested the legality of state surveillance through the courts, with mixed results, as will be discussed below.

Beyond these legislative changes, criminal proceedings against Asahara and his co-conspirators were also ongoing for charges including murder, attempted murder, manslaughter, kidnapping, and the illegal disposal of bodies. During the first months of detention, Asahara sent messages to his adherents via his lawyer to keep training.[14] In the trial proceedings, Asahara initially pleaded not guilty. As the hearings progressed, his comments became increasingly erratic and incomprehensible, before falling silent again for the remainder of the trials: whether this was voluntary or the result of deteriorating mental health has been fiercely contested.[15] Other accomplices in Aum's militarist programme received sentences ranging from several years in jail to life imprisonment and death by hanging. Many of those sentenced to death appealed the decision, but without success. For Inoue Yoshihiro, who led the ground-level operation in the Tokyo attack, the sentence was increased from a life sentence to the death sentence after the prosecution appealed against the initial verdict.

Besides their involvement in these criminal and civil trials, at an organisational level, Aum introduced a few organisational changes. Aum nominally replaced the official 'leaders' (*kyōso*) with Asahara's two young sons, changed Asahara's title to 'founder' (*kaiso*), and declared that it had banned the *Tantra Vajrayāna* doctrine that justified violence. However, few other substantive changes to its doctrines or practices were implemented.[16] Throughout this period, Aum's apparent lack of contrition, together with public anxieties stirred by sensationalist media reports and warnings by security agencies, contributed to hostile responses by civil actors. For instance, some school boards showed reluctance to admit some children of Aum members (including Asahara's children) from receiving compulsory education after Parent–Teacher Associations raised concerns.[17] In these cases, the children's legal representatives successfully reversed the Boards' decisions, but only after taking or threatening legal action. However, as I will discuss below, the issue of refusing educational opportunities to Asahara's children remained a recurring issue in the twenty-first century as well. Moreover, because discussions about the enactment of the ORA reignited interest – and, consequently, moral panic – about Aum, residents' associations organised demonstrations demanding Aum's expulsion from their neighbourhoods.

In general, during this period, Aum stagnated and struggled to find a new direction in the absence of its most charismatic and influential members. The group did not offer a public apology until December 1999 in anticipation of the imminent enactment of the ORA. The end of 1999 also saw the release of Aum's former spokesperson, Jōyū Fumihiro, from prison. Because Jōyū was stationed in Russia in the early 1990s, he was not implicated in Aum's most serious crimes. Soon after the Tokyo attack, he returned to Japan and appeared daily on television to defend Aum and accuse the state of religious persecution. He was arrested later in 1995 and was jailed for perjury and falsifying documents in relation to a land deal in 1990 (Jōyū 2012: 168). In addition to his skilful oratory skills and photogenic demeanour that earned him infamy on Japanese television, Jōyū was naturally poised to take up a leadership role as a '*Seitaishi*', the highest title awarded to disciples. He promptly took office as the new *de facto* leader of Aum before formally becoming its leader in 2002.

2000–2006: New beginning, old problems

The end of 1999 did not bring about the end of the world as Asahara predicted. Instead, the start of 2000 signalled the end of Asahara's central importance in Aum's activities. The beginning of Jōyū's tenure roughly coincided with the ORA coming into effect in early 2000. Around the same time, Jōyū announced the renaming of Aum Shinrikyō as Aleph. Aleph, the first letter of the Hebrew alphabet, signified a new beginning and a break from the past; some speculated that this was an attempt to escape the application of the ORA to the newly named group. Eager to differentiate Aleph from Aum and Asahara's symbolically polluting images, Jōyū opposed the application of the ORA to Aleph and began litigation proceedings, claiming an unconstitutional violation of freedom of religion.[18] The ORA was ruled constitutional and the state's surveillance of the group was upheld by the Tokyo District Court in 2001.[19] In terms of doctrines and training regimes, Jōyū also shifted the emphasis from becoming the 'guru's clone' to promoting physical and spiritual wellbeing through training techniques.

Books written by Jōyū in this period emphasise his image as the spiritual leader whilst omitting references to Asahara as an object of worship (Jōyū 2002a, 2002b).

Despite these changes, security agencies and civil society actors alike viewed the renaming of the organisation as little more than window dressing. In a typical response by security authorities, the PSIA spokesman emphasised in a news article from 2002 that Aleph 'is no less dangerous than it was seven years ago, in the sense that all of its members are under mind-control to worship Asahara' and that the size of the membership 'is sufficient (for the cult) to engage in terrorism on a grand scale' (Matsubara 2002). Residents living near Aleph's communes continued demonstrations calling for expulsion of Aleph from their community, fearing another terrorist plot. In some areas, local committees set up surveillance posts outside Aleph buildings and demanded the right to inspect any goods entering the premises, as Mori Tatsuya's documentary film *A2* captures (Gardner 2002; Mori 2001; Ushiyama and Baert 2016). 'Successful' cases of resident mobilisation did not lead to a fundamental resolution of social tensions either: even when Aleph members agreed to move out of the old neighbourhood, it would only start a new cycle of protests at their new destination.

Starting around 1999 and continuing into the 2000s, municipal governments also implemented policies to exclude Aum from local communities by declining to provide utility services and refusing to accept resident records (*jūminhyō*), which act as proof of address.[20] Although supported by many local residents, these decisions lacked a basis in law. Aleph was proactive in litigating against local governments' policy of exclusion, bringing cases to court in multiple prefectures for discrimination. In a landmark ruling, the Supreme Court ruled in 2001 that the annulment and refusal of Aum believers' resident records was unlawful.[21] Most district courts also ruled in Aum's favour and municipal governments were eventually forced to accept and process resident records and to pay compensation.[22]

Despite these legal victories, individuals associated with Aleph's difficult legacy continued to encounter challenges in being accepted in society. Between 2000 and 2001, in another iteration of moral panic surrounding Asahara's children, a school board in Ryūgasaki, Ibaraki Prefecture, refused to provide compulsory education to three of Asahara's children following strong pressures from local resident groups and Parent–Teacher Associations. In December 2000, a demonstration held by those opposing the children attending school gathered 1,000 participants.[23] The school board eventually agreed to admit the children, but only after the children's representatives took legal action for discrimination.[24] In a separate case, Asahara's third daughter Rika was denied admission to three private universities, despite having passed the entrance exams. She took legal actions against the universities to reverse their decisions, which resulted in rulings in her favour: she attended one of the universities, graduating with a psychology degree in 2008 (Matsumoto 2015). In all of these cases, influenced by strong demands from parents and local residents, school boards and universities continued to refuse admission of Asahara's children until legal action was taken against them despite lacking legal justification to do so.

Inside Aleph, Jōyū's reforms to de-emphasise Asahara as an object of worship led to a strong backlash from Asahara's immediate family. From 2003, he was placed under 'intense training', in which he was effectively quarantined from other followers. However, during this time, Jōyū formed a critical mass of followers that agreed with his direction. By 2005, around 200 followers had identified as the 'Jōyū-faction' or the 'representative faction' (*daihyō-ha*), distinct from the 'mainstream faction' (*shūryū-ha*), and began to organise its own events and to use separate facilities. In 2007, Jōyū reached a legal agreement with Aleph to separate and form a new group called Hikari no Wa, along with around 160 supporters (Public Security Intelligence Agency 2008).

2007–2018: Parting ways

Aleph

Since the split between Aleph and Hikari no Wa, Aleph has maintained a secretive profile, and their recent activities have been closed to outsiders (Baffelli 2012: 35). Following Jōyū's exit, Noda Naruhito, holding the rank of '*Seigoshi*', nominally served as the leader, but was later expelled from the organisation after rifts deepened between him and Asahara's family members (Noda 2010). Muraoka Tatsuko, who had co-run Aleph with Jōyū, also left Aleph several years later. Today, Aleph remains a 'world-rejecting' movement that seeks minimal contact with the outside world (Wallis 1984).

Although Aleph's website has made regular updates regarding the payment of reparations, the group has been reticent to act on other issues. For instance, the group has not made public statements on the executions of Asahara and the other 12 convicts. Sources of income are unclear, although the PSIA has reported that it has held yoga classes to recruit new members (Public Security Intelligence Agency 2017: 59, 2019: 63). Despite Aleph maintaining a low public profile, it has continued to rely on litigation as the main mechanism for seeking redress and protecting its legal rights. For example, it sued the state, unsuccessfully, to cancel the renewal and extension of the ORA in 2009.[25]

For Aleph, litigation has continued to be an important method of challenging the state for unlawful actions. In 2010, the Tokyo Metropolitan Police Department (*Keishichō*) held a press conference to mark the expiration of the statute of limitations for the shooting of the Chief of Police in March 1995, a week after the Tokyo sarin attack. Given the timing of the assassination attempt, Aum was initially suspected to be behind it, but no one from Aum or Aleph had been charged for the attempted murder. In a press conference, the head of the Public Security division named Aum as the culprits behind the attack without providing evidence. Aleph promptly sued the Tokyo Metropolitan Government for defamation and won both the District Court and High Court judgments, receiving a million yen (around USD10,000) in compensation.[26]

Aleph underwent another split in 2015 after disagreements intensified over who should be the next leader. The mainstream faction, led by Asahara's wife, supported Asahara's second son becoming Asahara's successor. By contrast, others who do not recognise the son as a legitimate heir have formed a smaller faction of around 30 people, which the PSIA call the 'Yamada *et al.* Group' ("*Yamada-ra no shūdan*") (Public Security Intelligence Agency 2018: 55–9). In 2018, the 'Yamada *et al.* Group' launched a legal challenge opposing PSIA's decision to place them under state supervision, which is still ongoing.[27]

Hikari no Wa

By contrast, Hikari no Wa has adopted a more conciliatory approach in its interactions with external stakeholders by emphasising its connections to the secular world (Baffelli 2012), arguably best described as 'world-accommodating' (Wallis 1984), insofar as it neither rejects nor fully integrates with the secular world. Although some members continue to live communally as 'full-time staff' similar to Aleph renunciants, Hikari no Wa has publicly and emphatically condemned Aum's criminal actions, renounced Asahara as guru, and stressed a fundamental break from Aleph. Although Jōyū has continued to act as its representative, the group holds that it does not have particular persons or deities that it worships, and its followers are described as 'members' (*kaiin*) not 'believers' (*shinja*). On the front page of the group's webpage, the caption below the banner image reads:

> "Hikari no Wa" is not a religion. It is a class for learning the wisdom, thought, and philosophy of happiness of East and West, including Buddhist thought, meditative methods and contemporary psychology without faith in particular founders, gods, or sects. You can study without joining. Please feel free to get in touch.[28]

According to the group's website and Jōyū's publications (Jōyū 2012; Jōyū and Tahara 2013), Hikari no Wa promotes a philosophy that breaks down the separation and opposition of 'us and them' by appreciating the connections between humans as well as connections between humanity and nature. Whilst continuing practices common to Aum such as yoga and meditation, Hikari no Wa also stresses connections to existing religious traditions. For instance, Hikari no Wa regularly hosts 'holy site pilgrimages' (*seichi junrei*) to sacred sites around Japan with members to appreciate the country's religious traditions and to raise funds that contribute towards the payment of reparations for victims of Aum's crimes.

Jōyū and other members have also emphasised the importance of an introspective, meditative practice called '*naikan*' ('Looking inward/introspection') (Hirosue 2016; Jōyū 2012; Munakata 2010). This meditative practice, held over several days, encourages participants to reflect on their personal lives with the guidance of an instructor external to Hikari no Wa. By reflecting on and reaffirming one's indebtedness to those closest to them, such as family, friends, and colleagues, the practice reaffirms one's inseparable connection to others. Jōyū and other members have highlighted this practice and the willingness to enter into dialogue with external actors as key dimensions that separate Hikari no Wa from Aleph. Indeed, the group has been proactive in speaking with members of the public online as well as in person through talks and events (Baffelli 2018). In recent years, in addition to regular 'seminars' aimed at Hikari no Wa members, Jōyū has also held talks aimed at members of the public, engaging in conversation with public figures on stage. The group's willingness to engage with researchers also illustrates its 'world-accommodating' stance, although critics, especially anti-cult activists who are mistrustful of Jōyū's former position as Aum's spokesperson, have dismissed its interactions with scholars as mere publicity stunts.

Jōyū has justified the continuation of the group as necessary, as it has a responsibility to look after elderly members and members and that reparations for victims may be difficult to pay as individuals (Jōyū 2012: 250, 2016). Nevertheless, some critics such as Takahashi Shizue, the representative of the Subway Sarin Incident Victims' Society, have dismissed the payment of reparations as a justification for the group's continued existence as 'outrageous' (Takahashi 2015). For Nagaoka Hiroyuki, the representative of the Aum Shinrikyō Families' Society, which represents parents of Aum members and ex-members, has also held that he considers Aleph and Hikari no Wa to be identical (Nagaoka 2015). Resident groups near Hikari no Wa's facilities have also continued to organise regular rallies calling for the group's disbandment.

Like Aleph, Hikari no Wa has sought to end the state's surveillance of the group. In late-2011, it set up an External Audit Commission to oversee its activities and report on potential illegal activities.[29] The first chair to serve on the Commission was Kōno Yoshiyuki, a survivor and a widower of the 1994 Matsumoto sarin attack, who later became a staunch advocate for the protection of human rights. In 2014 and 2017, the External Audit Commission published reports to provide information on the group's practices and to challenge the accuracy of ORA's justifications for the need to keep the group under surveillance.[30]

Litigation to challenge the legality of the ORA has also remained a consistent strategy shared by both Hikari no Wa and Aleph. In 2017, Hikari no Wa won a court decision in the Tokyo District Court that nullified the extension of the ORA in 2015.[31] However, the state appealed the decision and the Tokyo High Court reversed its decision in 2019.[32] In March 2020, the Supreme Court again upheld the High Court's judgment.[33] As the PSIA has already renewed the ORA for another three-year term in 2018, which Hikari no Wa has contested through a separate court case, the group will be under state surveillance until at least 2021, barring future court rulings in their favour.

Hikari no Wa attracted negative public attention in 2018 after a weekly tabloid magazine reported that Jōyū had been witness to a murder of a female adherent in 1991. The case was never brought to trial as Niimi Tomomitsu, one of the reported culprits who was executed in 2018, never made a formal confession. Jōyū has defended his silence on this issue, stating that he could not speak out of fear of retaliation from Aleph.[34] This revelation has fuelled criticisms that Jōyū may not have been entirely transparent and forthcoming about his activities as a devotee and his tenure as Aum's spokesperson.

Conclusions

Aum Shinrikyō, Aleph, and Hikari no Wa have all undergone significant organisational changes in the quarter-century since the Tokyo attack, and they have adopted various legal strategies in relation to external stakeholders. This chapter has shown that the legal disputes surrounding Aum following the Tokyo sarin attack are instructive for understanding how a minority religion that has committed multiple acts of violence has dealt with the legal, social, and political consequences of its actions. In this sense, this chapter has argued that it is important to study not just the causes of religious violence by minority religions, but also the social responses to it over the long-term.

Over the past quarter century, Aum has evolved relationally through interactions with external actors and the changing legal environment to ensure its survival and to protect its interests. Since the arrests of the culprits behind its violent crimes and terrorist attacks, Aum and its successor organisations have sought to survive in a society which has been categorically hostile to its very existence, a situation which has no doubt been exacerbated by Aum's initial reluctance to face up to crimes committed by its founder and the leadership. On the one hand, the law has undoubtedly been a constraint on the organisations' activities: the government initially attempted to disband Aum and, in failing to do so, opted to place it under surveillance through special legislation, possibly indefinitely. Aum's successor organisations also continue to bear financial responsibility for damages awarded to victims through class-action lawsuits. On the other hand, the judiciary has also provided Aum and its associated actors a vital avenue to pursue redress when rights violations have occurred. In cases where clear rights violations have occurred, these Aum plaintiffs have been successful in winning judgments in their favour, being awarded compensation, and reaching settlements. To this end, civil litigation has been and continues to be a valuable mechanism for Aum's successor organisations to challenge legal adversaries and to seek redress for perceived breaches of the law.

While much public and academic literature has rightly focused on religions like Aum as perpetrators of 'cult' violence, one must recognise that in some cases, Aum/Aleph have also been victimised by legal transgressions. In an isolated but important case in 2010, an Aleph member was stabbed to death by her estranged ex-husband, who had begrudged her for joining Aum/Aleph with their children. The man was handed a 13-year prison sentence.[35] To the author's knowledge, this is the second case since the murder of the lead scientist, Murai Hideo, that an Aum/Aleph member has been killed by external actors due to their membership. Given these cases of retaliatory violence against Aum/Aleph members and the voluminous examples of legal transgressions by public authorities and institutions including municipal governments, the police, school boards, and private universities, there are reasons to re-examine the aftermath of the Aum Affair as a problem of minority religions' rights.

Since Hikari no Wa's split from Aleph in 2007, their contrasting attitudes to external stakeholders have been pronounced. While Aleph continues to have minimal contact with the outside world, Hikari no Wa has engaged in more 'world-accommodating' practices such as hosting public talks and incorporating religious and philosophical ideas from outside of Aum's original teachings. Despite these differences, beyond academic discourse, attempts to understand Aum's trajectory towards terrorism and militarism beyond prevalent tropes of 'brainwashing/mind controlling cults' are still relatively rare (Ushiyama 2019a). As a result, public hostility towards both Aleph and Hikari no Wa is both prevalent and persistent.

The mass executions of Aum's death row convicts arguably brought a sense of closure for many people living in Japan. As the size of the remaining groups steadily decreases, and as the newsworthiness of Aum declines, it is likely that Aum Shinrikyō will be increasingly studied from the perspective of 'history of religions' and 'memory studies' as much as it will continue to be studied in sociology of religion.

Despite the Aum Affair's probable decline in significance in contemporary debates, the aftereffects of Aum's violence will continue to be relevant for a better understanding of minority religions' reactions to law as well as for tracing the historical evolution of late-twentieth-century minority religions into the twenty-first century. Furthermore, there are uncertainties about the future of Aleph and Hikari no Wa that merit consideration. The core membership, many of whom were in their twenties and thirties in the early 1990s are now entering their fifties and sixties. Because many Aum members' children were taken into care with the exception of Asahara's children, it is unclear how many second-generation members there are, if any. The total membership has also remained stagnant over the years at around 1,650 renunciant and lay members, despite PSIA claiming that Aleph and Hikari no Wa has gained around 100 new members per year (Public Security Intelligence Agency 2017: 54, 59, 2018: 58, 2019: 60). It is possible that old members are leaving at a similar rate to new converts, or, more likely, that new members are transient and leave after a short time. Given the age demographic of the 'old guard', it is unclear how long both organisations will survive in the coming decades. Nevertheless, it is also unlikely that they will completely disappear or disband soon. As Erica Baffelli has pointed out (2012: 32), there are also pragmatic 'exit costs' associated with disaffiliation; as the members get older, they may find it even harder to live independent lives outside of communes and leave behind what had provided them with clothes, food, shelter, and perhaps most of all, a sense of belonging.

Finally, there are ongoing legal controversies surrounding Aum's successor organisations and Asahara's surviving family members. After Asahara's execution, the government announced that Asahara specified his fourth daughter (who has used the alias Matsumoto Satoka) to be the custodian of his remains. In the past, Satoka had publicly denounced her father as a charlatan (Matsumoto 2010) and had legally cut off ties with her family. Following the execution, Satoka issued a statement through her lawyer that she intended to scatter Asahara's ashes in the Pacific Ocean to prevent his grave becoming a holy site for his devotees. Asahara's other surviving family members, including his second and third daughter, have disputed this account, arguing that Asahara was severely mentally ill before the execution and could not have made such decisions. In 2020, the Tokyo Family Court ruled that there was insufficient evidence that Asahara had explicitly specified the fourth daughter as the custodian of his remains, and awarded custody to the second and third daughter. The fourth daughter has appealed the decision.[36] These recent and ongoing disputes suggest that perhaps the 'Aum Affair' has not yet really ended and that new legal contests are likely to continue to arise with ever-shifting situations.

Notes

1 Following cultural and academic convention, all Japanese names appear surname first, with the exception of the author. Macrons (ō, ū) are used to indicate elongated vowels.

2 Asahara first used *'poa'* in 1988 to explain the death of a believer who 'accidentally' died during strenuous training. After Asahara completed the *'poa'* ritual, the body was secretly disposed of in a nearby lake (Watanabe 1998: 87).

3 Ministry of Justice (n.d.) <www.moj.go.jp/psia/habouhou-kenkai.html> Accessed October 2019.

4 *Yomiuri Shimbun* (1995) 'Shūkyō hōjin hō kaisei 83% ga sansei, tai Oumu habōhō tekiyō 79%', 23 November, p.1.

5 *Yomiuri Shimbun* (1995) '"Habōhō" Murayama shushō no taido itten; Yotō nai no shinchōron han'ei', 4 October 1995, p. 3.

6 *Yomiuri Shimbun* (1995) 'Habōhō no tetsuzuki wa shukushuku to susumeyo', 15 December, p. 3.

7 *Asahi Shimbun* (1995) 'Habōhō rongi wa uwasuberi da', 28 September, p. 5.

8 *Asahi Shimbun* (1995) 'Iken no utagai koi 'pandora' no hō' 18 December (Eve. Ed.), p. 7; *Yomiuri Shimbun* (1995) 'Oumu Shinrikyō ni taisuru habōhō tekiyō hantai seimei', 6 October, p. 19.

9 *Yomiuri Shimbun* (1995) 'Oumu ni habōhō tekiyō. Nennai nimo kaisan seikyū tetsuzuki', 14 December, p. 1; *Asahi Shimbun* (1995) '"Hō no ginen" kienu mama. Oumu Shinrikyō ni habōhō tekiyō e', 15 December, p. 2.

10 *Yomiuri Shimbun* (1997) 'Oumu Shinrikyō e no Habōhō tekiyō no seikyū Kōanshin ga kikyaku kettei', 31 January (Eve Ed.), p. 1.

11 Shūkyō hōjinhō no ichibu o kaisei suru hōritsu. 1995. Act No. 134.

12 Ministry of Education, Culture, Sports, Science and Technology (1996) 'Shūkyō hōjinhō no ichibu o kaisei suru hōritsu no sekō ni tsuite'. <www.mext.go.jp/b_menu/hakusho/nc/t19951226001/t19951226001.html>. 2 September, Retrieved January 2016.

13 Tokutei hasan hōjin no hasan zaidan ni zokusubeki zaisan no kaifuku ni kansuru tokubetsu sochihō. 1999. Act No. 148.

14 *Yomiuri Shimbun* (1995) 'Asahara hikoku ga gokuchū kara kyōdan ni soshiki gatame shiji Kōan chōsachō, habōhō tekiyō no konkyo ni' 2 October, p. 1.

15 For contrasting responses to Asahara's silence during the trials, see Aonuma (2007) and Mori (2012). Aonuma is confident that Asahara's silence was a sign of his attempt to evade responsibility, while Mori asserts that he was visibly mentally ill during the final hearings.

16 *Yomiuri Shimbun* (1996) Matsumoto hikoku no osanai chōnan, jinan ga "shin kyōso" ni' Oumu kyōdan ga happyō' 20 June, p. 35.

17 *Yomiuri Shimbun* (1995). 'Asahara hikoku no kodomo 4nin, Chiba,Kisarazu-shi ni jūminhyō utsusu; Jimoto PTA ga shūgaku kyohi yōsei', 13 September, p. 27; *Asahi Shimbun* (1996) 'Oumu Asahara hikoku no yonjo shūgaku, genjō dewa kyohi; fubo ra shomei teishutsu e', 22 January, Chiba Edition; *Yomiuri Shimbun* (1999) 'Oumu Shinrikyō shinja, shijo no shūgaku wo kyohi/ Saitama, Ikutogawa mura', 4 September, p. 39.

18 *Yomiuri Shimbun* (2000) 'Oumu Shinrikyō, kansatsu shobun no torikeshi motome gyōsei soshō e Jōyū kanbu ra kaiken', 2 February, p. 35.

19 *Asahi Shimbun* (2001) 'Oumu kansatsu shobun "gōken" Tokyo Chisai, torikeshi seikyū kikyaku', 13 June, p. 14.

20 *Yomiuri Shimbun* (1999) 'Kasoku suru "Oumu kyohi" 63-shichōson ga taisaku "kokyōno fukushi, saiyūsen"', 10 October (Saitama Ed.), p. 30.

21 *Yomiuri Shimbun* (2001) 'Jūmin tōroku torikeshi mitometa kettei o haki Oumu mōshitate mitomeru', 15 June 2001, p. 38.

22 For reports of different court judgements, see: *Yomiuri Shimbun* (2001) 'Oumu shinja no jūminhyō fujuri soshō Suitasshi ga kōso', 24 October (Osaka, Eve. Ed.), p. 12; (2001), 'Tennyū fujuri no torikeshi meijiru Oumu shinja shōso', 12 December (Eve. Ed.), p. 19; (2002), 'Oumu shinja no tennyū, Adachiku ga juri e', 31 October (Tokyo Ed.), p. 32; (2002) 'Oumu shinja tennyū todoke fujuri Miwachō mata haiso', 27 November (Ibaraki Ed.), p. 32; (2003) 'Oumu moto shinja tennyū todoke soshō kōsoshin Koshigayashi no shuchō mitome, baishō seikyū o kikyaku', 28 August (Saitama Ed.), p. 30.

23 *Yomiuri Shimbun* (2000) 'Oumu tennyū Ryūgasaki no jūmin 1000-nin ga hantai shūkai kyōdan to sesshoku, jittai kakunin e', 12 December (Ibaraki Ed.), p. 31.

24 *Mainichi Shimbun* (2001) 'Oumu Shinrikyō, Matsumoto hikoku kodomo no shūgaku mondai ga kecchaku – Ibaraki, Ryūgasaki-shi kyōi, ukeire hyōmei', 10 March, p. 30.

25 *Yomiuri Shimbun* (2009) 'Aleph ga shobun torikeshi motome teiso', 9 July, p. 35.
26 *Yomiuri Shimbun* (2013) 'Nishin mo "Aleph eno meiyo kison" Chōkan jūgeki dantei, To ni baishō meirei', 27 November (Evening Edition), p. 14.
27 *Mainichi Shimbun* (2018) 'Oumu bunpa: shobun no torikeshi yōkyū kuni o teiso', 17 October (Evening Edition), p. 7.
28 Hikari no Wa (n.d.) "Hikari no Wa" <www.joyu.jp/hikarinowa/> Accessed October 2019. Translation by author.
29 Hikari no Wa Gaibu Kansa Iinkai (n.d.) "Hikari no Wa Gaibu Kansa Iinkai" <http://hikarinowa-gaibukansa.jp/> Accessed October 2019.
30 Reports by the Audit Commission are available (in Japanese) at <http://hikarinowa-gaibukansa.jp/report/index.html> Accessed October 2019.
31 *Mainichi Shimbun* (2017) 'Kansatsu shobun ihō Hikari no Wa "Arefu to betsu dantai"', 25 September.
32 *Asahi Shimbun* (2019) 'Hikari no Wa, nishin de gyakuten haiso kansatsu shobun wa "tekihō" Tokyo Kōsai', 1 March, p. 38.
33 *Jiji Tsūshin* (2020) '"Hikari no Wa" gyakuten haiso kakutei. Oumu kōkei bunha no kansatsu shobun – Saikōsai'. <www.jiji.com/jc/article?k=20200311 01099&g=soc> Accessed June 2020.
34 *Daily Shinchō* (2019) '"Jōyū Fumihiro" ga hita kakushi! Keisatsu mo shiranai "Asahara Shōkō" no josei shinja satsugai'. 19 July <www.dailyshincho.jp/article/2018/07190557/> Accessed October 2019.
35 *Asahi Shimbun* (2011) 'Arefu moto tsuma satsugai chōeki 13-nen', 14 May, p. 37.
36 *Asahi Shimbun* (2020) 'Matsumoto moto shikeishū no ikotsu, jijo ni hikiwatashi Tokyo Kasai ga kettei', 17 September.

References

Aonuma, Y. 2007. *Ōmu saiban bōshōki*. Tokyo: Shōgakkan.
Baffelli, E. 2012. Hikari no Wa: A new religion recovering from disaster. *Japanese Journal of Religious Studies* 39(1), 29–49.
———. 2018. Aum Shinrikyō, in: L. Pokornyand F. Winter (eds), *Handbook of East Asian New Religious Movements*. Leiden: Brill, pp. 193–210.
Dorman, B. 2012. *Celebrity Gods: New Religions, Media, and Authority in Occupied Japan*. Honolulu: University of Hawai'i Press.
Edelman, B., & Richardson, J. T. 2005. Imposed limitations on freedom of religion in China and the margin of appreciation doctrine: A legal analysis of the crackdown on the Falun Gong and other 'Evil Cults.' *Journal of Church and State* 47(2), 243–67.
Gardner, R. A. 2002. A revisited. *Monumenta Nipponica* 57(3), 339–48.
Hardacre, H. 1989. *Shintō and the State, 1868–1988*. Princeton, NJ: Princeton University Press.
Hayakawa, K., and Kawamura, K. 2005. *Watashi ni totte Oumu towa nandattanoka*. Tokyo: Popurasha.
Hirosue, A. 2016. Author's interview with Hirosue Akitoshi, 29 July 2016, Tokyo.
Inoue, N. 2011. Shūkyō hōjin kaisan to Arefu/Hikari no Wa. in: N. Inoueand Shūkyō Jōhō Risāchi Sentā (eds), *Jōhō jidai no Oumu Shinrikyo*. Tokyo: Shunjūsha, 410–30.
Jōyū, F. 2002a. *Jōyū Fumihiro ga kataru: Kunō kara no kaihō*. Tokyo: Higashiyama.
———. 2002b. *Kakusei Shinseiki*. Tokyo: Higashiyama.

———. 2012. *Oumu jiken 17-nenme no kokuhaku*. Tokyo: Fusōsha.

———. 2016. Author's interview with Jōyū Fumihiro, 24 July 2016, Tokyo.

Jōyū, F., and Tahara, S. 2013. *Kiken na shūkyō no miwakekata*. Tokyo: Popurasha.

Kisala, R., and Mullins, M. (eds). 2001. *Religion and Social Crisis in Japan: Understanding Japanese Society through the Aum Affair*. Basingstoke: Palgrave.

Lifton, R. J. 1999. *Destroying the World to Save It: Aum Shinrikyō, Apocalyptic Violence, and the New Global Terrorism*. New York: Henry Holt and Co.

Matsubara, H. 2002. Aum grows again, Guru still revered. *The Japan Times Online*. 8 August, Retrieved from www.japantimes.co.jp/news/2002/08/08/national/aum-grows-again-guru-still-revered/

Matsumoto, R. 2015. *Tomatta tokei: Asahara Shōkō no sanjo Ācharī no shuki*. Tokyo: Kōdansha.

Matsumoto, S. 2010. *Watashi wa naze Asahara Shōkō no musume ni umareteshimatta noka: Chikatetsu sarin jiken kara 15 nenme no kokuhaku*. Tokyo: Tokuma.

Metraux, D. 1999. *Aum Shinrikyo and Japanese Youth*. Lanham, MD.; Oxford: University Press of America.

Mori, T. (dir.) 2001. *A2* [Documentary]. Independent Film. "A" Production Committee.

Mori, T. 2012. *A3*. Tokyo: Shūeisha.

Mullins, M. 2001. The legal and political fallout of the 'Aum Affair,' in: R. Kisala and M. Mullins (eds) *Religion and Social Crisis in Japan: Understanding Japanese Society Through the Aum Affair*. Basingstoke: Palgrave, pp. 71–86.

———. 2012. The Neo-Nationalist Response to the Aum Crisis: A Return of Civil Religion and Coercion in the Public Sphere? *Japanese Journal of Religious Studies* 39(1): 99–125.

Munakata, M. 2010. *Nijussai kara no 20 nen: "Oumu no Seishun" no Makyō o Koete*. Tokyo: Sangokan.

Nagaoka, H. 2015. Author's interview with Nagaoka Hiroyuki, 20 March 2015, Tokyo.

Noda, N. 2010. *Kakumei ka sensō ka: Oumu wa gurōbaru shihon shugi eno keishō datta*. Tokyo: Saizō.

Palmer, S. 2011. *The New Heretics of France: Minority Religions, la Republique, and the Government-Sponsored "War on Sects."* Oxford: Oxford University Press.

Pendleton, M. 2009. Mourning as global politics: Embodied grief and activism in post-Aum Tokyo. *Asian Studies Review* 33(3), 333–47.

Public Security Intelligence Agency. 2008. *Naigai Jōsei no Kaiko to Tenbō*. Retrieved from www.moj.go.jp/psia/kouan_naigai_naigai20_naigai20-00.html

———. 2017. *Naigai Jōsei no Kaiko to Tenbō*. Retrieved from www.moj.go.jp/psia/kouan_naigai_naigai20_naigai20-00.html

———. 2018. *Naigai Jōsei no Kaiko to Tenbō*. Retrieved from www.moj.go.jp/content/001252041.pdf

———. 2019. *Naigai Jōsei no Kaiko to Tenbō*. Retrieved from www.moj.go.jp/content/001252041.pdf

Reader, I. 2000a. *Religious Violence in Contemporary Japan: The Case of Aum Shinrikyō*. Richmond: Curzon.

———. 2000b. Scholarship, Aum Shinrikyo, and academic integrity. *Nova Religio* 3(2), 368–82.

————. 2012. Secularization, R.I.P? Nonsense! The 'rush hour away from the gods' and the decline of religion in contemporary Japan. *Journal of Religion in Japan* 1(1), 7–36.

Repp, M. 2011. Religion and violence in Japan: The case of Aum Shinrikyo, in: J. R. Lewis (ed.), *Violence and New Religious Movements*. Oxford: Oxford University Press, pp. 147–172.

Shimazono, S. 1995. In the wake of Aum: The formation and transformation of a universe of belief. *Japanese Journal of Religious Studies* 22(3/4), 381–415.

Takahashi, S. 2015. Author's interview with Takahashi Shizue, 6 April 2015, Tokyo.

Tsukada, H. 2011. Shinritō no undō tenkai to katsudō naiyō. In N. Inoue & Shūkyō Jōhō Risāchi Sentā (eds), *Jōhō jidai no Oumu Shinrikyō*. Tokyo: Shunjūsha, pp. 307–27.

Ushiyama, R. 2019a. Discursive opportunities and the transnational diffusion of ideas: 'Brainwashing' and 'mind control' in Japan after the Aum Affair. *The British Journal of Sociology* 70(5), 1730–53. https://doi.org/10.1111/1468-4446.12705.

————. 2019b. Latency through uncertainty: The 1994 Matsumoto sarin incident as a delayed cultural trauma. *International Journal of Politics, Culture, and Society* 32(1), 21–41.

Ushiyama, R., and Baert, P. 2016. Cultural trauma, counter-narratives, and dialogical intellectuals: The works of Murakami Haruki and Mori Tatsuya in the context of the Aum affair. *Theory and Society* 45(6), 471–99.

Wallis, R. 1984. *The Elementary Forms of the New Religious Life*. London: Routledge & Kegan Paul.

Watanabe, M. 1998. Religion and violence in Japan today: A chronological and doctrinal analysis of Aum Shinrikyo. *Terrorism and Political Violence* 10(4), 80–100.

11 Religious persecution and refugees

Legal and communication strategies of The Church of Almighty God in asylum cases

Massimo Introvigne and Rosita Šorytė

Introduction

The Church of Almighty God (CAG, whose name is written with a capital T in 'The') is the largest Chinese Christian new religious movement (Introvigne 2020). Chinese government sources claim that it has four million members (Ma 2014). Although some scholars think that the number may be inflated (Dunn 2015), Chinese police and intelligence departments are among the only agencies equipped to collect data on banned religious groups in China, and their evaluations should not be dismissed lightly.

The CAG was established in China in 1991. Its main teaching is that Jesus Christ has returned and incarnated as a Chinese woman, whom followers worship as Almighty God. While Jesus brought salvation and forgave our sins, Almighty God will eradicate the sinful nature of humans, whom will be thoroughly purified and usher in a millennial kingdom (Folk 2018).

As has happened to other fast-growing new religious movements, such as the Falun Gong, that refuse to be controlled by the regime, the CAG has been heavily persecuted in China (Introvigne 2020: 1–26, 37–42; Introvigne, Richardson and Šorytė 2019). The persecution has increasingly escalated since 2014, resulting in a flow of CAG refugees by the thousands, who have sought asylum in democratic countries.

Table 11.1 shows the situation of CAG asylum seekers as of September 2019.*

*Data obtained from asylum lawyers in various countries and from CAG officials.

The table, however, may be somewhat misleading. In countries such as South Korea and Japan, which are well known for granting asylum to a very limited number of refugees in general, the situation has not evolved. In other countries, more recent cases have a higher percentage of success than older ones. This shows that CAG refugees have implemented a partially

Table 11.1 CAG asylum seekers as of September 2019

Countries	Total applications	Asylum granted	Asylum rejected	Departure order	Deported
Germany	310	66	240	14	2
France	444	39	405	236	0
Italy	848	140	343	0	0
Greece	47	7	30	0	0
Netherlands	65	21	26	26	0
Czech Republic	40	3	23	0	0
Finland	39	37	2	0	0
Sweden	9	7	2	2	1
Switzerland	33	2	30	25	3
Portugal	12	0	10	0	0
Belgium	11	0	11	11	0
United Kingdom	8	2	3	0	0
Austria	9	2	7	1	0
Spain	528	0	0	0	0
Australia	233	7	29	0	0
New Zealand	62	53	0	0	0
Saipan	326	3	0	0	0
Japan	274	0	93	0	0
Canada	255	184	25	11	3
South Korea	1,023	0	671	180	0
United States	Around 1,000	27	1	1	0

successful strategy to overcome the main objections asylum seekers receive from administrative authorities and courts.

We will discuss the objections and how CAG refugees respond to them in the second part of this chapter. In the first part, we will present some general legal principles about religion-based refugee claims. Understanding them is necessary in order to place CAG's legal strategies in their proper context.

Religion-based refugee claims: general principles

The tragedy of World War II generated an unprecedented number of refugees in Europe. To confront this situation, the United Nations created in 1950 the office of the United Nations High Commissioner for Refugees (UNHCR). Its work with the European emergency was generally regarded as successful, and the UNHCR was awarded the Nobel Peace Prize in 1954.

The UNHCR also asked the United Nations to establish clear international law provisions regarding refugees. On 28 July 1951, the United Nations Conference of Plenipotentiaries on the Status of Refugees and

Stateless Persons convened in Geneva, Switzerland, under General Assembly resolution 429 (V) of 14 December 1950, and adopted the *Convention Relating to the Status of Refugees*, known as the 1951 Refugee Convention. Although some countries distinguish between 'asylum seekers' and 'refugees,' in the 1951 Convention, a refugee is simply an asylum seeker whose application has been accepted.

To this day, UNHCR regards this convention as "the key legal document that forms the basis of our work" (UNHCR 2017). However, the 1951 Convention was custom-tailored to solving the problem of post-war refugees in Europe, and some provisions were limited to such persons.

For this reason, a broader document was signed in New York in 1967, the *Protocol Relating to the Status of Refugees*. The United States, afraid of receiving too many refugees after World War II, did not sign the 1951 Refugee Convention but did sign and ratify the 1967 Protocol. Some 40 countries remain outside the Convention-Protocol system including Jamaica, Nigeria, Saudi Arabia and the Gulf States, India, Pakistan, Indonesia, Thailand, Vietnam, Mongolia, and Malaysia—as well as North Korea (although perhaps not many refugees would seek asylum there). China did sign and ratify the Protocol.

For the definition of a refugee, Article 1 of the 1967 Protocol refers to Article 1 of the 1951 Convention, which states:

> any person who, owing to well-founded fear of being persecuted for reasons of race, religion, nationality, or political opinion, is outside the country of his nationality and is unable or, owing to such fear or for reasons other than personal convenience, is unwilling to avail himself of the protection of that country or for reasons other than personal convenience, is unwilling to return to it.

The Universal Declaration of Human Rights, Article 14, already established that "Everyone has the right to seek and to enjoy in other countries asylum from persecution."

In general, these documents established that a refugee is a person who is outside his or her own country's territory owing to fear of persecution on protected grounds. 'Protected grounds' include race, caste, nationality, religion, political opinions and membership and/or participation in any particular social group or social activities.

Persecution, in turn, is the systematic mistreatment of an individual or a group by another individual or group. The most common forms are religious persecution, racism, and political persecution. The inflicting of suffering, harassment, imprisonment, internment, fear, or pain are factors that may establish persecution, but not all suffering will necessarily amount to persecution. The suffering experienced by the victim must be sufficiently severe. The threshold of severity, though, has been a source of much debate.

The worst form of persecution is torture. Torture is the act of deliberately inflicting physical or psychological pain in order to fulfil some desire of the torturer or to compel some action from the victim. Torture is prohibited by the 1987 United Nations *Convention Against Torture and Other Cruel, Inhuman or Degrading Treatment or Punishment* (ratified by 158 countries, including China in 1988).

Rendering true victims of persecution to their persecutors is an odious violation of a principle called *non-refoulement*. The 1987 Convention Against Torture, Article 3, stipulates that 'No State Party shall expel, return ("refouler"), or extradite a person to another State where there are substantial grounds for believing that he or she would be in danger of being subjected to torture.'

Two problems were, however, left open. The first was that there was no internal monitoring body for compliance with legally binding Conventions and their Protocols. UNHCR itself is not empowered to enforce the Convention. There is no formal mechanism for complaints against States, though they can be referred by another State to the International Court of Justice. An individual may lodge a complaint with the UN Human Rights Committee under the International Covenant on Civil and Political Rights or with the UN ECOSOC under the International Covenant on Economic, Social and Cultural Rights. At present, the only real consequences of violation are public shaming in the press and media and the verbal condemnation of the violator by the UN and by other countries.

The second problem is that interpreting provisions on religious persecution, a serious human rights problem, proved much less simple than international organizations originally believed. International courts were frequently involved and gave contradictory interpretations. Finally, in 2002, UNHCR and Church World Service, a Christian inter-denominational agency specialized in assisting refugees, convened an international roundtable in Baltimore. One of its conclusions was that UNHCR, as part of its mandate, could and should provide interpretive guidance on the provisions on religion included in the Refugee Convention and the Protocol. As a result, in 2004, UNHCR issued a document called *Guidelines on International Protection: Religion-Based Refugee Claims under Article 1A(2) of the 1951 Convention and/or the 1967 Protocol relating to the Status of Refugees* (UNHCR 2004).

The European Union waited for the official publication of the UNHCR Guidelines on 28 April 2004 and, the following day, 29 April, published in turn Directive 2004/83, known as the Qualification Directive, on the 'minimum standards' for being defined as a refugee. It was updated in 2011 as Directive 2011/95, known as the Recast Qualification Directive. Article 2 adopted the same wording as the Refugee Convention, mentioning a "well-founded fear of being persecuted for reasons of religion." The preamble mentioned, among the conditions for qualifying for refugee status, "the existence of a causal link between the reasons for persecution, namely [inter alia] religion [...], and the acts of persecution or the absence of protection against such acts."

That not all problems were solved by these definitions was proved by a number of high-profile cases before national courts, the Court of Justice of the European Union, and the European Court of Human Rights. Some of the main interpretive problems, relevant for the cases of CAG refugees, are discussed below.

What is a religion?

Defining religion is a notoriously intractable subject among scholars. An ambitious survey of existing scholarship sponsored by the European Union produced in 1999 a thick volume, concluding that academics offer many irreconcilable definitions of religion, and no agreement exists (Platvoet and Molendijk 1999). International institutions, however, tend to adopt as broad a concept of 'religion' as possible.

In 1993, as evidence of how difficult defining freedom of religion remains, the Human Rights Committee issued a *General Comment no. 22* as a set of guidelines for interpreting Article 18 of the Universal Declaration of Human Rights. Number 2 of *General Comment no. 22* is particularly important, as it deals specifically with new religious movements, often discriminated against as such:

> Article 18 protects theistic, non-theistic and atheistic beliefs, as well as the right not to profess any religion or belief. The terms 'belief' and 'religion' are to be broadly construed. Article 18 is not limited in its application to traditional religions or to religions and beliefs with institutional characteristics or practices analogous to those of traditional religions. The Committee therefore views with concern any tendency to discriminate against any religion or belief for any reason, including the fact that they are newly established, or represent religious minorities that may be the subject of hostility on the part of a predominant religious community.
>
> (Office of the High Commissioner for Human Rights 1993)

In light of *General Comment no. 22*, number 2, States have no right to deny refugee status based on the fact that the persecuted belief is related to a 'cult,' and 'cults' are 'not really religions' or are 'pseudo-religions.' Apart from the questionable status of such claims, it is clear that Article 18 UDHR protects beliefs not only *of* religions but also *about* religion. It protects the right to be nonreligious, that is, atheism, and it also protects the right to be differently religious, or spiritual, or holding unpopular or non-conventional beliefs about religion that the persecutors, or some, or even the majority, may regard as 'cultic' or 'not really religious.'

How religious should the refugee be?

The 2004 UNHCR Guidelines state in paragraph 9:

> It may not be necessary, [...] for an individual (or a group) to declare that he or she belongs to a religion, is of a particular religious faith, or adheres to religious practices, where the persecutor imputes or attributes this religion, faith or practice to the individual or group. [...] It may also not be necessary for the claimant to know or understand anything about the religion, if he or she has been identified by others as belonging to that group and fears persecution as a result.

Paragraph 10 specifies that even an infant born into a religion and persecuted as such, may qualify for refugee status based on religious persecution. This confirms that being conversant with the dogmas of the religion is not necessary. What counts is the attitude of the persecutor, not of the persecuted. The persecutor normally attacks all members of a banned community, without applying any theological test or verifying how many religious services they attend.

Paragraph 9 should be read together with paragraph 30, which states:

> Individuals may be persecuted on the basis of their religion even though they have little or no substantive knowledge of its tenets or practices. A lack of knowledge may be explained by further research into the particular practices of that religion in the area in question or by an understanding of the subjective and personal aspects of the claimant's case.

When a religious or spiritual group is persecuted, members qualify for refugee status irrespective of their knowledge of the religion, fervour in its practice, or age.

Credibility and sur place *claims*

Of course, claims to be religiously persecuted should meet a minimum standard of credibility to avoid frauds by those who simply want to emigrate for economic reasons and seek a refugee status under false pretexts. "Credibility is a central issue in religion-based refugee claims," states paragraph 28 of the 2004 UNHCR Guidelines. It calls for credibility to be assessed in a good faith dialogue, without placing an unnecessarily heavy burden of proof on the asylum seeker.

A particularly delicate case concerns fears of religious persecution arising from a conversion that happened after the applicant's departure from the country of origin. This is part of the so-called *sur place* claims, that is, requests that a refugee status is recognized because of events that happened not in the country of origin of the applicant but in the country where he or she now lives. A typical case concerns Muslims who left their country as economic migrants and converted to Christianity after settling in Europe. Some of them seek refugee status based on a credible fear of being persecuted as 'apostates,' should they return to their native country.

In the case of *sur place* claims, paragraphs 34–36 of the 2004 UNHCR Guidelines recognize that caution is justified by the fact that conversions may be simulated and only aimed at obtaining refugee status. On the other hand, these matters should be carefully investigated, as the existence of *sur place* conversions in good faith cannot be excluded.

How strong should the persecution be?

Defining persecution is not easier than defining religion. Very few countries, if any, forbid private religious belief. They only sanction the *manifestation* of such belief through public worship, missionary activities, or even wearing certain distinctive dresses or other signs.

Again, in the endeavour to limit the number of refugees, some national courts have argued that if persecution can be escaped by avoiding the public manifestations of one's religion, then refugee status can be denied. At least in Europe, this argument should be regarded as a thing of the past after a judgement rendered in 2012 by the Court of Justice of the European Union in the case of *Germany v. Y and Z*. Y and Z were Pakistani citizens, members of the Ahmadi community, which is regarded as heretic by mainline Islam and severely persecuted in some Islamic countries, including Pakistan. Germany had argued that if Y and Z would live privately their faith in Pakistan, without proclaiming it publicly or proselytizing, the risk would be low, and therefore refugee status in Germany need not be granted. The European Court found against Germany, concluding that 'the fact that a person could avoid the risk of persecution by abstaining from religious practices is, in principle, irrelevant. The authorities cannot reasonably expect the Applicant [for refugee status] to abstain from those religious practices' (Court of Justice of the European Union 2012). It is also not necessary to prove that an asylum seeker has been individually persecuted. The fact that persecution of his or her religion in a given country generates a reasonable *fear of persecution* is enough.

Accusations of common crimes

That certain religious movements are accused of common crimes is a delicate aspect of religion-based refugee claims and one especially relevant for the CAG. Some States claim that leaders or members of certain religious groups are not persecuted because of their religious beliefs but because of their behaviour, which has breached general laws that have nothing to do with religious discrimination. Russia, for instance, has banned or is threatening to ban several religious groups, including the Jehovah's Witnesses and Scientology, claiming that they are prosecuted not because of their religious beliefs but because they violate the Russian provisions against 'extremism' or carry on illegal commercial activities. Some states do not recognize conscientious objection and jail those who refuse to serve in the army because of their religious convictions (or for any other reason). China has a list of *xie jiao*, religious groups it claims are not really religions and are guilty of common criminal wrongdoings. Can a member or even a leader of one of these groups seeking refugee status claim that accusations of common crimes are a pretext and that prosecution is in fact motivated by religious beliefs?

The question is difficult, but precedents do exist. The 2004 UNHCR Guidelines, paragraph 26, state that "prosecution and punishment pursuant to a law of general application is not generally considered to constitute persecution," but immediately qualify this statement by adding that "there are some notable exceptions." An example is conscientious objection. Where the law does not recognize that a refusal to serve in the military may be based on genuine religious persuasions and does not offer alternatives (or only an 'excessively burdensome' alternative) in the form of non-military community service, those who flee the country may claim religious persecution and become eligible for refugee status.

There are significant precedents even outside the area of conscientious objections. Scientology is the object of legal limitations in various countries which claim that it is not really a religion, and it is not prosecuted for its beliefs but for different wrongdoings. In a well-known case in 1997, a United States Immigration Court granted asylum to a German Scientologist woman, concluding that German measures against Scientology qualified as religious persecution (Frantz 1997). In 2012, although on appeal after an initially unfavourable decision, the Australian Refugee Review Tribunal granted asylum in Australia to a Scientologist from Uzbekistan on similar grounds (Australian Visa Bureau 2012).

In 2005, the Swedish Supreme Court decided that asylum should be granted to Gregorian Bivolaru (Supreme Court of Sweden 2005). A Romanian citizen, Bivolaru is the founder of the Movement for Spiritual Integration into the Absolute (MISA), a new spiritual movement that teaches, inter alia, Tantric esoteric sexual techniques. He was sentenced to six years in jail for an alleged sexual relation with a minor, M.D. The crime was obviously not of a religious nature. However, Bivolaru argued that he could not get a fair trial in Romania because of the media campaigns against him as a 'cult leader.' M.D. herself testified before the Swedish Supreme Court that she was treated harshly by the Romanian police in order to compel her to confess a sexual relation that never existed.

The Swedish Supreme Court ruled that refugee status should be granted to a person accused of common crimes when it can be presumed that his or her religious opinion or teachings motivated the prosecution, that charges were trumped up, and that because of religious prejudice a fair trial could not be expected (Supreme Court of Sweden 2005).

This Swedish precedent is important for the claims of refugee status by members of new religious movements such as the CAG labelled as 'cults,' or *xie jiao* in China, by the regime and accused of common crimes. The Swedish case shows that the evaluation of evidence should be very careful and certainly cannot rely only on documents supplied by the country accused of persecution. The opinion of neutral scholars who have studied the movement should also be sought. And, as the Swedish case demonstrates, when it can be easily presumed that because of their religion, accusations against the defendants were fabricated, and they would not be granted a fair trial, recognizing that they qualify for refugee status is in order.

Legal answers and strategies by asylum seekers of The Church of Almighty God

CAG members seek asylum in countries that have signed and ratified the Convention and the Protocol and are bound by their principles. However, as mentioned earlier, except for a few, traditionally pro-refugee countries such as Canada, New Zealand, and Sweden (later followed by Finland), most of their applications have been rejected. This section investigates why the negative decisions occurred, and the efforts CAG refugees made trying to reverse the trend.

Some refugees escaped from China even before persecution escalated significantly in the second decade of the twenty-first century, and the number of CAG asylum seekers abroad went from the hundreds to the thousands. Based on our interviews with CAG refugees in a dozen different countries, the first CAG refugees (largely on the basis of their respective and different financial situations) either decided to hire their own lawyers or relied on lawyers provided for free by NGOs-assisting refugees or on court-appointed attorneys. A few refugees self-defended themselves. Some lawyers were well known in the field and tried their best to investigate the history and theology of the Church and the persecution in China. They mostly relied on documents supplied by the refugees themselves, as very little information from independent third parties existed at the time.

Western scholars had first started paying attention to the CAG in 2015, with the publication of a book by Australian scholar Emily Dunn (2015), who had previously authored some pioneer articles. Dunn, however, had not been able to interview any CAG member and had written her book based on Internet sources and information supplied by Chinese authorities only. CAG members found several inaccuracies in her text and advised their lawyers not to use her book to defend refugees.

In 2016, the CAG opened itself to studies by scholars of new religious movements, who were both familiar with and sceptical about the standard accusations against groups labelled as 'cults.' Scholars (and NGOs) were able to perform interviews, submit questionnaires, and access theological and other original materials of the CAG. This resulted in conference papers and articles based on independent studies as well as letters sent to authorities dealing with refugees in several countries, by the authors of this chapter, as well as such well-known scholars of new religious movements as J. Gordon Melton, James T. Richardson, David Bromley, Holly Folk, Eileen Barker, Susan Palmer, and Bernadette Rigal-Cellard. Several studies were published, and others are on their way (see, e.g., Folk 2017, 2018; Introvigne 2017a, 2017b, 2020; Introvigne and Bromley 2017; Introvigne, Richardson and Šorytė 2019). All these scholarly studies were collected by the CAG and given to the lawyers representing refugees, who used them in court. Some scholars also served as expert witnesses or executed affidavits for use in refugee cases.

Meanwhile, the CAG had started to send international human rights bodies and state institutions evidence about the persecution in China as well as confidential documents by the CCP (Chinese Communist Party) detailing the repression of the CAG. Some human rights organizations conducted independent investigations into these claims, including interviews with refugees who were subjected to detention and torture. In 2018, China had to undertake its Universal Periodic Review, an assessment of their human rights situation to which all member States of the United Nations should submit every five years before the UN Human Rights Council in Geneva. Based on their interaction with the CAG and their own research, a dozen NGOs were able to submit statements about the persecution of the CAG in China. These reports were published on the United Nations' website and mentioned in the general report about NGOs' submissions on China by the UN High Commissioner on Human Rights, former President of Chile, Michelle Bachelet (United Nations Human Rights Council 2018). Periodically, some NGOs also file written statements both with the UN Human Rights Council and the OSCE (Organization for Security and Co-operation in Europe) or intervene in oral discussions there, denouncing the persecution of CAG or the shortcomings of national authorities rejecting CAG asylum applications in democratic countries.

Furthermore, the CAG has persistently supplied documents about its persecution in China to American authorities. This has led to the magnitude of CAG persecution being denounced in official reports about human rights and religious liberty in China by the US Department of State (2019a, 2019b) and the US Commission on International Religious Freedom (2019). Again, all these documents were supplied to lawyers representing CAG refugees and filed as evidence in court cases in various countries.

The CAG also cooperates with other religions advocating religious freedom internationally, particularly through the International Religious Freedom Roundtables, originally established in Washington DC and now with branches in several countries. In March 2018, the Washington

Roundtable promoted, with the support of the US Department of State (which regularly works with the Roundtables), the Coalition to Advance Religious Freedom in China, where the CAG cooperates with representatives of Falun Gong, Uyghur Muslims, Tibetan Buddhists, Protestant House Churches, and secular advocates of democracy to denounce abuses of human rights by the CCP (Prososki 2019). The Roundtables were instrumental in collecting signatures for letters supporting CAG refugees in both the United States and Europe.

These coalitions of religions, scholars, and NGOs play an important role in the CAG refugee cases, which became apparent in the case of Zou Demei, a prominent CAG leader from China, who used to serve as a regional CAG leader in the four provinces of Yunnan, Guizhou, Chongqing, and Sichuan. This made her one of the CAG leaders most wanted by the authorities, with a substantial bounty placed on her head. To escape persecution, she entered the United States in 2017 with a false passport. She was arrested and an order of deportation back to China (where she would have faced a trumped-up accusation of espionage that might have led to the death penalty, in addition to being prosecuted as a leader of a banned religious group) was issued against her. The CAG hired a highly respected specialized lawyer for her, but also submitted Zou's case to, and sought support from, NGOs and scholars, who took the case to the American authorities (including President Trump) and the media. Their support was crucial in stopping the deportation order and allowing Zou to remain in the United States, although full asylum was not granted (Introvigne 2019).

Scholars and NGOs have greatly helped some CAG refugees in obtaining asylum. Yet, some countries such as South Korea and Japan still routinely reject all applications, and the situation remains very difficult in France, Switzerland, Belgium, and Germany. In most other countries, there are both positive and negative decisions. Keeping in mind the legal framework outlined in the first part of this chapter, we will now review the main problems still faced by CAG asylum seekers, and how the CAG tries to overcome them.

Outdated Country of Origin Information (COI)

In several cases, immigration authorities and courts that reject asylum applications by CAG members have relied on old documents in international COI (Country of Origin Information) data bases. These reports have not taken into account the existing scholarly literature on the CAG and simply mentioned articles in Chinese media, or in Western media that in turn quoted Chinese governmental sources. They include an old report from the Immigration and Refugee Board of Canada that although not an official UNHCR document, is available on the UNHCR data base (Immigration and Refugee Board of Canada 2014), other documents produced by the same Canadian Board, and a French report dated 2016 (DIDR 2016).

Although the Canadian reports were better than their French counterpart, these texts relied mostly on journalistic and anti-cult sources in turn compiling CCP information and articles by Evangelical groups vehemently hostile to the CAG. Some of the COIs also repeated that the CAG was responsible for the murder of a woman in a McDonald's diner in Zhaoyuan in 2014 and of gouging out the eyes of a six-year-old boy in the province of Shaanxi in 2013, while in both cases, scholars, by studying official Chinese sources and documents, had concluded that the perpetrators of the crimes were not CAG members (Folk 2017; Introvigne 2017a, 2018; Introvigne and Bromley 2017).

In South Korea and, partially, in Italy, court cases about CAG refugees often focused on the interpretation of Article 300 of the Chinese Criminal Code, which makes it a crime of being active in a *xie jiao*, a term often translated as 'evil cult' but meaning in fact 'heterodox teaching.' In fact, in China, a *xie jiao* is any movement the government decides to list as a *xie jiao* (Irons 2018). The CCP identifies any independent religious group that grows too fast and is perceived as hostile to the regime as a *xie jiao*. Together with a dozen Christian groups, including the Shouters and the All Range Church, the CAG has been included in the list of the *xie jiao* since 1995. While affidavits submitted by scholars insisted that Article 300 punishes *any* activity in a *xie jiao*, Chinese embassies became active in contacting refugee boards and courts and claiming that the article is only enforced against those members of *xie jiao* who 'commit crimes.' This interpretation of Article 300 found its way to some COIs. In 2019, the authors of this chapter together with well-known American scholar James T. Richardson authored a detailed study of Chinese court decisions against 200 CAG members, proving that Article 300 is in fact enforced to punish 'crimes' such as gathering for worship, trying to convert others to the CAG, and even keeping at home CAG books and brochures (Introvigne, Richardson and Šorytė 2019) (Figure 11.1).

Inaccurate COIs produced by governmental bodies remain a serious obstacle for CAG refugees because in several countries, the authorities regard them as highly reliable sources. Informed by the refugees of these problems, several scholars wrote to the agencies that had produced faulty or outdated COIs, urging them to reform the reports. Some results were obtained. On 25–26 April 2019, in Geneva, the Intergovernmental Consultations on Migration, Asylum and Refugees (IGC) held a closed-door China workshop focusing on the COIs about the CAG and the need to reform them. One of the authors (Introvigne) was invited to attend and present on the CAG. New and better-informed COIs were published in Canada on 24 October 2019 (Immigration and Refugee Board of Canada 2019). Italy produced two updated COI documents on the CAG in 2019

Figure 11.1 Members of The Church of Almighty God studying their Scripture.
(Picture courtesy of The Church of Almighty God)

(Commissione Nazionale per il Diritto d'Asilo 2019a, 2019b) and shared through the European data base EASO (European Asylum Support Office). The Netherlands produced a substantially accurate section on the CAG in their new COI on China of 2020, which was made available also in English (Ministerie van Buitenlandse Zaken 2020).

Accusations of being an 'evil cult'

The word 'cult' has been used in decisions denying asylum to CAG members in several countries. Crimes, including the McDonald's murder of 2014, have also been mentioned. CAG refugees have countered these accusations by supplying lawyers with scholarly literature denying that the group that perpetrated the McDonald's murder was part of the CAG. It has also mentioned in its material intended for lawyers that scholars of new religious movements tend to avoid the derogatory label 'cult,' that labelling rapidly growing groups as *xie jiao* and repressing them has been one of the CCP's usual tactics in repressing religion. CAG refugees have also pointed out that international conventions protect religious liberty irrespective of whether religious beliefs are regarded as orthodox or heterodox by other religionists or the governments and that the persecution of the CAG is a well-documented fact.

This strategy has been largely successful. By 2019, only a tiny minority of international decisions about CAG refugees mention the 'cult' issue or the McDonald's murder.

Knowledge of one's own religion

More dangerous, for CAG refugees, are accusations of not knowing their own religion. In such cases, authorities may doubt that the refugee is a genuine member of the CAG (despite certifications by the local CAG branches) and deny asylum.

In several cases, we have examined that the situation is somewhat paradoxical. CAG refugees are interrogated on their history and theology based on outdated or faulty COIs. In fact, their answers are correct, but the authorities regard the old COIs as more believable than the refugees' reconstructions of their religion.

In some countries, CAG asylum seekers have been accused of not knowing their religion because they refused to mention the name of the person CAG identifies with the incarnate Almighty God. This objection is based on a misunderstanding about CAG theology. As one of the refugees we interviewed told us, for CAG members, "it is more important to know the truth and God's substance through experiencing Almighty God's words than knowing the details of God's incarnated life." They claim that early Christians had a similar attitude with respect to Jesus Christ. CAG members do not discuss the person who is the incarnate Almighty God, nor do they mention this person's civil name (as they say, 'out of reverence for God'). Refugees also refer to Almighty God as 'him' rather than 'her' (while believing that God incarnated in our time in a female human body), as they want to emphasize that the present-day Almighty God is the same God who revealed himself as Jehovah in the Old Testament and Jesus in the New Testament. This also creates misunderstandings in refugee cases.

While not renouncing their theological principle that the civil name or biographical details about Almighty God should not be mentioned, CAG refugees have made an effort to explain their theology in terms understandable to refugee boards and courts, which are not composed of specialists of religion. Problems, however, remain.

Credibility

The UNCHR Guidelines do require credibility and are aimed at preventing that economic immigrants may claim religious persecution in order to be granted refugee status. Credibility (or lack thereof) is one key reason that CAG asylum applications are denied. One of the main factors is the communication barrier as well as the fact that authorities often do not know much about the CAG and the situation in China. The CAG has now established a reliable system where local branches are able to certify who is really a CAG member in good standing, but in some countries, authorities do not accept such certifications, preferring to rely on their own interviews with asylum seekers.

Refugee boards and courts sometimes find contradictions in the individual refugees' narratives. Some problems come from translation. Most refugees speak only Chinese, and the quality of court-appointed translators is often uneven. Notwithstanding the refugees' efforts, this problem is

difficult to overcome; as in most countries, refugees have to rely on translators appointed by the refugee commissions or courts and are not allowed
to bring their own.

In other cases, courts fail to recognize that the stories told by refugees are
fundamentally true, even if there may be contradictions in details, which
may be explained by the fact that asylum seekers newly arrived from China
answer interviewers in a situation of stress and fear. A case in point is the
story of Wang Xiumei, a CAG member who was denied asylum in Switzerland, accused of both not knowing her religion enough (once again, based on
available COIs) and of having told a contradictory story. Indeed, there were
some contradictions about details but these did not change the essence of her
story. Also, some contradictions might be explained by faulty translations
during the interview and her nervousness during the first interview, which
occurred only a few days after she had arrived in Switzerland. Nonetheless,
Wang had to go back to China where she was arrested. On 9 February 2018,
the Linshu County People's Court sentenced her to three and a half years in
jail for her activities in the CAG. Paradoxically, she was found guilty of ed-
iting CAG texts for theological correctness, while the Swiss authorities had
accused her of not knowing her religion enough (Introvigne, Richardson and
Šorytė 2019: 82–3).

Sometimes, credibility objections refer to persecution. It appears that
some authorities require evidence that the single asylum seeker has been
individually persecuted. This is against the prevailing international interpretation of the Convention and the Protocol, which regards it to be sufficient that the individual has *a credible fear of persecution*, even if he or she
managed to escape *before* being arrested. Reports by international bodies
and even the CCP-related media in China demonstrate that CAG members
are mercilessly hunted. If detected, every member of the CAG faces arrest
and imprisonment.

There are also those who were not CAG members in China and converted *sur place* in other countries. In this case, their conversions can also
be certified as genuine by local CAG branches, which can also supply evidence that some CAG members abroad, including those who converted *sur
place*, are often featured in CAG religious videos that are in turn routinely
examined by Chinese authorities. This circumstance was confirmed in one
of the new COIs produced by the Italian government in 2019 (Commissione Nazionale per il Diritto d'Asilo 2019b).

While the evidence that the CAG as a group is persecuted in China is
overwhelming, some refugee boards and courts consider the fact that the
refugee left China with a passport and a tourist visa as evidence of the
absence of such persecution. However, the control system of the Chinese
police is not infallible, data are not necessarily transmitted from one administration to another, and there are always alternative ways to obtain
passports and other documents, with one's own real or with an assumed
name, and cross the border: obviously, not all of these methods are legal.

Chinese authorities themselves routinely denounce the prevalence of corruption in their country (Wedeman 2012).

A good number of members of the CAG have not yet been identified as such by the authorities. Of course, they can be identified and arrested at any moment or denounced by neighbours interested in obtaining the rewards promised by the CCP; accordingly, they live in fear of persecution. But as long as they have not been identified, and if they do not have a criminal record, they are able to obtain a passport and leave the country.

Once abroad, however, the small communities of the CAG diaspora are easily kept under surveillance by Chinese agents. Unlike in China, most CAG activities abroad are public. They are also often filmed and the videos uploaded to the CAG websites and social network pages. The devotees who are active in the CAG abroad would be immediately arrested should they return to China.

Establishing credibility is an individual question. The CAG can only assist its refugees by urging them to consult reliable lawyers before being interviewed. Lawyers are in a better position to explain to CAG asylum seekers what parts of their stories commissions and courts are really interested in. The CAG has also supplied lawyers with affidavits by experts detailing how passports can be obtained in China, even by members of persecuted groups. However, some asylum applications continue to be denied on these grounds, as some courts rely on COIs inaccurately claiming that obtaining a passport in China for somebody in a situation of persecution is impossible. These courts regard such COIs, which most scholars of corruption in China would consider inaccurate, as more reliable than affidavits sworn by scholars.

In 2019, a new affidavit was given to lawyers internationally, sworn by a CAG member in the US who used to be a police officer in China, detailing the loopholes in the Chinese control systems and explaining how her co-religionists, although persecuted, may still be able to obtain a passport and escape. These documents have proved useful, although they would not overcome what some courts regard as contradictions in individual stories. The passport issue remains one of the most serious obstacles refugees have to overcome in order to obtain asylum.

Conclusion

Although claims by CAG refugees are not easily accepted, and some countries such as South Korea and Japan continue to reject most refugees in general (not only CAGs), our study demonstrates that the CAG has come a long way from when it was largely unknown in democratic countries or considered to be a criminal group based on the fake news about the McDonald's murder. CAG refugees have become more skilled in presenting their claims and have provided documents to scholars, lawyers, and governmental agencies demonstrating that every CAG member in China lives in constant fear of being arrested or worse. At least in some countries, these efforts have raised the percentage of asylum applications accepted, although problems remain. Some relate to specific CAG problems discussed in this chapter. Others derive from Chinese political influence or from a broader hostility towards refugees.

These are not easy times for refugees. From the United States to Europe, politicians may win elections by claiming that too many refugees are entering their countries, and something should be done to limit their numbers. Clearly, among those seeking refugee status, there are those who submit false or fraudulent claims, and therefore some caution by authorities is not unreasonable.

On the other hand, those persecuted for their religion have a genuine right to be recognized as refugees based on international laws and conventions. The social problems created in certain countries by the growing number of refugees are very real. But it is also true that religious liberty is a fragile and endangered right. Among the various categories of refugees, those who are genuinely trying to escape persecution because of their beliefs certainly deserve our generosity and sympathy.

Note

1 Easily accessible texts of international conventions are not included in the references.

References[1]

Australian Visa Bureau. 2012. Uzbek Refugee Proves Australia Visa Fraud to Gain Asylum. May 14. Accessed October 9, 2019. www.visabureau.com/news/uzbek-refugee-proves-australia-visa-fraud-to-gain-asylum.

Commissione Nazionale per il Diritto d'Asilo. 2019a. Persecuzioni per motivi religiosi in Cina, *Church of Almighty God*. March 28. Accessed October 9, 2019. https://coi.easo.europa.eu/administration/italy/PLib/2019_03_28_Cina_Chiesa_di_Dio_Onnipotente.pdf.

———. 2019b. Riconoscimento facciale in Cina; sorveglianza dei membri della Chiesa di Dio Onnipotente; video di propaganda della Chiesa di Dio Onnipotente. July 29. Accessed October 9, 2019. https://coi.easo.europa.eu/administration/italy/PLib/2019_07_29_Cina_Riconoscimento_facciale_Chiesa_Dio_Onnipotente.pdf.

Court of Justice of the European Union. 2012. *C-71/11 and C-99/11 Germany v Y and Z*. Grand Chamber, September 5. Accessed October 9, 2019. www.asylumlawdatabase.eu/en/content/cjeu-c-7111-and-c-9911-germany-v-y-and-z.

DIDR (Division Information Documentation Researches). 2016. *L'organisation millénariste Almighty God*. Paris: DIDR.

Dunn, Emily. 2015. *Lightning from the East: Heterodoxy and Christianity in Contemporary China*. Leiden: Brill.

Folk, Holly. 2017. 'Cult crimes' and fake news: Eye-gouging in Shanxi. *The Journal of CESNUR* 2: 96–109. DOI: 10.26338/tjoc.2017.1.2.5.

————. 2018. Protestant continuities in The Church of Almighty God. *The Journal of CESNUR* 2(1): 58–77. DOI: 10.26338/tjoc.2018.2.1.4.

Frantz, Douglas. 1997. U.S. Immigration Court grants asylum to German Scientologist. *The New York Times*, November 8. Accessed October 9, 2019. www.nytimes.com/1997/11/08/us/us-immigration-court-grants-asylum-to-german-scientologist.html.

Immigration and Refugee Board of Canada. 2014. China: The Church of Almighty God (*Quannengshen*), Also Known as 'Eastern Lightning,' Including Its Leaders, Location and Activities Attributed to It; Treatment of Members by Authorities (March 2013–September 2014). Accessed October 9, 2019. www.refworld.org/docid/546492804.html.

Immigration and Refugee Board of Canada. 2019. China: Update of CHN106256 of 23 September 2019 on the Church of Almighty God (CAG) (quan neng shen jiao; Quannengshen), also known as 'Eastern Lightning,' including its leaders, location and activities; treatment of members by society and authorities (2014-October 2019). Accessed December 30, 2019. https://irb-cisr.gc.ca/en/country-information/rir/Pages/index.aspx?doc=457950&pls=1.

Introvigne, Massimo. 2017a. 'Cruel killing, brutal killing, kill the beast': Investigating the 2014 McDonald's 'cult murder' in Zhaoyuan. *The Journal of CESNUR* 1: 61–73. DOI: 10.26338/tjoc.2017.1.1.6.

————. 2017b. Church of Almighty God. *Profiles of Millenarian & Apocalyptic Movements*, CenSAMM (Center for the Critical Study of Apocalyptic and Millenarian Movements). Accessed October 9, 2019. https://censamm.org/resources/profiles/church-of-almighty-god.

————. 2018. Gatekeeping and narratives about 'cult' violence: The McDonald's murder of 2014 in China. *Journal of Religion and Violence* 6(3): 370–87. DOI:10.5840/jrv20191960.

————. 2019. Church of Almighty God's Sister Zou Demei is free. *Bitter Winter*, June 13. Accessed October 9, 2019. https://bitterwinter.org/church-of-almighty-gods-sister-zou-demei-is-free/.

————. 2020. *Inside The Church of Almighty God: The Most Persecuted Religious Movement in China*. New York: Oxford University Press.

Introvigne, Massimo and David Bromley. 2017. The Lü Yingchun/Zhang Fan group. *World Religions and Spirituality Project*, October 16. Accessed October 9, 2019. https://wrldrels.org/2017/10/16/lu-yingchun-zhang-fan-group/.

Introvigne, Massimo, James T. Richardson and Rosita Šorytė. 2019. Would the real article 300 please stand up? Refugees from religious movements persecuted as *Xie Jiao* in China: The case of The Church of Almighty God. *The Journal of CESNUR* 3(5): 3–86. DOI: 10.26338/tjoc.2019.3.5.1.

Irons, Edward. 2018. The list: The evolution of China's list of illegal and evil cults. *The Journal of CESNUR* 2(1):33–57. DOI:10.26338/tjoc.2018.2.1.3.

Ma, Xingrui. 2014. 马兴瑞同志在省委防范和处理邪教问题领导小组全体成员会议上的讲话 (Comrade Ma Xingrui's Talk on the Meeting Open to All Members of the Provincial 610 Office). Reproduced on the Web site of the Association for the Protection of Human Rights and Religious Freedom. Accessed December 21, 2017. www.adhrrf.org/china-ma-xingrui-20140709.html.

Ministerie van Buitenlandse Zaken. 2020. Country of Origin Information Report China, May 2020. The Hague: The Ministry of Foreign Affairs of the Netherlands, Country of Origin Information Reports Section. Accessed September

30, 2020. https://www.government.nl/binaries/government/documents/reports/2020/07/01/country-of-origin-information-report-china-july-2020/COI+Report+China.pdf,

Office of the High Commissioner for Human Rights. 1993. CCPR General Comment No. 22: Article 18 (Freedom of Thought, Conscience or Religion). Accessed October 10, 2019. www.refworld.org/docid/453883fb22.html.

Platvoet, Jan G. and Arie L. Molendijk (eds). 1999. *The Pragmatics of Defining Religion: Contexts, Concepts and Contests.* Leiden: Brill.

Prososki, Paul 2019. New coalition demands China respect religion. *Bitter Winter,* March 6. Accessed October 10, 2019. https://bitterwinter.org/new-coalition-demands-china-respect-religion/.

Supreme Court of Sweden. 2005. Petition for extradition to Romania of Gregorian Bivolaru. October 21. English translation available on Gregorian Bivolaru's Web site. Accessed October 10, 2019. http://gregorianbivolaru.net/docs/asylum/Decision_Supreme_Court_Sweden_21_Oct_05.pdf.

UNHCR. 2004. *Guidelines on International Protection: Religion-Based Refugee Claims under Article 1A(2) of the 1951 Convention and/or the 1967 Protocol Relating to the Status of Refugees.* Geneva: UNHCR. Accessed October 10, 2019. www.unhcr.org/publications/legal/40d8427a4/guidelines-international-protection-6-religion-based-refugee-claims-under.html.

———. 2017. *The 1951 Refugee Convention.* Accessed October 10, 2019. www.unhcr.org/1951-refugee-convention.html.

United Nations Human Rights Council. 2018. *Summary of Stakeholders' Submissions on China: Report of the Office of the United Nations High Commissioner for Human Rights.* Geneva, Switzerland: United Nations Human Rights Council.

United States Commission on International Religious Freedom. 2019. *2019 Annual Report.* Washington, DC: United States Commission on International Religious Freedom.

U.S. Department of State. 2019a. *Country Reports on Human Rights Practices—China.* Accessed October 10, 2019. www.state.gov/documents/organization/289281.pdf.

———. 2019b. *International Religious Freedom Report 2018—China (Includes Tibet, Xinjiang, Hong Kong, and Macau).* Accessed October 10, 2019. www.state.gov/wp-content/uploads/2019/05/CHINA-INCLUSIVE-2018-INTERNATIONAL-RELIGIOUS-FREEDOM- REPORT.pdf.

Wedeman, Andrew. 2012. *Double Paradox: Rapid Growth and Rising Corruption in China.* Ithaca, New York, and London: Cornell University Press.

12 Minority religion reactions to the European Court of Human Rights[1]

Effie Fokas

Introduction

Within this volume's broader focus on religious minority reactions to the law, this chapter examines religious minority reactions to decisions of the European Court of Human Rights (ECtHR, or the Court), an institution which has brought about significant legal change regarding the protection of religious minorities in Europe and beyond. In the pages that follow, the relevance of this particular court to religious minority concerns is set out. A subsequent section presents the theoretical underpinnings of a study of grassroots level impact of the ECtHR in the domain of religion-related case law. Then, drawing on data from the latter study, the chapter explains the extent to, the ways in which, and the reasons why minority religions react, or do not react, to the ECtHR in its engagements with religion.

Why focus on the ECtHR?

There are several reasons why special attention to the European Court of Human Rights is worthwhile for a broader study of religious minority reactions to the law. First, this is a human rights court, offering recourse to individuals and groups who have a complaint against the states in which they reside for that state's failure to secure their human rights. It is a court of last resort for member states of the Council of Europe, under the auspices of which the ECtHR operates, so that if a legal claim has not been satisfied after having exhausted all national legal remedies (i.e., reaching a national high court), then a claim can be taken directly to the ECtHR. The ECtHR is thus by its nature counter-majoritarian, and in theory at least a resource for minority groups who may be vulnerable even in strong democracies because of course majoritarian rule does not always protect the needs of minorities.

Second, the Court is poised to protect religious sensibilities through a number of different rights guaranteed by the European Convention on Human Rights (ECHR), which the ECtHR defends. The first and foremost of these is **Article 9,** on "Freedom of thought, conscience and religion", which states that

1   Everyone has the right to freedom of thought, conscience and religion; this right includes freedom to change his religion or belief and freedom, either alone or in community with others and in public or private to manifest his religion or belief, in worship, teaching, practice and observance.

2   Freedom to manifest one's religion or beliefs shall be subject only to such limitations as are prescribed by law and are necessary in a democratic society in the interests of public safety, for the protection of public order, health or morals, or for the protection of the rights and freedoms of others.

Thus, the freedom of belief has no limitations. However, the right to manifest one's beliefs may be limited as long as such limitations are 'prescribed by law' and deemed 'necessary in a democratic society' based on reasons such as public safety, public order, and health

Another article frequently implicated in religion-related cases is **Article 10,** which protects the freedom of expression. The third article of the Convention much engaged by conscience-based groups in their claims against states in which they reside is **Article 11,** on the Freedom of assembly and association. According to this first paragraph of this article, "Everyone has the right to freedom of peaceful assembly and to freedom of association with others, including the right to form and to join trade unions for the protection of his interests". However, like Article 9, in the case of both Articles 10 and 11, the right is not absolute and is subject to restrictions to do with national security, public safety, prevention of crime and disorder and protection of health, morals and the rights of others.

Also, highly useful to religious minorities is **Article 14,** which prohibits discrimination on several bases, including religion. Finally, **Article 2 of the first Protocol** to the Convention guarantees the right to education and the right of parents to ensure such education and teaching "in conformity with their own religious and philosophical convictions". The latter phrase has been used by many conscience-based minorities in their complaints about mandatory religious education in a faith to which they do not belong and/or about the conditions for exemption from such religious education.

Beyond the wide remit that the ECtHR has through these several articles of the ECHR to address issues of concern to religious minorities, a further reason why the ECtHR is worthy of special attention is its wide geographic mandate. The Court's jurisdiction covers all 47 member states of the Council of Europe (CoE), including all European countries (save Belarus). This means that the Court bears relevance for over 800 million people. Specifically, any right won by a religious minority group or individual in any of these states automatically becomes a right which may be claimed by any other group or individual in any other member state.[2] This makes the Court an especially formidable player in the field of rights protection.

It should be noted that the Court was rather slow to engage actively with religion-related claims. The Court was established in 1959, but it was only in 1993 that the Court issued its first judgment finding a violation of religious freedom, in the case of *Kokkinakis v. Greece*. Minos Kokkinakis was a Greek Jehovah's Witness who had been arrested over 60 times for violating the Greek legal ban on proselytism elaborated in a 1938 law and embedded in the Greek Constitution. *Kokkinakis* was a watershed case for the ECtHR. After *Kokkinakis* 'broke the ice', the Court went from 0 decisions based on Article 9 between 1959 and 1993 to seven within the next decade (notably, six of these seven judgments in which violations of religious freedom were found were against majority Orthodox states). Today, the Court has issued over 85 judgments in which it has found violations of Article 9 and far more such condemnatory judgments regarding other religious minority rights (e.g., assembly, non-discrimination). This suggests a rapidly developing judicialization of religion by the Court.[3]

In *Kokkinakis'* aftermath, the ECtHR has evolved into an arena where some of the most challenging debates around European religious pluralism take place, and its case law has centrally contributed to shaping the terms of such controversies. The Court increasingly deals with matters touching a nerve of European Christian, Muslim, secular and atheistic publics alike, with its decisions regarding, for example, the right to a religiously neutral education versus a state's right to display the crucifix in public schools (Italy – the *Lautsi* case of 2011), and the right to manifest one's faith in the wearing of a burqa versus a state's right to protect its notion of 'living together' (France – the *S.A.S.* case of 2014). Notably, the rights claims of conscience-based minorities in these two cases (an atheist family in Italy and a Muslim woman in France) were *not* vindicated by the Court. And, as we shall see below, it *matters* in which cases the Court does or does not vindicate minority religious rights. But certainly, the Court has expanded minority religious rights through a robust body of relevant case law.[4] This makes the Court an important point of consideration for such groups, both as a potential resource for their own potential legal recourse, and more generally because of legal changes, the Court's decisions may bring about in the states in which they reside.

Also important for religious minorities are certain 'messages' that the Court communicates through the texts of its judgments. In its *Kokkinakis* judgment, the Court developed for the first time, in clear terms and cited repeatedly in later case law, its conception of, and what might be considered its 'mantra' on, religion in relation to pluralism:

> As enshrined in Article 9 (art. 9), freedom of thought, conscience and religion is one of the foundations of a 'democratic society' within the

meaning of the Convention. It is, in its religious dimension, one of the most vital elements that go to make up the identity of believers and their conception of life, but it is also a precious asset for atheists, agnostics, sceptics and the unconcerned. The pluralism indissociable from a democratic society, which has been dearly won over the centuries, depends on it.

(*Kokkinakis v. Greece*, 1993, ECtHR, para. 31)

Through subsequent case law, one may identify at least two further 'mantras' especially prevalent in case law on religious minority rights and emphasizing the importance of pluralism.[5] In one, special attention is paid to the concept of state neutrality. As expressed in *Manoussakis and Others v. Greece* (1996) and subsequently in several other cases:

> The Court has frequently emphasised the State's role as the neutral and impartial organiser of the exercise of various religions, faiths and beliefs, and stated that this role is conducive to public order, religious harmony and tolerance in a democratic society. Thus, the State's duty of neutrality and impartiality is incompatible with any power on the State's part to assess the legitimacy of religious beliefs or the ways in which those beliefs are expressed, and the Court considered that this duty requires the State to ensure mutual tolerance between opposing groups. Accordingly, the role of the authorities in such circumstances is not to remove the cause of tension by eliminating pluralism, but to ensure that the competing groups tolerate each other.
>
> (cited here from *Ebrahimian v. France*, 2016, para 55)

The third mantra is embedded first in a 1976 freedom of expression case (*Handyside v. UK*), but subsequently in several cases regarding religious minority rights:

> Pluralism, tolerance and broadmindedness are hallmarks of a "democratic society". Although individual interests must on occasion be subordinated to those of a group, democracy does not simply mean that the views of a majority must always prevail: a balance must be achieved which ensures the fair treatment of people from minorities and avoids any abuse of a dominant position (see ...). Pluralism is also built on genuine recognition of, and respect for, diversity and the dynamics of cultural traditions, ethnic and cultural identities, religious beliefs and artistic, literary and socio-economic ideas and concepts. The harmonious interaction of persons and groups with varied identities is essential for achieving social cohesion (see ...). Respect for religious diversity undoubtedly represents one of the most important challenges to be faced today; for that reason, the authorities must

perceive religious diversity not as a threat but as a source of enrich-
ment (see…).

(Cited here from *Izzettin Dogan and
Others v. Turkey*, 2016, para 109)

Together, these three mantras entail clearly powerful statements in support
of religious minority rights (even if they have not *always* been referenced in
cases in which the Court decided in favour of the religious minority group
or individual in question).

   In summary, this Court should matter to religious minorities for several
reasons. First, because it has a strong set of tools at its disposal (including
but not limited to the five ECHR articles presented above) to adjudicate
religious minority legal claims. Second, it has proven itself as a friend of
religious minorities through its broad-ranging case law on religion. Third,
the Court should matter to religious minorities because it has controversially *not* supported religious minority rights in other cases. It is a resource
available to *any* group or individual with a religion-based claim arising in
47 different states. Also, its precedence from judgments in these 47 states
is potentially relevant for over 800 million individuals. Finally (in this not
exhaustive list), the Court should matter to religious minorities because it
has produced powerful messages – through its judgments – in support of
religious pluralism.

Indirect or 'radiating' effects of the ECtHR

We have established, then, that the ECtHR should matter to religious minorities, *and* it *has* mattered to religious minorities, as demonstrated by the
large body of case law through which the rights and freedoms of various
religious minority groups have been supported. But to what extent does the
Court's jurisprudential pattern matter for your 'average Joe Blow' religious
minority individual? This question was addressed empirically through
the Grassrootsmobilise research programme (2014–2019), which sought
to understand the grassroots level impact of ECtHR religion-related case
law. By 'religion-related', I mean not only issues of religion *per se* (e.g.,
religious education, freedom of religious expression, right to worship),
but also socio-bioethical issues which tend to mobilise religious people
in particular. These include campaigns against abortion rights or against
same-sex marriage or assisted reproductive technology. Also included are
atheist, secularist or humanist concerns regarding religious oaths, religious
symbols in public spaces and other issues related to church–state separation. The Grassrootsmobilise programme conducted research in four
different countries – Greece, Italy, Romania and Turkey – and included
in-depth interviews with approximately 200 (in total) representatives of
religious minority groups, religious majority groups, NGOs dealing with

religion-related issues, lawyers handing religion-related cases and government officials engaging with religion-related concerns. The research effort sought insight into the extent to and ways in which grassroots level social actors know and make use of ECtHR religion-related case law in their pursuit of their own rights – in other words, the indirect or 'radiating' effects of that case law.[6]

What are indirect or radiating effects of case law? Beyond the direct effects, the Court has by bringing about legal change (or, in some cases, controversially *not* calling for legal change), courts in general and this court in particular also carries great potential *indirect effects*.[7] The latter entail a broad set of influences beyond the strictly legal domain, including influence on groups' and individuals' understanding of their rights, their discourse about their rights and their social and political mobilizations around those rights (Galanter 1983; McCann 2004). A 'decentered' approach to the impact of courts shifts attention from the direct effects of case law and recognizes that court decisions can significantly facilitate the placement of issues on the public agenda and thus serve as catalysts for significant social change – what legal scholar Stuart Scheingold (1974) calls the development of a 'politics of rights'. According to Scheingold, perceptions of entitlement associated with particular court decisions may lead marginalized groups to capitalize on those decisions by initiating and nurturing political mobilization. This process of 'rights consciousness raising' is, according to socio-legal scholar Michael McCann "perhaps the most significant point at which law matters" (2004: 510).

The indirect effects of courts may also be effectively described with the use of Marc Galanter's (1983) term, 'the radiating effects'. According to Galanter, limiting our attention to 'direct' effects of courts entails a drastic and imprudent narrowing of our purview of the Court's influence. Courts resolve by authoritative disposition only a small fraction of all disputes that are brought to their attention, and these are only a small fraction of all disputes that might conceivably be brought to court and an even smaller fraction of the whole universe of disputes. The broader 'radiating effects' of courts are largely down to the dissemination of information: 'Courts produce not only decisions, but messages. These messages are resources that parties use in envisioning, devising, pursuing, negotiating, vindicating claims (and in avoiding, defending, and defeating them)' (1983: 126). The impact of these messages is largely contingent on who receives what messages from the court, who is in a position to evaluate and process those messages, how he or she processes the information and who is in a position to use that information. Drawing then on research looking into these points, this chapter addresses the question (Fokas 2016; Fokas and Richardson 2018), to what extent do the ECtHR's messages on religion 'trickle down' to religious minorities at the grassroots level and to what effects?

The view from the grassroots level: factors influencing reactions – or lack thereof – to the ECtHR

As Michael McCann notes, legal knowledge "does not simply trickle down on citizens and state officials in a unidirectional, determinate fashion" (1992: 733). Rather, it goes through some kind of diffusion process, and this process varies significantly from one context to the other. Hence the need to study grassroots level impact of the ECtHR in different country contexts and across different conscience-based minority groups.

The research underpinning the present study has yielded insight into several factors and mechanisms influencing grassroots actors' reactions (or lack thereof) to decisions rendered by the ECtHR. These can be divided into (at least) three categories which are independent and yet have some degree of overlap. Included are factors that come to the fore through cross-country comparison, those considering different conscience-based groups in relation to one another and those considering one individual in relation to the other from the perspective of their access to legal expertise.

Country differences

Considering the results of the research conducted across the four country case studies, five structural factors in particular stand out as critical for how messages of the ECtHR are diffused to the grassroots level. One is **variation in national legal and political opportunity structures**: the potential effectiveness of lobbying politicians versus that of taking one's complaints to court varies from one national context to the other. In some cases, the national-level court system is extremely cumbersome and expensive to navigate. Where this is the case, there tends to be less hope placed in courts to resolve one's problems – and by extension, less hope in the ECtHR, and by further extension, thus less *attention* to the ECtHR. In other words, from most of the respondents' perspectives, the ECtHR – as all courts – are of interest only directly proportionally to their potential to help their own problems. The potential 'indirect effects' of the ECtHR are not considered much by most grassroots actors (see below though for nuance).

A second factor influencing levels of awareness and interest in the ECtHR is **where the Court stands in the 'national legal order'** in the given case. In some countries, precedence set by the Court automatically overrides relevant national law – the ECtHR's decisions entail the 'final word' on a given matter. In other countries, there are significant limitations on how easily the Court's decisions may override relevant national law. In the case of Italy, the status quo in this domain changed during the course of the research. In an Italian Constitutional Court judgment of 2015, the court narrowed the domestic impact of the ECtHR case law by calling on domestic judges to refrain from applying the ECtHR's case law where: (a) there is a high degree of jurisdictional creativity, which implies that the new principle is not well settled in case law; (b) there are inner conflicts within the ECtHR's jurisprudence; (c) the principle is promulgated by a Chamber rather than Grand Chamber decision; (d) the ECtHR judgment displays a misunderstanding of the Italian legal context; and (e) the decision is accompanied by dissenting opinions (Pin and Tega 2015). As a result, the Court provides lesser bargaining power before Italian national courts. In the words of one Italian lawyer, in the context of an interview for the Grassrootsmobilise programme:

> In the end, we always come back to the fact that it is a task of the national state. The European instrument is essential, it is absolutely crucial, but the European instrument does not help you to change your laws, if you do not want to. That is, if the national legislature and the regional legislatures do not make those principles their own, we can go as many times as we want to the ECtHR, but we will never reach a definitive solution.

The third factor arising through cross-country comparison is the role played by **where the majority faith stands in the 'national *religious* order'**. Realistically, in all country contexts, there is some degree of privilege afforded to one belief system over others (or to a selection of belief systems). The extent to which religious minorities are interested in what the ECtHR 'has to offer' is to some extent contingent on the degree of privilege and dominance of a 'majority faith'. In the Italian context again, for example, there is a sense that the Roman Catholic Church is a force that even the ECtHR cannot ignore.

A further relevant factor which has to do with the country context is **the national track record in relation to the ECtHR**. In the Turkish case, for example, in the domain of religion, the Court has issued a relatively large number of judgments finding the Turkish state in violation of religion-related rights. The combination of the large number of such judgments (e.g., on rights of Alevis), on the one hand, and the tendency of the Turkish state *not* to implement legal change called for by many of these judgments has brought extra attention to this Court amongst stakeholder social actors. In the Greek case, largely *because* of where Orthodoxy stands within the national religious – its constitutional enshrinement as the 'prevailing faith' in the Greek Constitution and the various privileges that flow from the latter – the Greek state has attracted several ECtHR judgments finding violations of religious freedom. But, unlike the Turkish context, there has been no social or political activism around this case law, only continued legal activism until particular violations of religious freedom have come to an end, in practice if not in legal terms. For example, after *Kokkinakis*, the Greek ban on proselytism was not removed from the law books but, as one Greek Ombudsman's representative notes,

'*Kokkinakis* is in the drawer' at Greek police stations, as a reminder to police that they may not arrest people merely because they are talking about their faith to others. Kokkinakis' persistence in this case, both in sharing his faith and in taking his case to the ECtHR, led to a change in practice, if not in law.

Finally, **the place of the country in relation to the Europeanisation process** is also a relevant structural factor in the particular case studies in Grassrootsmobilise. The case studies include the 'older democracy' of Italy with its greater length of its participation in the European unification project. The selection also includes the relatively younger (modern-day) democracy of Greece, with its membership in the European Communities/Union since 1981. Romania is a country more recently acceded to the EU and a newer (post-communist) democracy, and the (currently flailing) democracy of Turkey is in a continued intermittent membership negotiation process with the EU. The stage of relationship of a country with the EU is a particularly critical factor. All members of the EU are required to be signatories of the European Convention on Human Rights and are thus bound by the Court's jurisdiction. However, the Romanian and Turkish accession processes have entailed rather stringent requirements for human rights provisions, including training of national judges in ECtHR case law and linking of judges' promotion to citations of ECtHR relevant case law in the Romania case (Ozgul 2019; Popa and Andreescu 2019: S84). The more that national courts reference ECtHR case law, the greater potential, at least, one can imagine for a trickle-down effect to grassroots social actors.

Group differences

The data generated through research on grassroots level impact of the ECtHR religion-related case law also reveals notable differences in levels of awareness of and engagement with the Court's jurisprudence from one conscience-based group to another. In part, this has to do with where in particular each conscience-based *minority* group stands within the national religious order and, to an extent related to the latter, where religious freedoms fall in the priorities list of each such group. The treatment of atheist groups and levels of discrimination against them is different, for example, in the Romanian, Greek and Turkish cases, from the treatment of members of the Catholic Church. The extent to which religion-related rights violations are high on their agenda varies accordingly.

There are additional, in some cases related, factors relevant to group differences. For example, Jehovah's Witnesses are a religious minority group with a strong record of their own case law before the ECtHR and, in general, have a relatively high propensity to pursue their rights-related claims in courts. They also tend to employ in-house lawyers. Both these facts lead to notably higher levels of awareness of the ECtHR and its case law amongst representatives of this religious group. The same applies to the Church of Scientology though this group's own case law before the ECtHR is not as voluminous.

Islam has a prominent place in the Court's religion-related case law, but perhaps more as the results of strategic litigation rather than as a reflection of Muslim groups' attention to and engagement with the Court's case law. For example, *S.A.S. v France* and *Molla Sali v. Greece* were both cases which had behind them legal actors actively seeking ways to bring an end to a particular status quo: the French ban on the full-face veil from *all* public spaces and the Greek application of Sharia law to all Muslim minorities in the region of Thrace. Muslim respondents from Greece and Italy, most of them first or second-generation immigrants, tend to see legal pursuit of religion-related rights as an especially confrontational act. Several Muslim respondents express a sense in which taking their respective states to the ECtHR would render them even 'less welcome' (see Giorgi and Anicchinno 2017).

It should be noted, though, that the perception of litigation before the ECtHR as a particularly confrontational act is not limited to Muslim minorities. Majority Muslims in Turkey express that "we are sons of this country" and thus do not want to accuse the Turkish state at the ECtHR. Similarly, a Protestant believer in Romania indicates that "we do not want to wash our dirty laundry all over Europe".

Atheist, humanist and secularist respondents in those same countries, on the other hand, seem to be 'freer' of such concerns. They are already perceived as (or conceive of themselves to be perceived as) 'anti-nationals', regardless of legal complaints against their respective states, by dint of their 'rejection' of majority religion. These groups, then, are less restrained in their approaches to the Court and express a relatively keen interest both in learning about its case law and in potential litigation before it.

Down to the individual...

Though the country and group differences presented above do provide some insight into observable trends, they are of course not predictors of who understands what about the ECtHR religion-related case law and what he or she will do with that understanding. Looking at the individual level, a central determining factor is some degree of legal expertise or close proximity to such – that is, membership in a religious community which employs an in-house lawyer. As Frances Zemans notes, legal competence is "an active and searching awareness of the opportunities offered by law for enhancing one's position in society" (1982: 1009–10), and lawyers in the continuous employment of those whose rights they represent can serve as the client's rights consciousness by providing for their clients that "active and searching awareness of the opportunities offered by law" (1982: 1013).

This first point hides another perhaps more important one: the research reveals a fairly widespread presumption that all things legal (e.g., ECtHR decisions) are matters directly accessible and comprehensible solely to law-yers. Respondents with no legal expertise often shied away from questions to do with particular ECtHR cases and deferred instead to lawyers for such questions.

That said, some respondents rather bravely entered the world of ECtHR unarmed with such legal knowledge: for example, one Romanian Ortho-dox priest and one Romanian high-school teacher more or less taught themselves all they needed to know before they embarked on an ulti-mately successful mission to reach the ECtHR with their own religion-re-lated rights claims (see Popa and Andreescu 2017: 305–7, 2019: S92–4). The research also revealed a large role played, in terms of respondents' perceptions and understanding of the Court, by a small number of cases. Conclusions are often reached regarding whether the Court is friendly or not to one's causes based on (sometimes rather vague) knowledge of one or two particular judgments of the Court.

Assessments: how *do* minority religions react to the ECtHR?

Certainly, across all cases, minority religious individuals show fairly lit-tle knowledge of particular ECtHR cases – even those on issues of direct relevance to them. The same applies more or less to other categories in-terviewed, including *majority* religious individuals, and even government representatives who work on religion-related issues and, to a lesser extent, representatives of NGOs dealing with religion-related issues. And in terms of the few cases they know by name or theme, these *tend* to be limited to cases against the interviewees' own states. Here then again, the factor of the state's own track record in relation to the Court makes a difference.

Mostly, we find a combination of the above-presented factors at play influencing varying levels of social actors' awareness of and engagement with ECtHR case law and to differing effects. For example, in the Greek context, where Jehovah's Witnesses pioneered in ECtHR case law on re-ligious freedoms: after *Kokkinakis*, the subsequent several violations of religious freedoms found by the Court were in cases against the state of Greece. As a result, several respondents in the research conducted in Greece reflected a conception of the Court as a friend of 'fringe' religious minority groups and thus welcomed by some and criticized by others. In this, Jehovah's Witnesses seem to have a 'filtering effect' over Greek re-spondents' conceptions of the Court (Markoviti 2017).

Similarly, in the case of *Lautsi v. Italy* (2011), the Court left what the Italian reseachers in the Grassrootsmobilise research project have called a 'long shadow' over social actors' expectations of the Court. In this case, the Court ruled that the display of the crucifix on Italian school walls does not, in and of itself, entail a violation of Article 2 of Protocol 1 on the right to education in accordance with one's own religious or philosophical beliefs.

Many Italian respondents read in this case an indication that the privileges enjoyed by the Roman Catholic Church would not (ever) be challenged by the Court.

Lautsi is amongst the few cases that travelled across national lines into the consciousness of religious minorities in other country contexts. In relation to this case, we find evidence of Galanter's claim that "a single judicial action may radiate different messages to different audiences" (1983: 126). The grassroots-level actors consulted for this study displayed several different interpretations of the same case – interpretations influenced both by personal, group and national specificities. For example, in Greece, a predominant message received from this case by grassroots actors was that the authority on these issues remains at the national level, and the icons of the Virgin Mary or Jesus currently in all public school classrooms are allowed (though this is a rather gross misinterpretation of the Court's actual judgment). Meanwhile, social actors in Romania read in the *Lautsi* verdict a blow to any minority religious claims. Only in Turkey, amongst the cases examined here, did *Lautsi* not reverberate much of anything amongst grassroots actors.

Though, as we have seen, there are significant variations in the ways and extent to which grassroots actors react to ECtHR case law, what is clear is that – viewed from the perspective of indirect effects – the Court is a severely *underused* resource. The Court's path-breaking case law which is favourable to religious minorities carries great but unfulfilled potential to inspire *further* rights claims by religious minority groups and individuals across 47 countries – a potential which is hampered by a mere lack of awareness of this case law. This chapter entails a loud cry for better forms of communication of the Court's messages, in lay terms and tailored to grassroots actors' specific areas of interest.

Notes

1 This chapter draws on research conducted under the auspices of the Grassrootsmobilise Research Programme (2014–2019), funded by the European Research Council (ERC; Grant Agreement No. 338463), and with the support of the London School of Economics Hellenic Observatory, of which the author is a Research Associate, and that of the Henry Luce/Leadership 100 project on Orthodoxy and Human Rights (Orthodox Christian Studies Center, Fordham University), of which the author is a participant.

2 *Note bene*: the right to make a claim (signified also by the Court's acceptance of a case as admissible) does not however necessarily lead to the establishment of the same right in other national contexts. The Court may and often does deem the particulars of a given case as not generally applicable, thus limiting the precedential value of a given judgment.

3 Specifically, violations of Article 9, the main article dealing with religious freedom; there are of course far more if we broaden the gamma to include violations of the right to assembly of religious groups (Art. 11), the right to non-discrimination based on religion (Art. 14), and others.

4 See 'Guide on Article 9 of the European Convention on Human Rights', updated 31 August 2019 (available at: www.echr.coe.int/Documents/Guide_Art_9_ENG.pdf), for an overview of some such; and see also special issue of *Politics and Religion*, Vol. 12, Sup. 1, for an overview related specifically to religious education case law, and a special issue of *Religion, State and Society*, Vol. 64, No. 1, for an overview related to legal status-related case law.
5 This discussion of 'mantras' is informed by that in Fokas (2020), a text for which I examined patterns in ECtHR case law on religion in relation to the concepts of pluralism, secularism and tolerance.
6 The research also entailed a study of mass media representations of ECtHR religion-related engagements; a study of national high courts' references to relevant ECtHR case law; and a macmi study of mobilisations prior to and in the aftermath of one particular ECtHR case in each country case study.
7 This discussion of the indirect effects of the European Court of Human Rights draws heavily on Fokas (2015), in which the Grassrootsmobilise research programme (see note 1) is presented.

References

Fokas, Effie. 2015. Directions in religious pluralism in Europe: Mobilizations in the shadow of European Court of Human Rights religious freedom jurisprudence. *Oxford Journal of Law and Religion* 54: 54–74.

———. 2016. Comparative susceptibility and differential effects on the two European courts: A study of grasstops mobilizations around religion. *Oxford Journal of Law and Religion* 5: 541–74.

———. 2020. Messages from the European Court of Human Rights on tolerance, secularization and pluralism, in: Vyacheslav Karpov and Manfred Svensson (eds), *Secularization, Desecularization and Toleration: Cross-Disciplinary Challenges to a Modern Myth*. Cham, Switzerland: Palgrave Macmillan, 2020, pp. 279–298.

Fokas, Effie, and James T. Richardson (eds). 2018. *The European Court of Human Rights and Minority Religions: Messages Generated and Messages Received*. London: Taylor and Francis.

Galanter, Marc. 1983. The radiating effects of courts, in: Keith O Boyum and Lynn M Mathe (eds), *Empirical Theories about Courts*. London: Longman, pp. 117–42.

Giorgi, Alberta, and Pasquale Anicchinno. 2017. 'Genuine' religions and their arena of legitimation in Italy – the role of the ECtHR. *Religion, State and Society* 45(3–4): 284–96.

Markoviti, Margarita. 2017. The 'filtering effects' of ECtHR case law on religious freedoms: legal recognition and places of worship for religious minorities in Greece. *Religion, State and Society* 45(3–4): 268–83.

McCann, Michael. 1992. Reform Litigation on Trial. *Law & Social Inquiry* 17(4): 715–43.

McCann, Michael. 2004. Law and social movements, in: Austin Sarat (ed.), *Blackwell Companion to Law and Society*. London: Blackwell, pp. 506–22.

Ozgul, Ceren. 2019. Freedom of Religion, the ECtHR and Grassroots Mobilization on Religious Education in Turkey. *Politics and Religion* 12(S1): S103–S133.

Pin, Andreas, and D. Tega. 2015. Mini symposium: Pin and Tega on Italian Constitutional Court judgment. No. 49/2015. Available at: www.iconnectblog.com/2015/04/mini-symposium-on-cc-judgment-49-2015/

Popa, Mihai, and Liviu Andreescu. 2017. Legal provisions, courts, and the status of religious communities: A socio-legal analysis of inter-religious relations in Romania. *Religion, State and Society* 45(3–4): 297–316.

———. 2019. Religion and education in Romania: Social mobilization and the 'shadow' of the European Court of Human Rights. *Politics and Religion* 12: 79–102.

Scheingold, Stuart. 1974. *The Politics of Rights: Lawyers, Public Policy and Political Change*. New Haven: Yale University Press.

Zemans, Frances. 1982. Framework for analysis of legal mobilization: A decision-making model. *American Bar Foundation Research Journal* 7(4): 989–1071.

13 Minority religions respond to the law

A theoretical excursus

James T. Richardson

Introduction and overview

This collection presents examples of how minority religious groups have responded to efforts by governmental authorities, including executive branches, lawmakers, and judicial systems, to manage them and other belief-based groups. That management can vary from a positive, welcoming approach (rare) to overt efforts to repress (regrettably not as rare). How minority religious groups have responded to official postures towards them varies greatly in substance and outcome, as shown in this volume. This concluding chapter will attempt to present relevant theoretical concepts and ideas that help us understand how and why those responses by minority religions have occurred.

All minority religious groups must find ways to function within the society in which they have chosen to operate. Therefore, it is crucial to understand the societal context in which the interactions between minority religions and various arms of the state, as well as other non-state entities, take place. To this end, concepts and ideas from 'The Sociology of Religious Freedom' literature (Richardson 2006) will be offered to aid our understanding. These will include discussion of historical, structural, and demographic characteristics of a society, along with an assessment of how the legal/judicial system of the society treats minority religions. Theories from the sociology of law offered by Donald Black and his students (Black 1976, 1999; Black and Baumgartner 1999; Cooney 1994) and by William Chambliss and others (Chambliss 1964, 1979; Chambliss and Zatz 1993) offer useful ideas to aid understanding of the societal context within which religious groups must operate.

Occasionally, minority religions have within their ranks legal prowess to defend themselves or even take the offensive in dealing with efforts of governmental representatives to manage or control them. Examples offered in this collection by the Jehovah's Witnesses, the Church of Scientology, as well as some of the other groups, demonstrate that this type of approach can sometimes be quite successful. However, more often than not, minority religious groups do not possess the political and legal expertise to defend themselves or to promote their values and way of life within the society in which they are attempting to operate. In such situations, if the group is to survive, it must be creative and learn how to function within sometimes unfriendly environs. Religious groups in such situations, such as several highlighted in this volume, may seek to form alliances with others who might be able to assist them because of their own status within the society. Again, theories from the sociology of law mentioned above, particularly from Black's work, offer ideas useful to explain how such weaker, less popular religious groups might occasionally prevail within the legal and political arena. Such ideas also help us grasp why and how more successful religious groups in the legal arena, such as Scientology and the Jehovah's Witnesses, have been able to prevail in a number of different societies and legal systems.

The concept of 'cause lawyering' from the social movement literature is a useful tool to augment theories from the sociology of law. Cause lawyering is the practice of law by legal professionals who seek to use legal means to support movements for social change (Marshall and Crocker Hale 2014; Sarat and Scheingold 1998, 2005, 2006). Some legal professionals and their organizational entities work to achieve change that would recognize a more pluralistic contemporary society. Thus, cause lawyering can help explain how some minority religions have been able to attract the assistance they need to function within legal systems. One aspect of cause lawyering involves dedicated NGOs which focus their attention and resources on specific causes such as legal actions on behalf of minority religious groups. Examples of cause lawyering and the functioning of NGOs are demonstrated in some of the chapters presented in this collection. Lawyers for such groups have intervened in cases before various judicial tribunals, assisting behind the scenes, sometimes with direct intervention such as furnishing legal representation or filing *amicus* briefs on behalf of a party in a legal case (Burli 2017; Lehmann 2016; van den Eynde 2013, 2017).

The sociology of religious freedom and minority religions

The idea of religious freedom is a relatively new concept in human history (Richardson 2006). Although there were hints of tolerance for different religious traditions in some older societies, the concept in its more modern form was born out of efforts to resolve costly religious wars in the European area several hundred years ago. The United States Constitution, approved in 1789, contained the first clear constitutional-level statement concerning religious freedom with its 'free exercise' clause. This clause was included as something of a political compromise reached between several religious groups that had settled different parts of the continent. This politically motivated social construction has been much-copied in other constitutions since, but is often honoured in the breech, as minority faiths are not always welcome in societies where there is a dominant religion or no official religion at all. Thus, there are many versions of what is called religious freedom, and it can ebb and flow, depending on changing societal conditions as shown in this collection.

There are several key conditions that foster the development of religious freedom in contemporary societies. Included are (1) the presence of religious pluralism in the society, (2) no exclusive theocratic or atheistic state or powerful dominant religion, (3) separation of powers among branches of government, including a strong and independent judicial system, (4) the spread of 'constitutionalism' among nations with religious freedom included in constitutions and statues, and (5) development of institutional structures, including both governmental and NGOs, that protect personal freedoms, including religious freedom.

There are also contextual cultural and political factors that taken together support the development of religious freedom in the contemporary world. One is for key individuals and institutions to value religious pluralism and promote it within the society. This is best indicated by the clear statement of such a value in founding documents or legislation, as exemplified by the free exercise clause that now appears in most constitutions and by laws and practices that implement that value. The institutional structure of the state should also be supportive, with all branches of government taking actions supportive of the religious freedom value. Transnational entities such as the United Nations (UN), the Council of Europe (CoE), and the Organization for Security and Co-operation in Europe (OSCE), along with other such entities, also play an important role supportive of religious freedom by adopting positions and taking actions that protect this freedom. Nations that are parties to such international entities, and the treaties and compacts that establish them, are encouraged if not required to support the mandate of those organizations, which offers external support to those promoting religious freedom. Such entities can also furnish a check on actions that violate important values such as religious freedom, as exemplified by the way that decisions by the CoE's European Court of Human Rights can, through its decisions, encourage or even require changes in member nations' approach to religious groups.

Minority religions and legal and judicial systems

As noted above, a crucial aspect of establishing and maintaining religious freedom in a society is the presence of a reasonably powerful institution that can promote and protect the religious freedom for minority religious groups. This would usually be the role of the judicial system in a society that had separation of powers and which granted the judicial system at least a modicum of *autonomy* as well as some power over executive and legislative branch actions. This is important because both the executive and legislative branches may be more prone to support majoritarian perspectives in their actions simply because of how they are chosen within a democratic society. But if founding documents include protections for religious freedom, and those can be enforced by the judicial system which has a reasonable degree of autonomy, then religious freedom for minorities can be more effectively protected. However, if the judicial system is dominated by either the legislative or executive branch, perhaps by virtue of how judges are selected, compensated, and removed from office, then judicial power to protect religious freedom will be diminished, if not non-existent. Similarly, if there is a dominant religious or anti-religious ideology underpinning the society, or if the military is the major power in a society, then those considerations too can overcome a possible positive role of the judiciary in protecting religious freedom of minority religious groups.

Although the degree of autonomy of a judicial system is the most important consideration when analysing the role of the legal system in a society, there are other issues that can affect how those systems operate (Richardson 2001, 2006). The *pervasiveness* of the legal system is of import. Are all elements of the society governed by the dominant legal system or are there some societal groups that are exempt or have some independence from the dominant system of law? Are some religious groups allowed to establish their own rules for some aspects of life (such as domestic or family affairs)? A related important consideration is how *centralized* the legal system is. Are there geographic enclaves where the dominant legal system seems not to operate as effectively? Are there areas where the law, or certain laws, seem not to be adhered to or enforced? Thus, pervasiveness and degree of centralization are important issues to consider when seeking an understanding of how religious freedom might develop and be maintained.

The type of legal system – *adversarial* or *inquisitorial* – also matters. In adversarial legal systems, those caught up in the system can usually assume that they have the right to be defended in court. Assuming that resources are available, whether privately or because of public policy, an entity (individual attorney or an organization such as the American Civil Liberties Union or some other NGO) may be retained to defend the person or group within the legal system. In an inquisitorial system, this right to a defence is not guaranteed, and the rights of individuals or groups needing to defend themselves in legal proceedings are much more limited. This distinction is important, but note that the adversarial system can only function as described if other institutional structures within a society allow the legal profession and NGOs to operate. If those entities which might engage in a defence for a party charged with lawbreaking are precluded from doing so, such as is the case now in China and Iran, then there is no effective way that the party charged can defend themselves.

One other major consideration concerns the *normative role of the judiciary*. Assuming a reasonable degree of autonomy of the judiciary in a given society, what values does the judiciary promote and protect? If the judiciary is not dominated by other branches of government or by a dominant religion or the military, then it can better protect minority religious groups from exploitation and allow them any rights that are guaranteed under the society's governing documents. But, if members of the judiciary do not espouse values that include religious freedom, then rulings in favour of minority religions may be rare. Conditions are sometimes optimal for judicial systems to offer protections for religious freedom of minority religions. Such a situation might be referred to as the 'judicialization of religious freedom' (Richardson 2015), which refers to a dominant role played by the judiciary in promoting and defending religious freedom. However, such is not always the case, even in western democracies, and sometimes other institutional structures within society overwhelm or impede efforts to protect minority faiths (Maryl 2018). This situation now obtains in France to a considerable extent as has been detailed in several of the chapters herein.

Sociology of law theories relevant to minority religions

Donald Black and William Chambliss, although quite different in their theoretical approaches, have both had a significant impact on understanding how law develops and operates in society. First, some relevant ideas from Black will aid in understanding how legal systems function when minority religious groups are involved, either to defend themselves from various charges or, as such groups attempt to use the legal system, to protect themselves and promote their beliefs and practices.

Donald Black's theories and minority religions

Black's concepts of *status* and *intimacy* are important building blocks for his theories of how law operates within society (Black 1999). Status refers to where the party to a legal action is located within the social hierarchy of society. The higher the status, the easier it usually is for a person to work his/her will within the legal system. The same obtains for organizations of course, and usually, there is no higher status organization in a society than the government itself. Higher status also usually implies that the party has access to needed resources to use the legal system to defend their interests. And higher status also typically means that the party may be a 'repeat player' with experience in using the legal system for their own ends. Having intimate ties with key institutional leaders within a legal system refers to a sharing of values with societal leaders and perhaps even having social ties with them. When a party to a legal action shares such ties with a judge, for example, the judge may be more sympathetic to the position of the party, if only because the judge and the party may share a common vocabulary and values.

By definition, most minority religious groups, including those discussed in this volume, do not have high status within society; therefore, they would typically lose when involved with the legal system, especially if brought to that system by a high-status player such as a governmental entity. Most minority religious groups and their leaders also do not share intimate ties with decision-makers in the legal system. Indeed, there may be a very wide gulf between the values of the religious group and those of decision-makers within the legal system. The two entities do not share a universe of discourse and may even have great difficulty communicating. So, how can minority faiths cope and perhaps even sometimes prevail in legal actions in which they become involved?

One important consideration of course is whether decision-makers within the judicial system value religious freedom and take such considerations into account as they make decisions. However, no matter the proclivities of the judicial decision-makers, an important avenue for minority religious groups involved in the legal system is to seek allies to assist in their efforts. Black and Baumgartner (1999) propose the concept of *third-party partisans*, by which they mean situations in which a party uninvolved in a legal action decides to enter the dispute on the side of one of the parties. This can be done in a number of ways, including such things as direct financial support for the legal action, offering behind the scenes legal advice, making public statements on behalf of a party to the action, filing an *amicus* brief when a judicial decision is appealed, or offering expert testimony on behalf of the religious group.

If an unpopular minority religion is involved in legal action and a higher status entity with intimate ties to decision-makers in that system decides to assist them, this can shift the odds of success dramatically. Such a development is more likely to be able to occur with an adversarial system of justice, which means that the minority religion might manage to retain a high-status lawyer or attract support from an NGO with experience and intimate ties to key players within the justice system. There are a number of potential third-party partisans that might be able to assist a minority religion caught up in legal actions. There are well-known NGOs such as the American Civil Liberties Union in America, Amnesty International, and organizations such the United Nations that might enter into or comment on various legal matters involving minority religions. Also, an individual attorney might decide to take a case for personal reasons, or individual political figures might enter the fray on behalf of a minority religion. Mass media also can play a third-party partisan role if decisions are made to present the group in a more favourable light than is typical with coverage of unpopular minority faiths.

Indeed, an argument can be made that even courts might be thought of a third-party partisan if they accept cases and rule in favour of a minority religion in a regular fashion. The interaction between the United States Supreme Court and the Jehovah's Witnesses over the years might fit such a definition, as the JWs have won over 50 cases before that court and the Court used some of those cases to extend its authority over states and local governments. A similar argument might be made about the European Court of Human Rights, which has ruled in favour of the JWs is over 50 cases as well as over two dozen 'friendly settlements'. In taking so many cases from Witnesses, the Court used some of those cases to expand its authority over newer members of the Council of Europe from Central and Eastern Europe (see Richardson 2017 for details).

Of course, third-party partisans can also align themselves *against* the interests of minority religions and work with those who would limit or repress such groups. For example, some private 'anti-cult' groups in Russia and in France have been welcomed by government officials interested in controlling minority faiths. Some such groups have even gained public funding for their efforts and been allowed to file legal actions against minority religious groups, with the support of the legal arms of those governments. In America and some other countries, some (but certainly not all) representatives of the mental health profession, as well as a few other professional and academics, have aligned themselves with those who would limit the freedom of minority religious groups to operate. These professional individuals and organizations have, for example, promoted much-criticized pseudo-scientific 'brainwashing' theories or focused on alleged harm to children in such groups to advance their agenda (Anthony 1990; Palmer and Hardman 1999; Richardson 1993, 1999).

Mark Cooney, a former student of Donald Black, develops another element derived from Black's theoretical work that is useful to understanding of what happens when minority religions get caught up in legal processes (Cooney 1994). Cooney describes the social process of producing evidence and notes that those in charge within the legal system get to decide what evidence is produced and presented in court or to other important decision-making groups, such as commissions, legislative committee, or governmental agencies. Judges and those who sit on those other tribunals then get to decide whether to accept or reject the evidence that has been produced. Clearly, there are many decision points where discretion enters the process of socially constructing and making use of evidence in decisions that are made concerning minority religions which find themselves caught up in legal processes. There are several instances described in this volume's chapters where the production and acceptance of certain types of evidence played a role in ultimate decisions rendered by courts of other important bodies.

Perhaps, the most notorious demonstration of the position expounded by Cooney in the realm of minority faiths concerns the use of the 'brainwashing' metaphor in attacks against minority religions in various countries, including the Unification Church described in one chapter of this volume. Much effort was made first in the United States but then elsewhere, including western Europe, Russia, and China, to convince the general public, mass media, and, ultimately, judges in civil and even criminal actions involving some minority religions that brainwashing was a scientific term and that it was readily practiced on unsuspecting potential followers by leaders of those minority faiths. Scholars readily debunked these claims (Anthony1990; Anthony and Robbins 2014; Barker 1984; Richardson 1991, 1993), but such claims were accepted for well over a decade in American courts, and the concept still is accepted in some quarters around the world. These claims undergirded, for example, the idea of 'mental manipulation' that has played a major role in efforts to control or repress minority religions in France, one of the countries referred to in several of the chapters herein.[1]

William Chambliss' theories and minority religions

Whereas Donald Black focuses on what happens after an individual or group becomes a party to a legal action, William Chambliss is more interested in how laws develop initially, especially laws that involve major shifts in policy for a society. He adopts a dialectic approach that eschews mechanistic or reifying theories which leave human volition out of explanations of human affairs. Instead, he offers a more humanistic approach, focusing on choices made to resolve *contradictions, conflicts,* and *dilemmas* that arise in specific historical contexts.[2] The focus is on law as a process which seeks to resolve contradictions that occur when extant laws are being applied within a given historical context. Sometimes, such resolutions lead to further contradictions and conflicts which pose further dilemmas for societal leaders. Those dilemmas lead in turn to further efforts to resolve difficulties, demonstrating the continuing dialectic nature of law making. Simply put, laws that were thought to resolve a problem at one point in time may lead to yet other unexpected problems or conflicts, meaning that societal leaders are faced with new dilemmas which demand further resolution.

Chambliss' ideas have a clear application to the situation concerning minority religions because many different nations are attempting to deal with the increasing number of new religions that have developed within their societies or whose believers have migrated into the society from elsewhere. Also, some nations have seen internal political changes that have led to major efforts to exert new controls over minority religions. Institutional leaders in such situations seem to have decided that older laws or traditions whereby religious groups were regulated are no longer adequate and are contributing to difficulties and conflicts. In some cases, minority religions have become a political target used by politicians to further their own interests. Therefore, new approaches were developed to resolve perceived dilemmas in those societies. Thus, in recent times, a plethora of new laws (or creative applications of older laws) have been developed in various nations attempting to grapple with developing conflicts over religion within the society.

Examples of new laws designed to manage or control minority religious groups abound in the countries represented in this volume. Scientology has experienced news laws being promulgated in several countries such as Australia and has also seen laws governing psychological services and commercial activities applied to the organization in innovative ways. The Jehovah's Witnesses have seen a very strained but apparently successful (so far) effort to apply post 9/11 laws against extremism passed in Russia against the group. The entire organization has been dissolved with the blessing of the highest courts in Russia.[3] Austria's efforts to dissuade the Unification Church from operating within that country led to development of new laws specifically focused on that group, leading to years of effort before the group was successful in gaining at least some recognition as a religious community. Japan passed a new law in an effort to respond to the deadly actions of Aum Shinrikyo, and the remnants of the group described herein have been forced to operate under those laws even as they challenge them. And, as detailed in the chapter on apostasy groups, throughout the world, those attempting to organize such groups, particularly those rejecting Islam, have had severe difficulty with the application of apostasy laws that exist in many Muslim countries.

China represents a special case where all religions not accepting the dominance of the Chinese Communist Party are subject to severe harassment that has included imprisonment, torture, and even death for members of some minority religious groups, including the Church of the Almighty God described in the chapter in this volume. New laws and governmental agencies have been developed in China to facilitate this extreme level of control (Edelman and Richardson 2003; Introvigne, Richardson and Soryte 2019), and the situation there for minority religions has worsened considerably in recent years under the new regime of President Xi Jinping.

France, also a special case, has passed laws to control or repress minority religions based on questionable logic and science (Anthony and Robbins 2004; Beckford 2004; Duvert 2004) and also developed a list *in camera* of 172 groups that political leaders considered a threat to France's way of life and culture. France also has made creative use of tax laws in an effort to force the dissolution of several religious groups. A decision was made to treat contributions to certain groups as gifts which meant that a 60 per cent tax rate applied. Thus, the JWs were presented with a bill for past due taxes of over $50 million. Legal efforts within France to dissuade the French government of this tactic were unsuccessful, but a case filed with the European Court of Human Rights did eventually (after over ten years) succeed in stopping this effort for the JWs and for two other religious groups. It is within this negative atmosphere towards minority religions that the efforts of the Japanese group Tenrikyō described herein were forced to operate if it wanted to remain in France. And the Essene group described in another chapter actually felt compelled to leave France and establish itself in Canada, but not without also encountering creative efforts to exert control over them in their new somewhat more welcoming environs. Canada also developed new legal structures in an effort to grapple with the actions of the Sons of Freedom Doukhobor group that migrated to Canada to escape persecution in their home country.

Chambliss, in one of his first demonstrations of the efficacy of his ideas, carefully explained the derivation of laws against vagrancy as they were developed in early English history to force people to work (Chambliss 1964). Each of the examples mentioned above, drawn from chapters in this volume, might offer enough details about the application of law to that particular group to help readers understand how the theoretical approach of Chambliss might apply to the experience of the group being discussed. Such detailed historical sociological analyses that recognize the crucial volitional elements of effort to exert control over minority religions is important for understanding how minority religious groups are affected by the law.

Cause lawyering and minority religions

There are many ways minority religious groups may find themselves involved in the legal and political systems of society, as made clear in the chapters of this volume. Often, the legal action is an effort to defend themselves from efforts to regulate, control, or even repress the organization and its practices. Thus, minority religions may be either defendants in a case brought by a governmental authority or private person or plaintiffs who have brought a case in an effort to change a law or practice of authorities in the society (Richardson 1998b).

As indicated above, minority religious groups vary greatly in their access to competent legal assistance when they become involved in the legal system. Some religious groups have long had legal expertise within their ranks: the jurisprudential records of both Scientology and the Jehovah's Witnesses prove that this can be very effective. Some other groups such as the Unification Church have also decided to promote legal and political training among members because of difficulties encountered by the group in dealing with the greater society and its agencies. Lawyers from both situations meet the definition of cause lawyering, as they are trying to effect major changes in law and public policy through their actions concerning religious freedom for minority religious groups (Marshall and Crocker Hale 2014; Sarat and Scheingold 1998, 2005, 2006).[4]

However, many if not most minority religions do not have ready access to legal expertise, and thus, they must rely on others to help defend themselves within the legal system and the political arena. Often, such groups are forced to take whomever they can get, and thus, they may end up with someone with no experience of handling cases involving religious freedom issues. This usually ends up with a bad result from the perspective of the minority religion. However, on occasion, such groups are able to attract 'third-party partisans' (Black and Baumgartner 1999) to assist them with legal matters and also with other institutional structures such as the media, legislatures, and agencies of the executive branch.

Those third-party partisans might be individual attorneys (or even non-attorneys) who are able to assist in significant ways as the minority religion defends itself in court or promotes its cause as a plaintiff in a legal action as well as in other forums. Or, the partisan might be an organization that has chosen to involve itself in a legal matter to promote values that it espouses and wants to protect. A number of NGOs are interested in promoting religious freedom in various parts of the world, and they sometimes choose to get involved in cases of interest within their society and may also work internationally, filing briefs, giving advice, and assisting in cases in the United States, in Europe, and elsewhere. Some of the Jehovah's Witness cases before the United States Supreme Court and in Europe that were submitted to the ECtHR have attracted *amicus* briefs from various interested parties. Some recent religion cases before the ECtHR also have attracted considerable support from mass media organizations and others such as the United Nations in their effort to defend themselves and promote their values within various legal arenas.[5]

How minority faiths go about attracting the interest of potential third-party partisans is an issue worthy of research. Black and Baumgartner (1999) use the term 'strange attractor' to suggest that this is basically an unknown process; hence research is needed to help us understand how this process operates and what happens when a third party chooses to get involved in an action not of their own making. Obtaining the interest and support of a high-status third party with intimate ties with those in the power structure of the society obviously will increase the chances that the minority religion might prevail in legal action as well as with public opinion.

One example known about by this writer will perhaps illustrate how some 'third parties' developed in one important area of litigation over minority religions that has ramifications for several of the groups discussed in this volume. For several decades in America, major legal battles were fought over the 'brainwashing' claims mentioned above which were being lodged against some of the religious groups in civil actions for damages filed by former members or their parents. A number of scholars doing research on new religions (including both editors of this volume) were concerned and even offended by presentation of such claims in court as being valid science (see Anthony 1990; Barker 1984; Richardson 1991, 1993). That concern was compounded when it became clear that those claims were sometimes accepted by judges and juries, with devastating results for the religious group which might be ordered to pay large amounts of damages. Some scholars became involved in offering advice, occasionally serving as expert witnesses in cases, and in helping draft *amicus* briefs if the case was lost at the trial court level but then appealed to a higher court. Indeed, some scholars even participated in convincing several major professional scholarly organizations to enter the fray and file briefs opposing brainwashing claims, briefs that were prepared with assistance by some of those scholars. Thus, this was a situation where potential third-party partisans actually sought out or volunteered to assist because they were so offended at what was happening in some important court cases involving minority religious groups accused of brainwashing their participants. The battle was a long and trying one, but was eventually successful (Richardson 1997). The eventual outcome was to have such claims disallowed in American courts and in most other courts in western countries.

Conclusions

In this concluding chapter, I have attempted to apply relevant theoretical approaches from the sociology of religion and the sociology of law to help us understand the ways that minority religious groups have responded to applications of the law. Theories from the sociology of religion literature that have focused on the historical, structural, and demographic aspects of the 'sociology of religious freedom' are useful in helping us understand the context in which the minority religions discussed herein must operate. Also, very useful are the contrasting theoretical positions of two prominent sociology of law theorists, Donald Black and William Chambliss. Black focuses on what happens after minority religions are involved in legal actions, and his work (and that of some of his students) is especially helpful in grasping the outcomes of actions taken against minority groups. This approach helps us understand why minority faiths often lose in the judicial arena but also helps us grasp why they sometimes manage to prevail. Chambliss focuses on how laws and other regulations that might affect minority religions get developed initially, making us aware of these crucial processes involved in efforts to manage and control minority religions. His work is quite helpful because there has been a plethora of new laws developed around the increasingly pluralistic world to manage and control minority religions. Minority religions must learn how to deal with those new efforts of social control and also even to attempt to influence how these new laws and regulations are developed.

Last but not least, this chapter closes with a discussion of cause lawyering, and how this type of legal representation has affected various types of minority religions as they try to deal with regulatory systems in the various societies in which they try to function. The concept of cause lawyering interacts, of course, with ideas from the sociology of law that have been discussed because when minority religions get involved in the legal system, they often need assistance. How that assistance is obtained, what kind of assistance is accessed, and to what effect is crucially important. Understanding the role of cause lawyers interested in religious freedom battles will grow in importance as societies become more pluralistic, leading to increased efforts by governmental authorities to manage various expressions of religion that are developing within contemporary societies.

Notes

1 Note that China also made use of the 'brainwashing' concept in its efforts to control minority faiths, but, after the tragedy of 9/11, China and also some other countries found that defining selected minority religions as terrorist organizations was more acceptable to the general public and therefore more effective as a means of social control.

2 See Richardson (2014) for a more detailed explication and application of Chambliss' theories to development of laws concerning the spread of *Shari'a* in the United States, Canada, and Australia. The chapter also offers a critique and extensions of Chambliss' theorizing.

3 Over 30 cases from Russia submitted by the JWs are now before the European Court of Human Rights, but those cases have not been adjudicated as of this writing. See Richardson (2017) for details.

4 Two of the most famous cause lawyers in the history of the United States are Thurgood Marshall, who headed up the legal arm of the National Association for the Advancement of Colored People (NAACP) and Ruth Bader Ginsburg, who successfully championed women's rights for decades. Interestingly, both ended up being appointed to the United States Supreme Court themselves.

5 In the interest of full disclosure, it should be stated that this writer has occasionally served as an expert witness or in other capacities (such as offering advice) to minority religious groups involved in legal actions, especially cases that involved accusations of 'brainwashing' but also, even less frequently, accusations of child abuse (Richardson 1998a).

References

Anthony, Dick. 1990. Religious movements and brainwashing litigation: Evaluating key testimony, in: T. Robbins and D. Anthony (eds), *In Gods We Trust*. New Brunswick, NJ: Transaction Books, pp. 295–344.

Anthony, Dick, and Thomas Robbins. 2004. Pseudoscience versus minority religions: An evaluation of the brainwashing theories of Jean-Marie Abgrall, in: J.T. Richardson (ed.), *Regulating Religion: Case Studies from around the Globe*. New York: Kluwer, pp. 127–49.

Barker, Eileen. 1984. *The Making of a Moonie: Brainwashing or Choice?* Oxford: Basil Blackwell.

Beckford, James A. 2004. 'Laïcité,' 'Dystopia,' and the reaction to new religious movements in France, in: J.T. Richardson (ed.), *Regulating Religion: Case Studies from around the Globe*. New York: Kluwer, pp. 27–40.

Black, Donald 1976. *The Behavior of Law*. New York: Academic Press.

———. 1999. *The Social Structure of Right and Wrong*. New York: Academic Press.

Black, Donald and M.P. Baumgartner. 1999. Toward a theory of the third party, in: D. Black (ed.), *The Social Structure of Right and Wrong*. New York; Academic Press, pp. 95–124.

Burli, N. 2017. *Third Party Interventions before the European Court of Human Rights*. Cambridge: Intersentia.

Chambliss, William. 1964. A sociological Analysis of the law of vagrancy. *Social Problems* 12: 46–67.

———. 1979. On lawmaking. *British Journal of Law and Society* 6: 149–72.

Chambliss, William and Marjorie Zatz (eds). 1993. *Making Law: The State, the Law, and Structural Contradictions*. Bloomington: Indiana University Press.

Cooney, Mark. 1994. Evidence as partisanship. *Law and Society Review* 28: 833–58.

Duvert, Cyrille. 2004. Anti-cultism in the French Parliament, in: J.T. Richardson (ed.), *Regulating Religion: Case Studies from around the Globe*. New York: Kluwer, pp. 41–52.

Edelman, Bryan, and James T. Richardson. 2003. Legal social control of the Falun Gong in China. *Nova Religio* 6: 312–313.

Introvigne, Massimo, James T. Richardson, and Rosita Soryte. 2019. Would the real Article 300 please stand up? Refugees from religious movements persecuted as *Xie Jiao* in China: The case of the Church of Almighty God. *The Journal of CESNUR* 3(5) Sept-Oct. issue, an on-line journal.

Lehmann, K. 2016. *Religious NGOs in International Relations*. London: Routledge.

Marshall, Anna-Maria and Daniel Crocker Hale 2014. Cause lawyering. *The Annual Review of Law and Social Science* 10: 301–20. doi: 10.1146/annurev-lawsocsci-102612-133932.

Maryl, Damon. 2018. The judicialization of religious freedom: An institutionalist approach. *Journal for the Scientific Study of Religion* 57: 514=30

Palmer, Susan, and Charlotte Hardman (eds). 1999. *Children in New Religious Movements*. New Brunswick: Rutgers University Press.

Richardson, James T. 1991. Cult/brainwashing cases and the freedom of religion. *Journal of Church and State* 33: 55–74.

———. 1993. A social psychological critique of 'brainwashing' claims about recruitment to new reli: gions, in: J. Hadden and D. Bromley (eds), *Handbook of Cults and Sects in America*. Greenwich: JAI Press, pp. 75–97.

———. 1997. Sociology and the new religions: 'Brainwashing', the courts, and religious freedom, in: P. Jenkins and S. Kroll-Smith (eds), *Witnessing for Sociology*. New York: Praeger, pp. 115–37.

———. 1998a. The accidental expert. *Nova Religio* 2: 31–43.

———. 1998b. Law and minority religions: 'Positive' and 'negative' uses of the legal system. *Nova Religio* 2: 93–107.

———. 1999. Social control of new religions: From 'brainwashing' claims to child sex abuse accusations, in: S. Palmer and C. Hardman (eds), *Children in New Religious Movements*. New Brunswick: Rutgers University Press, pp. 172–186.

———. 2001. Law, social control, and minority religions, in: Pauline Cote (ed.), *Frontier Religions in Public Space*. Ottawa: University of Ottawa Press, pp. 139–65.

———. 2006. The sociology of religious freedom: A structural and socio-legal analysis. *Sociology of Religion* 67(3): 271–94.

———. 2014. Contradictions, conflicts, dilemmas, and temporary resolutions: A sociology of law analysis of *Shari'a* in selected western societies, in: A. Possamai, J. T. Richardson, and B. Turner (eds), *The Sociology of Shari'a: Case Studies from around the World*. New York: Springer, pp. 237–52.

———. 2015. Managing religions and the judicialization of religious freedom. *Journal for the Scientific Study of Religion* 54(1): 1–19.

Richardson James T. 2017. Update on Jehovah's Witness cases before the European Court of Human rights: implications of a surprising partnership. *Religion, State, and Society* 45: 232–248.

Sarat, Austin, and Stuart A. Scheingold (eds). 1998. *Cause Lawyering: Political Commitments and Professional Responsibilities*. New York: Oxford University Press

———. (eds). 2005. *The Worlds Cause Lawyers Make*. Stanford: Stanford University Press.

———. (eds). 2006. *Cause Lawyers and Social Movements*. Stanford: Stanford University Press.

Van den Eynde, Laura. 2013. An empirical look at the *amicus curiae* practice of human rights NGOs before the European Court of Human Rights. *Netherlands Quarterly of Human Rights* 32: 271–313.

———. 2017. Encouraging Judicial dialogues: The contribution of Human Rights NGOs' briefs to the European Court of Human Rights, in: A Muller and E. Hege (eds), *Judicial Dialogues and Human Rights*. Cambridge: Cambridge University Press, pp. 339–97.

Index

ACM *see* anti-cult movement
Ahmadiyya Community 6–7, 20, 194
Aleph 170, 175–83, 185; *see also* Aum Shinrikyo
alliances 109, 157, 222
Al-Muhajiroun 13
alternative service *see* conscientious objection
America *see* United States of America
American Civil Liberties Union (ACLU) 15, 81, 224, 226
American Constitution 43–4, 48–50, 53, 85, 89
amicus curiae 14, 22, 81, 222, 226, 231, 232
Amnesty International 226
Ananda Marga 4
anarchist 10, 116–17, 129–30
anti-cult movement (ACM) 80, 98–9, 100–1, 104, 108–11, 153, 155, 165, 170, 174, 180, 199, 227; *see also* FECRIS; and MILS; and MIVILUDES
archangels 157, 161, 116–7
Article 300, Chinese Criminal Code 7, 199; *see also* China
Armenia 39–40
arson 116, 118–21, 128
Article 300, Chinese Criminal Code 199; *see also* China
Asahara Shōkō 12, 169, 171–2, 175–9, 183; *see also* Aum Shinrikyo
Association Culturelle Franco-Japonais de Tenri 138–40, 142
Asylum 6, 15, 188–90, 193–204
ATF *see* Bureau of Alcohol, Tobacco and Firearms
Attorneys 3, 26, 81–8, 88–90, 100, 102, 106, 122–3, 125–6. 131, 196, 224, 231

Aum Shinrikyo 3, 12, 169–83; *see also* Aleph; and Asahara; and Hikari no Wa
Australia 15, 31, 60–2, 127, 189, 195, 196, 229
Austria 14, 38–9, 72, 97, 99, 104–10, 112, 189, 229

Baha'i 7, 15, 28, 67
Bandera and others v. Italy (1997) 59; *see also* Church of Scientology
Baumgartner, M.P. 221, 226, 231
Beckford, James A. 139, 146, 149, 153, 155–7, 229
Belgium 8, 66–7, 189, 198
Berg, David 'Moses' 11; *see also* Family International
Black, Donald 221–2, 225–8, 231–2
blood, transfusion 8, 25–6, 33, 50–2
Boko Haram 2
Bolshevik 10
Bomb 3–4, 116, 119–21, 128, 166
brainwashing 84, 95, 101, 110, 155, 182, 227–8, 231–3
Branch Davidians 3, 153, 231
Bruenner, Christian 106, 110
Bromley, David 79, 84, 86–7, 153, 158, 165
Bureau of Alcohol, Tobacco and Firearms (ATF) 3, 204

Caesar 25, 37–8, 40, 42, 44, 47, 49–50, 52–3
CAG *see* Church of Almighty God
Canada 7, 10, 38, 44–5, 48–51, 115–20, 123, 125–31, 152, 159–67, 189, 196, 198–9, 205, 230, 233
cause lawyering 14, 222, 230, 232–4
Chambliss, William 221, 225, 228, 230, 232

Children 3–4, 6, 9–11, 25–26, 42, 47, 49, 51, 74–5, 85, 87, 104, 115–17, 120–8, 130, 145, 158, 176–8, 182, 227, 233
Children of God *see* Family International, The
China 5–6, 8, 12, 15, 100, 109, 128, 188, 190–1, 195–203, 224, 227, 229, 233–4
Chinese Communist Party (CCP) 5, 197, 229; *see also* China
Christian Essene Church *see* Essenes
Church of Almighty God (CAG) 5–6, 15, 188–9, 192, 194, 196–205, 229
Church of the Flying Spaghetti Monster 8–9
Church of Jesus Christ of Latter-day Saints 9, 11, 16, 67, 107
Church of Scientology 8, 13, 58–73, 76, 101, 105, 195, 216, 221–2, 229–30
civil rights 2, 53, 81, 83, 85
COI *see* Country of Origin Information
conscientious objection *see* Military Service
conservatorship 80, 84–5
Constitution *see* American Constitution
Convention Relating to the Status of Refugees (1951) 190
Cooney, Mark 221, 227
Council of Europe 58, 72–5, 77, 207–8, 223, 227
Country of Origin Information 198–200
Cours de Japonaise de Tenri 140
Czech Republic 19, 189

Denver 115–16, 121–6, 128, 130–1
deprogramming 80, 84–5, 108
disfellowshipping 49, 50
Doukhobors 10, 115–21, 123–4, 126, 128–31, 230
Druze 10
Dunn, Emily 188, 196

ECHR *see* European Convention on Human Rights
ECtHR *see* European Court of Human Rights
education 6–7, 9, 13, 27–28, 31, 47–9, 61, 64, 74, 77, 79, 87, 93, 104, 107, 124, 130, 139–40, 145, 149–50, 174, 176–7, 184, 208–9, 211, 217, 219
Essenes 7, 152–3, 155–68, 230

Estonia 10, 23–34
European Convention on Human Rights (ECHR) 39, 53, 55, 68, 71, 75, 110, 207–8, 211, 215, 219
European Court of Human Rights (ECtHR) 8, 14, 23, 38–40, 50, 53, 56–7, 71, 74, 192, 194, 207–20, 223, 227, 229, 231, 233
European Federation of Centres of Research and Information on Cults and Sects *see* FECRIS
Evangelische Zentralstelle für Weltanschauungsfragen (EZW) 101, 109, 111
evidence, social production of 227–8
Exclusive Brethren *see* Plymouth Brethren Christian Church
extremism 1, 8, 195, 229
EZW *see* Evangelische Zentralstelle für Weltanschauungsfragen

Falun Gong 6, 15–16, 188, 198, 234
Family Federation for World Peace and Unification (FFWPU) 13, 79, 86–8, 90, 92–5, 106, 109, 112; *see also* Unification Movement
Family Federation for World Peace and Unification International, et al. v. Hyun Jin Moon (a/k/a Preston Moon), et al 87–90; *see also* Family Federation for World Peace and Unification (FFWPU); *and* Moon Hyun Jin (Preston); *and* Unification Movement
Family International, The 5, 11–13
FBI (Federal Bureau of Investigation) 3
FECRIS (European Federation of Centres of Research and Information on Cults and Sects) 98, 108–10
Federal Family Ministry (Germany) 104
Finland 189, 196
flag, saluting 4, 8, 42, 47–9; *see also* manifestation of belief
FOREF (Forum for Religious Freedom–Europe) 14, 98–9, 106, 108, 110–11
France 7–8, 12, 38, 65, 72–5, 97, 100–2, 109–10, 134–48, 152–66, 189, 198–9, 209–10, 216, 225, 227–30, 234
Freedomites *see* Sons of Freedom
French National Gendarmerie Intervention Group (GIGN) 156–7

Germany 4, 6, 38–9, 53–4, 69–71, 97–105, 108, 110–13, 138, 189, 194–5, 198, 205
Gesellschaft zur Vereinigung des Weltchristentums see Society for the Unification of World Christianity
GIGN *see* French National Gendarmerie Intervention Group
Global Peace Foundation (GPF) 14, 90; *see also* Moon, Hyun Jin; and Unification Movement
Guidelines on International Protection: Religion-Based Refugee Claims 191–5, 201; *see also* UNHCR
GVW *see* Society for the Unification of World Christianity

Hak Ja Han *see* Moon, Mrs
Handyside v. UK 210
Hikari no Wa 12, 170, 175, 178–83, 185; *see also* Aum Shinrikyo
Holy Spirit Association for the Unification of World Christianity (HSA-UWC) 79, 82, 86, 86–7, 90–5, 101, 113; *see also* Unification Movement
HSA-UWC *see* Holy Spirit Association for the Unification of World Christianity
HSA-UWC v. Tax Commission of New York City (1982) 82–3
HRC *see* United Nations Human Rights Committee
HRWF (Human Rights Without Frontiers) 41, 109
Hubbard. L. Ron 76–7; *see also* Church of Scientology
Humanism 73, 76, 211, 216, 228
human rights 14–16, 23, 37–41, 48, 50, 53, 62, 66, 68, 71, 73–6, 98–9, 101–2, 108–9, 123, 125–6, 128, 180–1, 190–2, 197–8, 207, 215, 223, 227, 229; *see also* European Court of Human Rights; and European Convention on Human Rights

INALCO (*Institut National des Langues et Civilisations Orientales*) 137–8
Intergovernmental Consultation on Migration, Asylum and Refugees (IGC) 199

Interministerial Mission in the Fight Against Cults *see* MILS
Interministerial Mission of Vigilance and Combat against Sectarian Aberrations *see* MIVILUDES
Internal Revenue Service (IRS) 8, 64–5, 72, 81, 94, 142; *see also* taxes
International Coalition for Religious Freedom 99
Intimacy 225
IRS *see* Internal Revenue Service
ISIS (Islamic State of Iraq and Syria) 2
Islam 5–7, 12–13, 15, 28, 31–2, 73, 109, 111, 194, 198, 209, 216, 229
Italy 58–60, 77, 189, 199, 202, 209, 211, 213–18

Japan 12, 41, 79–83, 87–8, 108, 127, 134–49, 169–74, 176, 179, 182–3, 188–9, 198, 203, 229, 230
Jedi Order 8
Jehovah's Witnesses 4–5, 7, 10, 13, 23–6, 33–54, 76, 105, 195, 201, 209, 215, 217, 221–2, 226, 229–31
Jews *see* Judaism
Jiba 135, 142
Jonestown *see* Peoples Temple
Jōyū, Fumihiro 176; *see also* Hikari no Wa
Judaism 4, 7, 10, 24, 28, 31–3, 83
judicialization 209, 225
judicial system 50, 66, 68, 83, 93, 159, 163, 181, 218, 221–6, 232

Katz v. Supreme Court 85, 94
Kokkinakis v. Greece 209–10, 214–15, 217
Korea *see* North Korea; *and* South Korea
Ku Klux Klan 2

Larson v. Valenti 83–4
Lautsi v. Italy 209, 217–19
licensing laws 8–9, 43–4, 84, 91
Lord's Resistance Army 2

Maavalla Koda 27–34
manifestation of belief 38, 42, 48, 194; *see also* flag, saluting
Manitara, Olivier 7, 152, 156–7, 159, 165–7; *see also* Essenes
Manoussakis and Others v. Greece 210
Maple Village 152, 160, 162–4

McDonald's murder 199–200, 203
McVeigh, Timothy 3
medical treatment 10, 25–6, 38, 50–2, 67, 70
Messianic Community 6
military service 4–5, 10, 24–5, 37–42, 54, 106, 116–18, 195
MILS (Interministerial Mission in the Fight Against Cults) 155, 165–6
MIVILUDES (Interministerial Mission of Vigilance and Combat against Sectarian Aberrations) 109, 155, 165–6
Molla Sali v. Greece 216
Moon Hyun Jin (Preston) 14, 87–9, 93, 94, 95; *see also* Global Peace Foundation (GPF); and Unification Movement
Moon, Hyung Jin (Sean) 14, 87–8, 91–4; *see also* Sanctuary Church; and Unification Movement
Moon, Mrs 13, 79, 87, 91–3, 95, 97–105, 108–10, 112–13; *see also* Unification Movement
Moon, Sun Myung 2, 13–14, 79–82, 85–9, 91–4, 97–105, 109–10, 112; *see also* Unification Movement
Mormon *see* Church of Jesus Christ of Latter-day Saints
MOVE, the 4
Muslim *see* Islam

Nakayama Miki 135
Nakayama Shōzen 135, 137
Native Religions 9, 23, 27–30, 33–4
Netherlands, The 31–2, 45, 71, 189, 200
New Zealand 60–1, 77, 189, 196
NGOs (Non-Governmental Organisations) 16, 72–3, 87, 109, 196–8, 211, 217, 222–4, 226, 231
normative role of judiciary 224
North Korea 84, 190
nudity 10, 116, 118–21

Office of Religious Affairs (*Kultusamt*) 105–6, 108
Oklahoma bombing 3
Order of the Solar Temple *see* Solar Temple

PACE *see* Parliamentary Assembly of the Council of Europe

Parliamentary Assembly of the Council of Europe (PACE) 72–5
Paganism 10, 34; *see also* Native Religions
Pastafarians 8, 9
Peoples Temple 3, 15
permits *see* licencing laws
persecution 6, 15–16, 24, 44, 68, 99, 104–5, 109, 117, 130, 155, 172, 174, 176, 188, 190–8, 200–4, 230
peyote 9
Plymouth Brethren Christian Church 12
Portugal 189
Prison 4, 13, 23, 38, 41, 67, 81, 116–17, 120, 123, 125, 128, 130, 176, 182

Quakers 4
Quebec 44–5, 56, 152, 159–61, 164

radiating effects 211–12, 218
Rajneesh 3
RCMP *see* Royal Canadian Mounted Police
refugees 188–204
Republic of Korea *see* South Korea
ritual slaughter *see* slaughter
Royal Canadian Mounted Police (RCMP) 115–16, 121, 123
Russia 5, 8, 10, 46, 50, 52–4, 71, 100, 110, 115–20, 126, 130, 176, 194–5, 227, 229, 233

Saipan 189
Salles, Rudy 72–5, 78
Sanctuary Church 14, 18, 90–2, 95
Santo Dame 10
Schengen 97–104, 108, 110, 112
Scientology *see* Church of Scientology
seditious libel 44
shechita *see* slaughter 32, 33
Shincheonji 15
slaughter 10, 24, 30–3
Spain 4, 68–9, 97, 101, 189
Society for the Unification of World Christianity (*Gesellschaft zur Vereinigung des Weltchristentums*) (GVW) 105–6; *see also* Unification Movement
sociology of law 221–2, 225, 232
sociology of religious freedom 221–2, 232
Solar Temple 101, 152–3, 155–6, 166
soliciting by-laws 43, 45, 80, 83–4

Sons of Freedom 10, 115–16, 119, 120–2, 125–30, 230
South Korea (ROK) 40–2, 135, 188–9, 198–9, 203; *see also* North Korea
Spain 4, 68, 69, 97, 101, 112, 189
surveillance 81, 156, 170, 175–7, 180–2, 203
Sweden 26, 31, 71, 189, 195–6
Switzerland 90, 189–90, 198, 202

taxes 8, 14, 37, 44, 60–1, 64, 71, 80–3, 106–7, 110, 152, 160–3, 173, 229; *see also* Inland Revenue Service
Tenrikyō 12, 134–49, 230
Terranova Village 156–8, 162
third-party partisans 14, 226–7, 231–2
torture 4, 109, 130, 174, 191, 197, 229
Twelve Tribes *see* Messianic Community

UCI *see* Unification Church International
UNHCR (United Nations High Commissioner for Refugees) 189–91, 193–5, 198; *see also* Guidelines on International Protection
Unification Church (UC) *see* Unification Movement
Unification Church International (UCI) 87–90; *see also* Unification Movement
Unification Church, Nikkuni, et al. v. INS (1982) 83; *see also* Unification Movement
Unification Movement 1, 5, 13–14, 17, 79–95, 97–8, 101–7, 109–10, 112–13, 227, 229–30; *see also* Global Peace Foundation (GPF); and Moon,

Sun Myung; and Moon, Mrs; and Sanctuary Church
United Kingdom (UK) 13, 26, 62–3, 102, 110, 189, 210
United Nations 99, 101, 123, 189, 191, 197, 223, 226, 23; *see also* UNHCR
United Nations Convention Against Torture (1987) 191; *see also* torture
United Nations High Commissioner for Refugees *see* UNHCR
United Nations Human Rights Committee (HRC) 41, 42, 102, 197
United States of America (US; USA) 2, 8–9, 11, 15, 38, 42–4, 47–8, 50, 59–60, 64, 72, 79–81, 83–7, 91–4, 99–100, 102, 142, 153, 189–90, 195, 197–8, 203–4, 222, 226–7, 231, 233
United States v. Sun Myung Moon (1982) 80–2; *see also* Moon, Sun Myung; *and* Unification Movement

Vagrancy 131, 230
Ventura, Marco 65, 71
Verigin, Peter 117–20
Victims of Aum Shinrikyo *see* Aum Shinrikyo

Waco *see* Branch Davidians
Wang, Xiumei 202
Ward, Lord Justice 11
Ward v. Conner 85
Watchtower Bible and Tract Society *see* Jehovah's Witnesses

xie jiao 5, 8, 15, 195–6, 199–200

Zoning by-laws 152, 160–1
Zou, Demei 198

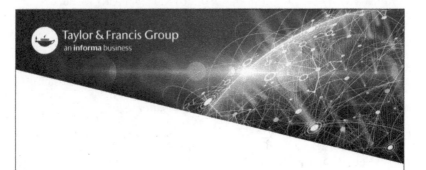